Satisficing and Maximizing
Moral Theorists on Practical Reason

How do we think about what we will do? One dominant answer is that we select the best available option. When that answer is quantified it can be expressed mathematically, thus generating a maximizing account of practical reason. However, a growing number of philosophers would offer a different answer: Because we are not equipped to maximize, we often choose the next best alternative, one that is no more than satisfactory. This strategy choice is called satisficing (a term coined by the economist Herbert Simon).

This new collection of essays explores both these accounts of practical reason, examining the consequences for adopting one or the other for moral theory in general and the theory of practical rationality in particular. It aims to address a constituency larger than contemporary moral philosophers and bring these questions to the attention of those interested in the applications of decision theory in economics, psychology, and political science.

Michael Byron is Associate Professor of Philosophy at Kent State University.

Nothing is good enough for someone to whom enough is little.
— Epicurus

Satisficing and Maximizing

Moral Theorists on Practical Reason

Edited by

MICHAEL BYRON

Kent State University

CAMBRIDGE
UNIVERSITY PRESS

PUBLISHED BY THE PRESS SYNDICATE OF THE UNIVERSITY OF CAMBRIDGE
The Pitt Building, Trumpington Street, Cambridge, United Kingdom

CAMBRIDGE UNIVERSITY PRESS
The Edinburgh Building, Cambridge CB2 2RU, UK
40 West 20th Street, New York, NY 10011-4211, USA
477 Williamstown Road, Port Melbourne, VIC 3207, Australia
Ruiz de Alarcón 13, 28014 Madrid, Spain
Dock House, The Waterfront, Cape Town 8001, South Africa

http://www.cambridge.org

First published 2004

Printed in the United States of America

Typeface ITC New Baskerville 10/13 pt.   *System* LaTeX 2_ε [TB]

A catalog record for this book is available from the British Library.

Library of Congress Cataloging in Publication Data

Satisficing and maximizing : moral theorists on practical reason / edited by Michael Byron.
p. cm.
Includes bibliographical references and index.
ISBN 0-521-81149-X – ISBN 0-521-01005-5 (pbk.)
1. Decision making – Moral and ethical aspects. 2. Practical reason. I. Byron,
Michael, 1964–

BJ1419.S28 2004
170′.42–dc22   2004043584

ISBN 0 521 81149 X hardback
ISBN 0 521 01005 5 paperback

Learning Resources
Centre

12691674

Contents

Contributors

Michael Byron is Associate Professor of Philosophy at Kent State University, where he has been teaching since 1997. His research interests include ethical theory, rational choice theory, and the history of ethics; he is the co-author (with Deborah Barnbaum) of *Research Ethics: Text and Readings*, published by Prentice-Hall, and articles in ethical theory and theory of rationality.

Tyler Cowen is Holbert C. Harris Professor of Economics at George Mason University. He has published extensively in economics and philosophy journals, including *American Economic Review, Journal of Political Economy, Ethics*, and *Philosophy and Public Affairs*. His *In Praise of Commercial Culture* and *What Price Fame?* were published by Harvard University Press, and his latest book, *Creative Destruction: How Globalization Is Changing the World's Cultures*, was published in 2003 by Princeton University Press. He is currently writing a book on the concept of civilization and its relation to political philosophy.

James Dreier is Professor of Philosophy at Brown University. He has been a visiting lecturer at Monash University and John Harsanyi Fellow at the Social and Political Theory program at the Research School of Social Science at the Australian National University. His main work is in meta-ethics and practical reason.

Thomas Hurka is Jackman Distinguished Chair in Philosophical Studies at the University of Toronto. The author of *Perfectionism* (1993), *Principles: Short Essays on Ethics* (1993), and *Virtue, Vice, and Value* (2001), he works primarily on perfectionist views in ethics, political philosophy, and the history of ethics.

Jan Narveson is Professor of Philosophy at the University of Waterloo in Ontario, Canada. He is the author of more than two hundred papers in philosophical periodicals and anthologies, mainly on ethical theory and practice, and of five published books: *Morality and Utility* (1967), *The Libertarian Idea* (1989), *Moral Matters*, (1993; 2nd ed. 1999) and *Respecting Persons in Theory and Practice* (2002); and, with Marilyn Friedman, *Political Correctness* (1995).

Henry S. Richardson is Professor of Philosophy at Georgetown University. He is the author of *Practical Reasoning about Final Ends* (Cambridge University Press, 1994) and *Democratic Autonomy* (Oxford University Press, 2002) and co-editor of *Liberalism and the Good* (Routledge, 1990) and *The Philosophy of Rawls* (5 vols., Garland, 1999). Building on "Beyond Good and Right: Toward a Constructive Ethical Pragmatism," *Philosophy & Public Affairs* 24 (1995), he is working to articulate a moral theory centering on non-maximizing, non-satisficing modes of moral reasoning.

David Schmidtz is Professor of Philosophy and joint Professor of Economics at the University of Arizona. His *Rational Choice and Moral Agency* (Princeton University Press, 1995) expands upon his chapter reprinted in this volume. He co-edited *Environmental Ethics: What Really Matters, What Really Works* (Oxford University Press, 2002) with Elizabeth Willott and co-authored *Social Welfare and Individual Responsibility* (Cambridge University Press, 1998) with Robert Goodin. His current projects are *The Elements of Justice* (Cambridge University Press, 2005) and *The Purpose of Moral Theory*.

Michael Slote is UST Professor of Ethics and Professor of Philosophy at the University of Miami, Coral Gables. He was previously Professor and Chair of the philosophy department at the University of Maryland, and before that he was Professor of Philosophy and a Fellow of Trinity College, Dublin. The author of many articles and several books on ethical theory, he is currently completing a large-scale study of "moral sentimentalism." He is a member of the Royal Irish Academy and a former Tanner lecturer.

Christine Swanton teaches at the University of Auckland, New Zealand. Her field is virtue ethics, in which she has recently published a book with Oxford University Press, entitled *Virtue Ethics: A Pluralistic View*. She is currently working in role ethics, Nietzschean virtue ethics, and Humean virtue ethics.

Mark van Roojen is Associate Professor of Philosophy at the University of Nebraska–Lincoln. He has taught philosophy as a visitor at Brown University and at the University of Arizona. His main research interests are in meta-ethics, ethics, and political philosophy.

Michael Weber is Assistant Professor of Philosophy at Yale University. His research and teaching are in moral and political philosophy, focusing on practical reason, rational choice theory, and ethics and the emotions. His papers have appeared in *Ethics, Philosophical Studies,* and the *Canadian Journal of Philosophy.*

Introduction

Michael Byron

It is testimony to the breadth of thought of Herbert Simon, the man who conceived the idea of 'satisficing', that the concept has influenced such a wide variety of disciplines. To name a few: Computer science, game theory, economics, political science, evolutionary biology, and philosophy have all been enriched by reflection on the contrast between choosing what is satisfactory and choosing what is best. Indeed, these disciplines have cross-fertilized one another through the concept. So one finds satisficing computer models of evolutionary development, satisficing economic models of international relations, satisficing applications of game theory within economics, and philosophical accounts of all of these.

Philosophical interest in the concept of satisficing itself represents a convergence. The fecund and appealing idea of choosing what is satisfactory finds a place in the theory of practical reason, or thinking about what to do. The appeal of the concept derives partly from the fact that what is satisfactory is, well, satisfying. Satisfaction is generally good, and goods of this generality feature prominently in any account of practical reason. More noteworthy is the fact that the concept of satisficing finds application from so many perspectives, even within the relatively narrow confines of moral theory.

In any conversation of this complexity it is always in point to ask whether the participants are talking about the same thing. So of course this issue arises with respect to the essays collected in this volume. I will not try to resolve that issue here; instead, I would like to explore the starting points that have led the authors to their views about satisficing. As so often happens in any theoretical enterprise, where one begins has a crucial – and often decisive – impact on where one ends up, at least if one's conclusion follows from one's premises.

Simon Says

Among the first statements of his account of satisficing is Simon's essay "A Behavioral Model of Rational Choice."[1] Several contributions in this volume summarize Simon's argument, so I will be brief. After characterizing the choice situation and defining his terms, Simon contends that in typical choice situations the application of classic rules of choice such as "max-min," the "probabilistic rule," and the "certainty rule" involves calculative and cognitive skills that no human being possesses. Maximizing expected utility – or choosing one's actions so that they are most likely to bring about states of affairs that one prefers – seems out of reach for people like us. Simplification seems to be in order.

Simon simplifies rational choice along two dimensions. One is the value function. Maximization requires rational agents to assign a utility, or numerical index of preference, to each possible outcome of every available alternative action. Everything that might happen after one acts must be rated on a common numerical scale. Putting the point this way already seems daunting. Simon's model allows agents instead to use a simpler evaluation function in two values, (1,0), corresponding to "satisfactory" and "unsatisfactory."[2] So rather than, for example, having to decide exactly how much better two heads are than one, we might simply say that both are satisfactory, and zero heads would be unsatisfactory.

The second dimension of simplification appears in Simon's satisficing rule itself. According to that rule, rationality requires an agent first to identify the set of all satisfactory outcomes of the choice situation, and then to choose an alternative all of whose outcomes are in the set of satisfactory outcomes. More briefly, it's rational to choose any action that guarantees a satisfactory outcome. That way, whatever happens, one will be satisfied. This rule is simpler than maximizing in virtue of eliminating probabilities from rational choice. For when I maximize, I must weight the utility of each possible outcome by the probability that it will occur.

An example might help make the simplification more evident, mainly by exposing the complexity of maximizing. Suppose that I am at the racetrack planning to make a bet. I am prepared to make one of three choices: no bet, a $10 bet on Toodle-oo, or a $10 bet on Beetlebaum. The guaranteed outcome of no bet is that I lose nothing and keep my

$10. The odds on Toodle-oo are 4:1, which means the payoff if the horse wins would be $50 ($40 plus the $10 bet). The odds also indicate that in the oddsmakers' judgment the horse has a 0.2 probability or 20 percent chance of winning. Beetlebaum, on the other hand, is the long shot, paying 24:1. My $10 bet would yield $250 if Beetlebaum won, but there's only a 0.04 probability or 4 percent chance of that. Let's call these options N (no bet), T ($10 on Toodle-oo), and B ($10 on Beetlebaum).

We can then calculate the expected utility of each of these options according to the following formula:

$$EU(A) = [P(O_1/A) \times U(O_1)] + [P(O_2/A) \times U(O_2)] + \ldots + [P(O_i/A) \times U(O_i)]$$

Each of the O_i represents a possible outcome of the act A, $U(O_i)$ is the utility of that outcome, and $P(O_i/A)$ is the probability of O_i given A.[3] We can thus calculate the expected utilities of each of our three acts. Let's assume that utility is convertible with dollars.

$$EU(N) = P(\text{no loss}) \times U(\text{no loss}) = 1 \times 10 = 10$$
$$EU(T) = [P(\text{T wins}) \times U(\text{T wins})] + [P(\text{T loses}) \times U(\text{T loses})]$$
$$= [0.2 \times 50] + [0.8 \times -10]$$
$$= 10 - 8 = 2$$
$$EU(B) = [P(\text{B wins}) \times U(\text{B wins})] + [P(\text{B loses}) \times U(\text{B loses})]$$
$$= [0.04 \times 250] + [0.96 \times -10]$$
$$= 10 - 9.6 = 0.4$$

Clearly, if that's all there is to the choice situation, then the maximizing choice is not to bet. But I have probably omitted an element of the second two alternatives, namely the enjoyment of betting. Suppose that the excitement alone is worth $10 to me; in that case, I should add 10 to the expected utilities of T and B (but not to N, where I make no bet), and the bet on Toodle-oo emerges as the best choice. In any case, the complexity of the calculation – even for this simplistic example – is evident.

Now contrast Simon's satisficing approach. First, I rate the outcomes as satisfactory or unsatisfactory. Suppose I rate as satisfactory winning more than $100 or losing $10 (because that would mean I had had a chance to win); no loss or gain (the outcome of not betting) is an unsatisfactory outcome. In that case, N would be irrational according to the satisficing rule, because it would guarantee an unsatisfactory outcome. T would also be eliminated by the rule, because it has a possible outcome that is unsatisfactory (namely, winning $50). Hence, the satisficing rule identifies B

as the rational choice, because all of its possible outcomes are satisfactory. Notice that I have assigned no utilities or probabilities and performed no calculations. I have, of course, evaluated the outcomes, but only to the extent that I have rated them as "satisfactory" or "unsatisfactory."

Simon's satisficing rule can also function in another way. Suppose you find yourself searching for alternatives because they are not all in view. In that case, it is impossible to apply expected utility theory to all the alternatives, because they aren't known. Simon's satisficing rule can be employed as a "stopping rule" in this kind of choice situation. That is, it can provide a principled way to stop searching for alternatives. So if you were looking for a suitable wine to serve with dinner, you might adopt as a rule the idea of stopping your search upon finding a satisfactory wine – one that is "good enough." This approach is consistent with the other sort of satisficing, inasmuch as you use a simplified valuation function (satisfactory, unsatisfactory) instead of assigning utilities to every possibility, and you choose a course of action that is guaranteed to be satisfactory.

The computational tractability and theoretical simplicity of satisficing are its most attractive features for Simon. And, at least initially, he presents the model of rationality as both normatively and descriptively more adequate for human beings than a maximizing conception. It is more normatively adequate in making rationality feasible for creatures like us. How could we be required to maximize, when in most cases we cannot? A maximizing conception of practical rationality entails that virtually all of our actions are irrational, and that consequence seems counterintuitive. Yet defenders of maximizing insist that their conception sets a standard against which human choices can be judged: Our choices are rational *to the extent that* they approximate the ideal established by the maximizing conception. Moreover, maximizing theories are most defensible when they incorporate constraints (time, money, cognitive resources, etc.). Such theories propose as the normative standard not bare maximizing, but maximizing within given constraints. This debate has implications for maximizing conceptions of rationality, such as rational choice theory, because if a satisficing model is normatively superior, then rational choice theory loses its claim to be the best account of practical reason.

On the other hand, satisficing models can claim to be descriptively adequate, as when they contend to be better accounts of the way people actually choose. Does anyone actually rate all the possible outcomes along a single scale of utility? Don't many of us think, upon reaching a particular outcome, "Well, that'll do"? As many of the contributions will remind us, satisficing is rational as a time- and other resource-saving strategy: Given our limited resources, we sometimes settle for what's good enough in order to devote resources elsewhere. We could hold out for the best price when buying or selling a car, but that could consume a lot of time and energy that we would prefer to spend elsewhere. And so we take an offer that is good enough. Defenders of maximizing have a response to this claim of descriptive superiority; I'll return to it later.

Supererogation

The concept of supererogation has for many years been at home in "common sense morality." Meaning "above what is required," supererogatory acts exceed some threshold, typically a threshold of moral duty. Heroic and saintly acts are often regarded as "above and beyond the call of duty," and they are paradigm examples of morally supererogatory types of action. Morality might require me to assist a stranger in an emergency if the situation presents little or no cost or risk to me, for example by calling 911. But I am probably not morally required to risk my life to assist someone I don't know. Not required, but if I choose to help anyway, that's something especially admirable, something supererogatory.

Michael Slote has argued that the concept of supererogation can be applied analogously in the context of practical reasoning.[4] Just as we are often not required to do the *morally* best action, so we are often not required to do the *rationally* best action. Slote goes to considerable lengths to spell out the analogy, arguing by reference to a range of cases which he finds intuitively satisfying that in many contexts one might rationally decline to do an action that one judged better than the action one in fact chose. His satisficing conception of rationality emerges as a competitor to a maximizing account in virtue of capturing the appealing idea that rationality does not always require us to do and choose the very best of everything.

An interesting feature that emerges from Slote's view – and a point of contention among defenders of the satisficing conception of rationality – is that it can be rational to choose an option that one judges to be *inferior*. Suppose I prefer Zinfandel to Shiraz, and suppose I have a bottle of each. Other things equal, one might expect that I would choose the Zinfandel, in virtue of the fact that I prefer it. Yet Slote contends that I need not – that rationality does not require me to, that it would not be irrational of me not to – choose the bottle that I prefer. If the Shiraz is satisfactory, then I can rationally choose it.

To see why this position is puzzling, remember that when I say, "I prefer Zinfandel," that means I prefer it at the moment of choice, and so I'm not indifferent between the two. I might prefer Shiraz under some circumstances, but those don't apply (or I wouldn't have the preference that I do have at the moment of choice). The concept of preference is closely linked to choice: Ordinarily, many theorists suppose, preference determines rational choice, so that to prefer something is to be disposed to choose it when the time comes. True, the Shiraz is satisfactory; but, according to the story, I *prefer* the Zinfandel. My preference presumably captures all the reasons that I have for choice. Tote them all up, and I like the Zinfandel better. So how could it be rational to choose the Shiraz? The fact that it is satisfactory doesn't seem to do the trick.

But things are not necessarily as bad as they might seem for Slote and others who defend this kind of strong view of satisficing. The line of thinking that problematizes satisficing depends on a particular conception of 'preference' and an assessment of actions in terms of their outcomes. This thinking is, crucially, consequentialist, because it evaluates actions by how well they succeed in bringing about preferred consequences. Yet, as the discussion of supererogation might suggest, it is possible to think of rationality more in terms of duties than consequences. The concept of supererogation – of actions above and beyond what duty requires – is at home in deontology, not consequentialism, which is typically understood as a family of theories embodying a maximizing conception of the good. If right action is the best, how could one go "above and beyond" that? We might understand rationality to impose certain cognitive and practical duties on us, duties that are related to our preferences but not necessarily cashed out in consequentialist terms. Our rational duties might thus impose a threshold on our actions, such that if we fail to meet or exceed that threshold we act irrationally. Yet it does not follow, on this view, that rationality demands always seeking the most preferred outcome. Our duties need not be that stringent – indeed, many theorists argue that they are not so for moral duties. The details of this sort of view would have to be spelled out; some of the contributions in this volume approach, in interestingly different ways, this task.

Moderation

An idea that appears several times in this volume is the notion that the adoption of satisficing as a strategy of rational choice exhibits a virtue, especially the virtue of moderation. This point seems to apply a kind of moral evaluation to rational choice. Maximizing and optimizing can seem greedy: Those who maximize are by definition always seeking more, indeed as much as possible. Misers maximize their money, gluttons maximize their food, sadomasochists maximize pain, and hedonists maximize pleasure. In each of these cases, and perhaps generally, maximizing appears to be morally objectionable. We need not think it is maximizing alone that is morally objectionable in these vices; gluttony and greed might be wrong for other reasons as well. But they each involve maximizing, and some theorists claim that this feature contributes to their wrongness.

In contrast, moderation has from antiquity been regarded a virtue. True, theorists have defined the term differently – Aristotle's *sophrosune* is distinct from the moderation of genteel British society praised by Victorian novelists, for example. Yet when contrasted with maximizing, the points of overlap among these concepts might be more significant than their differences. For essential to any concept of moderation is the idea of steering between excess and deficiency: neither too much nor too little. And to have application, the idea of avoiding excess must generally eschew maximizing. Those who pursue moderation might thus be led to embrace a model of practical rationality given in other than maximizing terms.

Moderate folks – or anyone else who pursues the virtue of moderation – might prefer to understand practical rationality in terms of satisficing rather than maximizing. For in satisficing one need not always seek the best or the most. To seek what is good enough – especially when the best is an option – might emerge as an expression of the virtue of moderation. In the cafeteria line, I might see that I could take three pieces of chocolate cake and maximize my enjoyment. But I might on reflection decide that three pieces are too many, and that one is enough and so the rational choice. This kind of deliberation embodies the intuitive appeal of a satisficing account of rationality for proponents of the virtue of moderation.

Notice that the form of argument here is distinct from that linking supererogation with satisficing. There, it was an analogy that provided the conceptual link. Rationality is supposed to be akin to morality in imposing practical duties. These duties are such that some actions meet them, others exceed them, and still others fall short of meeting them. Maximizing is analogous to morally supererogatory actions in exceeding the duties imposed by rationality. Satisficing is akin to morally permissible actions that are not heroic or otherwise supererogatory: In satisficing we fulfill our rational obligations while recognizing that it is possible to be "super-rational" and maximize. The argument here, in contrast, is that the pursuit or exercise of a virtue rationally leads one to choose in a distinctive way. The moderate choice is a satisficing choice; and in general a satisficing conception of practical rationality seems more moderate. Satisficing emerges as, if not itself a virtue, a strategy of choice that we might often use in the service of or to express a virtue.

Not everyone finds this line of thinking persuasive. David Schmidtz, for one, has challenged the notion that moderation and satisficing exhibit any interesting conceptual connection (see Chapter 2). He points out that the contrast class of the moderate is the immoderate, not the maximizing. The satisficer as such is satisfied with a certain bundle of goods, but nothing in the idea of satisficing ensures that the satisfactory bundle is moderate. I might find three dozen cookies a satisfactory serving, but my doing so does not make that quantity moderate. Similarly, moderation need not be satisfactory in every case. Moreover, the maximizer could end up with a moderate amount, if time and other resource limitations make further pursuit of the good at stake too costly.

Finally, we might note that the form of argument here is odd. Why should theorizing about practical rationality be responsive to moral virtues like moderation? Some theorists would certainly approve of this connection: Those who discover a substantial connection between rationality and morality – like a Kantian who identifies practical rationality as the criterion of morality – would insist that any adequate account of practical reasoning will have to end up endorsing all (and perhaps only) moral actions. Such an approach might be correct, but it seems to beg the question against instrumentalists, who often defend maximizing conceptions of practical rationality. That is, the defender of satisficing claims that employing the strategy is rational in virtue of its expressing certain virtues, whereas an instrumentalist might challenge the rationality of "virtuous" action that fails to maximize ("If you're so smart, why ain't you rich?"). This approach to defending satisficing thus seems at home in a larger defense of a more substantive conception of practical reasoning, one that links rationality and morality in substantive ways.

Consequentialism

In an early paper on satisficing, Michael Slote challenged the intuitive connection between consequentialism and maximizing.[5] From James Mill and Jeremy Bentham, utilitarians and other consequentialists have embraced a maximizing conception of right action. John Stuart Mill's principle of utility, for example, declares an action right "in proportion as it tends to promote happiness," or pleasure and the absence of pain.[6] It is easy to see the appeal of such a view, once we recognize that the fundamental insight of consequentialism is to make the world a better place. Given a choice, it makes sense to choose the best. Once we make the consequentialist move and declare that the only features of actions relevant to moral evaluation are their consequences, we seem to have every reason to strive to bring about the best consequences we can, whether 'best' is cashed out in terms of pleasure, preference satisfaction, or agent-neutral value.

Slote presents satisficing consequentialism as an alternative conception of morality. His argument claims several virtues for the conception, including the capacity to account for supererogation. It's difficult to see how a maximizing conception of morality can allow room for supererogation: If I'm required in every case to choose the best available option, how could I ever do *more* than morality required? What would supererogation mean in a maximizing context? So a possible objection to maximizing consequentialism is that it leaves no conceptual room in moral theory for supererogation. Satisficing consequentialism allows for supererogation by, in principle, leaving a gap between a morally permissible action that is good enough and one that is the best, allowing that in some cases the two might coincide.

Notice that the earlier section on supererogation focused on the idea of rational, rather than moral, supererogation. There, we came to the idea of satisficing through the theory of rationality, and the point was to introduce the concept of rational supererogation and to build a theory around that idea. Here, the concept of moral supererogation is supposed to be intuitive, and we entertain the idea of an alternative to traditional maximizing consequentialism in order to account for moral supererogation.

It is, of course, open to defenders of a more traditional consequentialism to jettison the concept of supererogation. Though intuitive, the idea of supererogation does not hook up well with the idea of rational choice. Given a choice between A and B, if A is better, why choose B? The point is especially pressing if the values are moral: If A is morally better, on what moral ground could one choose B? Defenders of maximizing consequentialism might point out that the notion of supererogation is most at home in a deontological theory, where the concept of duty plays a significant role. Once the idea of duty is in place, it's easier to make

sense of how an action can be "above and beyond" duty. Because consequentialism has traditionally found less place for the idea of duty (and
deontology's correlative evaluation of action in terms of motivation), it
might make sense to resist the idea that supererogation ought to play
a significant role in consequentialist thought. If that's right, part of the
intuitive motivation for satisficing consequentialism goes away.

Incommensurability

Here's a general approach to arguing that satisficing is not a distinctive
choice strategy, but rather just one kind of optimizing strategy. First ask:
In virtue of what is an alternative "good enough"? The satisficer as such
chooses an alternative because it is, in some way, good enough, whether
or not it is the best. Assume that doing so is rational, in some sense. But
something about the alternative must rationalize or justify the choice: It
is presumably some feature of the alternative that makes it good enough.
However the chooser answers this question, the feature(s) mentioned
can be built into a conception of good, utility, or whatever according to
which the choice is optimizing. Or so holds this line of thought.

This strategy takes advantage of the conceptual connection discussed
earlier between preference and choice. Where preference is clear, it
seems to determine choice. What would it mean to prefer A over B but
to choose B? Such choice is surely *possible*: One might be under a spell,
or in the grip of a passion, or otherwise impaired and prevented from
executing a rational choice. But such instances are hardly paradigms of
rationality. For the choice of B over A to be rational, it must be superior
to A in some respect, or at least equal to A on balance. One's initial description of the choice situation might be inadequate or incomplete in
some respect relevant to understanding the choice as rational. So, the
proponent of this view will argue, once we take into account the entire
picture, B emerges as the maximizing choice.[7]

For example, suppose that I decide to buy a certain model of car to
drive to work, and suppose I do so because it is "good enough." What
makes it good enough? I might value the reliability of the car, its purchase price being within a certain range, the style and comfort, and so
on. In all of these respects, the model I settle on is satisfactory. Now, if we
understand my preferences that pertain to the car purchase to include
budgetary preferences (both time and money), then it's possible to por-
tray this choice as maximizing over all of my preferences. Sure, the car is
"good enough" with respect to reliability and style. But I do not wish to

spend any more time or money making this purchase than I must, and so within those constraints the choice of the first model with satisfactory features along other dimensions emerges as the best overall. That's how this view collapses all satisficing into optimizing: If rational choice is to be intimately linked to an account of rational preference satisfaction, then satisficing is rational only if optimific. The present instance illustrates the general strategy for reducing satisficing to a kind of optimizing.[8]

One obvious way to resist this kind of strategy would be to claim that the rational preference account is a mistake. That kind of account presupposes that all values are commensurable, so that we might always weigh any two alternatives against each other pairwise to determine which is better. In the face of value incommensurability, it will not necessarily be possible to place every pair of alternatives on a common scale such as utility. And if not, then traditional maximizing approaches – which after all are mathematical functions that depend on some common scale of measurement – will fail to yield an account of rational choice.

This is not the place to survey all the different ways of understanding value incommensurability or of incorporating limited or widespread incommensurability into the account of rational choice. For now, it is enough to observe two quite distinct responses to value incommensurability. One perspective can be found in Michael Weber's paper (Chapter 5). In it, he argues that we can understand our lives from two distinct and incommensurable temporal perspectives: that of the moment and that of a whole life. In some instances, an alternative might be best from one perspective and suboptimal from the other. Weber contends that the incommensurability of the perspectives might yield a *rational permission* to satisfice with respect to one of them. This permission is supposed to parallel an agent-centered moral permission in moral theory to do other than what would maximize agent-neutral well-being. On some consequentialist accounts it is moral, for example, to save the life of my child in preference to saving two strangers, and we might account for this discrepancy from the model of maximizing agent-neutral value in terms of an agent-centered permission that conditions the demands of maximizing. Similarly in the theory of individual rational choice, the whole-life and momentary perspectives might condition each other, for instance with respect to career ambitions. One might, from the whole-life perspective, aspire to career greatness and yet at any particular moment be unwilling to sacrifice leisure, family, or other ends to do what greatness requires. In this instance the values of the momentary perspective condition those of the whole-life perspective, yielding a rational permission to seek less than what is optimal. Incommensurability thus underwrites a form of rational satisficing, on Weber's account.

Henry Richardson (Chapter 6) also argues from a standpoint that recognizes value incommensurability, yet he reaches a conclusion quite different from Weber's. The heart of Richardson's argument is the observation that a satisficing conception of practical rationality places incompatible demands on the theory. On the one hand, the notion of "tradeoffs" implicit in the idea of settling for what is "good enough" suggests that satisficing will be a rational strategy only when applied to relatively local pursuits, such as buying a car or choosing one's clothes. One cannot satisfice with respect to one's global goal of pursuing the good, because the global context would not provide any constraints such that an alternative would be good enough. In the global context, one chooses the best option, though locally satisficing can be rational. That said, the theorist of satisficing must provide some metric along which to assess some alternatives as good enough and others as not that good. Ordinarily, the metric is utility or preference satisfaction, and these notions are quite global. Richardson thus identifies a tension within the theory of satisficing: Although applicable only to local ends, its metric is a global one. This global metric, moreover, runs afoul of value incommensurability of the sort we confront every day, according to Richardson, who has his own non-optimizing, non-satisficing theory of rationality. In this case, it seems, incommensurability is a reason to reject a satisficing theory.

No doubt it is too quick to oppose Weber and Richardson in this fashion. Weber addresses incommensurable perspectives, and Richardson treats incommensurable values. And yet their contributions can speak to each other: The value incommensurability that drives Richardson's account might be accommodated differently by Weber's diverse temporal perspectives. The latter's account of choice in terms of temporal perspectives might be built into different values by Richardson. Theorists of rational choice will benefit from these reflections on incommensurability and how to handle it.

Notes

1. H. A. Simon, "A Behavioral Model of Rational Choice," *Quarterly Journal of Economics* 69 (1955): 99–118.
2. Alternatively, one might adopt a three-valued function, (1,0,−1), corresponding to "win, draw, or lose." This nuance of Simon's discussion need not concern us.

3. For an excellent and straightforward introduction to expected utility theory, see Michael D. Resnik, *Choices*. Minneapolis: University of Minnesota Press, 1987.
4. Michael Slote, *Beyond Optimizing: A Study of Rational Choice*. Cambridge, Mass.: Harvard University Press, 1989.
5. Michael Slote, "Satisficing Consequentialism," *Proceedings of the Aristotelian Society* 58 supp. (1984): 139–163.
6. J. S. Mill, *Utilitarianism, Second Edition*. Indianapolis: Hackett, 2001, p. 7.
7. Notice that this argument does not depend on a so-called "revealed preference" account, according to which we reveal our actual preferences through our choices. Rather, it explains the initial expression of preference as perhaps only partial, and thus one that incompletely or inadequately characterizes the alternatives under consideration.
8. I develop this argument in Michael Byron, "Satisficing and Optimality," *Ethics* 109 (1998): 67–93.

1

Two Views of Satisficing

Michael Slote

The title of this essay should naturally put knowledgeable readers in mind of a certain kind of disagreement about the nature of (rational) satisficing. Many economists, philosophers, and others have held that satisficing makes sense only in relation to a larger overall maximizing or optimizing perspective, and on such a view it is rational to seek less than the best one can only if for example one is in circumstances where maximizing is impossible or where local satisficing is a means to overall optimality. For convenience, let us call this the instrumental conception of satisficing.

It is also possible to conceive satisficing as sometimes being *non-instrumentally* rational, as a form of decision making that is sometimes, as we can say, *inherently* or *intrinsically* rational. This has been and still is decidedly the minority view on the rationality involved in satisficing, but the disagreement between those who maintain that all rational satisficing is instrumental and those who maintain that satisficing can sometimes be rational on non-instrumental or intrinsic grounds has been an interesting feature of the recent philosophical landscape.[1] That interestingness may well be one reason for the existence of the present book, but I don't propose to continue this particular debate in my contribution to this volume. In fact, I know of others who will be carrying it forward here, and I very much look forward to seeing what they have to say.

What I want to do here is consider a rather different distinction having to do with satisficing. Although some significant criticisms of intrinsically rational satisficing have been made elsewhere and in the present volume, I shall here be assuming that there can be non-instrumental justifications for satisficing (or being moderate in one's desires). I will be doing so because it is only against the backdrop of such an assumption that one can raise the issue that I *do* want to consider here, one that I have not explicitly raised in any other venue and that may help us better understand the nature and implications of intrinsic satisficing. The question of intrinsic versus instrumental satisficing is one concerning the kind of rationality involved in satisficing. But satisficing, maximizing, and optimizing are all naturally conceived as occurring *in relation to* options or outcomes that are good for individuals, and the issue I want to raise has to do with the connection or lack of it between intrinsically rational satisficing and the personal goods with regard to which the satisficing occurs.

Roughly speaking, the question is whether personal goods like pleasure are in an appropriate sense *independent* of the satisficing, optimizing, or maximizing that may occur with respect to them or whether, and alternatively, such goods are partially *constituted by or dependent on* the decision-making attitude an individual takes with respect to them. That, at any rate, is the still somewhat obscure or inchoate question I wish to pose and consider, and I hope that, when I have had a chance to say more about the question and about how one might answer it, the reader will see why it is important to consider it. We need to think about whether satisficing should be conceived intrinsically or instrumentally, but a differently focused discussion of what we should say about the relationship between personal goods and non-instrumental satisficing may actually help us decide that other issue. However, the question of the relationship between personal goods and satisficing also raises large issues about the relationship between rational virtue and human good or flourishing, questions about the viability and promise of virtue ethics, and questions about the *kind* of virtue ethics, if any, we ought to be pursuing.

I raise all these issues in what follows, though not at the length that they ultimately deserve; but I want to begin by laying some groundwork for subsequent discussion. After briefly rehearsing some of the considerations that I think favor intrinsically rational satisficing, I situate the problem of the relationship between such satisficing and human good(s) within a set of larger issues about the nature and viability of virtue ethics. Having done that, and having said what I think can be said in favor of the virtue-ethical view that satisficing and a degree of moderation are partly constitutive of certain personal goods, I hope finally to show that certain Platonic diologues anticipate the view I will have been describing and defending. But let us begin.

Satisficing, Moderation, and Teleology

One thing that led me to believe that satisficing is or can be intrinsically rational is the seeming reasonableness of being satisfied with less good than one might seek to have or enjoy. If I have enjoyed a good meal, I might enjoy eating more, but I may be satisfied with what I have already had and so turn down the chance for more food. In order to do this, I don't have to think of the enjoyment of the additional food as *not really a good thing*. Feeling that things are fine as they are doesn't necessarily mean that they couldn't be any better, and I think one kind of moderation involves being satisfied with what one takes to be good enough and fine and *not wanting, not feeling the need for, anything more or better*.

This kind of moderation involves being moderate in one's desires or needs, and it stands in marked contrast with the instrumental moderation praised, for example, by the Epicureans, moderation that involves *not giving in* to some desire when one knows, for example, that it would harm one or harm others if one did. People who don't eat because they don't want to ruin their appetite for dinner or in order to avoid gaining weight show self-control, but people moderate (or modest) in their desires don't eat because they don't *desire* any more food. And, as I said, this doesn't require such moderate people to think that additional food wouldn't be a good thing (momentarily) in their lives. So there is an important difference between the kind of instrumental moderation, or satisficing, that demonstrates control or mastery over one's desires and an intrinsic moderation, or satisficing, that consists in (to some extent) *lacking desires that need controlling*.

The distinction also applies outside the sphere of gustatory pleasures. You can limit your career ambitions, for example, because you want to spend a good deal of time with your children and because you think that you (and your children) will on the whole be better off if you don't try to be the best lawyer you can be. But such self-limitation is an example of instrumental moderation or satisficing that seeks the best or most good overall while choosing less than the best in one area or in one respect. However, one might simply have modest ambitions and have no aspiration beyond, say, being a really fine lawyer like one's mother. The fact that one doesn't strive for anything better than that may not reflect self-control that reins in a desire in order to maximize overall happiness or desire-satisfaction but may simply indicate a limit to one's aspirations (a point of improvement beyond which one feels no desire or need to go).

Now these descriptions seek to be true to how people in general (people not influenced by economic or philosophical theory) think about their goals, decisions, and actions. But there are and have been many objections to simply accepting the foregoing "manifest image" of (much of) human thought, desire, and activity. However, for purposes of this paper, I won't engage with those objections and will simply assume that human lives exemplify the distinction between intrinsic and instrumental satisficing (or moderation). The question, then, that I want to pose in the light of that (large) assumption concerns the relation or connection between intrinsically satisficing moderation and the putative goods with respect to which a person satisfices or demonstrates moderation. (From now on, my talk of satisficing will refer to the intrinsic kind unless I indicate otherwise.)

Within certain limits, it is natural to think of enjoyment and pleasure as at least momentary goods in people's lives. A philosopher can get people to wonder whether a sadist benefits even momentarily from enjoying the unhappiness of others, but when it comes to ordinary human pleasures, we naturally think of them as good. But the thought that something would be enjoyable or momentarily good for us doesn't automatically make us want the thing, and that means that it makes at least some sense to suppose that things like pleasure and enjoyment may count as potential personal goods independently of our attitude toward them.

As described previously, satisficing about career achievements or gustatory enjoyment involves satisficing with respect to goods that count as such independently, for example, of whether we want them. This is not really hedonism, because even if the description of gustatory satisficing involved a kind of automatic assumption that (normal, nonsadistic) enjoyments constitute good things in our lives, a satisficing attitude toward advancement, achievement, or success in one's career doesn't have to assume that these things constitute personal goods only to the extent that they bring us pleasure or enjoyment. (I shall say more about this shortly.) Even so, we have some tendency to think of achievement and the like as good things *independently of our desire for them*, and when one combines such thinking with an attitude of tolerance or acceptance toward those who have limited aspirations toward achievement or success, one ends up (as I in effect ended up previously) thinking of rational moderation or satisficing as an attitude one can have to goods whose status as such is independent of the attitude one takes or has taken toward them. On such a conception, rational satisficing involves (on non-instrumental grounds) taking less rather than more of what is or would be good for one, and if maximizing counts as immoderate and even perhaps *irrational* or *lacking in virtue*, one is then being immoderate, irrational, or unvirtuous with respect to things or experiences whose status as good is independent of how immoderate (and so forth) one is being.

Such a view resembles so-called teleological theories in ethics, which (according to Rawls and others) treat the concept of the good as prior to the concept of the right. The concept that is primarily at issue in discussions of the rationality of satisficing versus maximizing may be the concept of rationality rather than the notion of the (morally) right, but differing views about whether satisficing or maximizing is rational are all analogous to (different forms of) teleological theories of morality to the extent that they too regard the concept of the good (understood as personal good or well-being) as prior to that of rationality.[2] My earlier description and defense of rational satisficing to that extent assumed a teleological understanding of rationality, even as it called into question an assumption that most teleologists of rationality have assumed, namely, that practical individual rationality involves seeking and doing what is overall *best* for oneself.

Now defenders of *maximizing* individual rationality make or defend an additional assumption to the effect that what is best for one is what involves obtaining the *most* of some good or weighted set of goods. But as I argued in the book referenced earlier, many philosophers have thought that what is *best* for one may not be some *greatest sum or amount* of anything, and such philosophers have gone on to argue that rationality doesn't involve maximizing, even if it does involve *optimizing* with respect to one's own good. The idea of satisficing challenges both maximizing and the more inclusive class of optimizing conceptions of practical rationality, but, given the arguments and considerations canvassed previously, a satisficing conception of individual rationality agrees with these other conceptions in assuming that practical reason is teleological at least to the extent of focusing on independently conceived goods. What I want to suggest now, however, is that satisficing needn't be "teleologized" in this way and that if we really want to understand the significance, the rationality, or virtue of satisficing moderation, we may have to give up on the teleological element that all of the theories of rationality discussed here so far have in common. If we take (certain kinds of) virtue ethics seriously enough, we may be led to think of appetitive and other human goods as owing their status at least in part to the presence of rational and other virtues. Value judgments about virtue, far from depending on value judgments about what is good, may turn out to be the main *basis* for claims about what is good.

Virtue Ethics

We clearly want to be able to distinguish personal goods from what a person (most) wants. If we couldn't, then deliberate self-sacrifice would be ruled out on conceptual grounds, given that a person was doing what, in the circumstances, he or she most wanted to do. But this doesn't mean that we have to view what is good as having that status entirely independent of all attitudes to what counts as good, and as I have just indicated, certain forms of virtue ethics encourage us to question that assumption.

It is difficult to give a strict or accurate definition of everything we want to count as virtue ethics. Most typically, however, we conceive virtue ethics as either playing down issues of right and wrong or – and I believe more promisingly – as offering something different from consequentialist and deontological theories of right and wrong. Virtue ethics doesn't base the moral evaluation of actions in moral rules, law, or principles, and it also doesn't make good consequences the touchstone of its act-evaluations. More can certainly be said, though the more one says about what we mean by 'virtue ethics', the greater the risks of saying something inaccurate (or worse).

But in addition to the differences in how they understand rightness and wrongness, virtue theories – at least most of those dominant in the ancient world – can be seen as having distinctive ideas about the *relation* between rightness and human good or well-being. Classical utilitarianism sees rightness as reducible to facts about well-being: The fact that they produce well-being is what *makes* acts right or morally better. This reduction is possible because well-being is conceived as specifiable independently of the right, in the manner characteristic of all so-called teleological theories; and if we think of well-being in hedonist terms as consisting in pleasure, we assure such independence.

Kant clearly doesn't think rightness or virtue can be reduced to facts about well-being, but neither does he think that a conception of well-being can be grounded in a conception of rightness or virtue. Rather, he thinks that rightness (or virtue) and well-being are "entirely heterogeneous" concepts.[3] Kant is thus a *dualist* regarding the categories of well-being and virtue or rightness. But many virtue ethicists – arguably Plato, Aristotle, and the Stoics – have a quite different view of the relation between virtue (or rightness) and well-being. They don't seek to reduce all virtue to well-being in the manner of certain forms of consequentialism, but neither do they, like Kant, assume dualism with respect to the facts associated with these two concepts. Instead, they can be thought of as monistically understanding well-being in terms of virtue, and this in effect stands utilitarianism on its head.

It would be a bit misleading, however, to say that the Stoics or Plato *reduce* well-being to virtue, because we naturally think of virtue as a higher aspect of our psyches than our capacity to enjoy personal goods. I have elsewhere coined the term "elevates" for how ancient virtue ethics tends to view well-being in relation to virtue (it is difficult to find any less barbarous term that is equally accurate).[4] This term helps to convey the idea that, just as utilitarianism (or ancient Epicureanism) takes virtue "down a peg" by seeing it as embodied totally in facts about human well-being, ancient virtue ethics gives us a more *exalted* view of well-being than we are perhaps accustomed to by claiming that all well-being involves or is equivalent to virtue.[5]

Now not all forms of virtue ethics are elevationist in the sense just mentioned. Epicureanism is as *reductionistic* and *hedonistic* about human good as utilitarianism is, and in the modern world there are forms of virtue ethics which either make no assertions about the connection between well-being and virtue or else accept a kind of Kantian dualism about well-being and virtue.[6]

But Stoicism definitely *is* elevationistic and monistic about the relation between virtue and well-being. It *identifies* well-being with independently understood virtue, says that well-being or a good life *consists in* being virtuous. Such a view taxes our patience, as it taxed Aristotle's, for one thing because of its wildly implausible implication that someone being tortured on the rack but still possessed of virtue is as well off as it is possible to be. However, not all elevationist forms of virtue ethics are as implausible as Stoicism. Aristotle too can be said to have an elevationist conception of the relation between virtue and well-being, even as he rejects the thesis of sheer identity between them that is so distinctive of and implausible about Stoicism. But for reasons too complicated to enter into fully here, I think Aristotle's elevationism isn't all that much more plausible than Stoicism's[7]; and in recent years I have sought to formulate a form of virtue-ethical elevationism that doesn't commit one to saying anything highly implausible and that really can account for the full range of what is good in and about our lives.

Interpreted as elevationist, Aristotle holds that nothing is any good for us unless it is consistent with virtue *taken as a whole*. (Let us leave what is bad for us aside, to simplify our discussion.) This seems a bit extreme (it was certainly thought so by Kant), because it entails, for example, that thieves enjoying their ill-gotten gains don't really benefit from or have anything intrinsically good as a result of those gains. For this and other reasons, I believe it would be preferable to argue that the basic elements of our well-being need only be consistent with or involve *individual* virtues, with different virtues being tied to different elements or aspects of that well-being or a good life.

I have recently argued that Plato has something like this view in mind in certain of his dialogues; and in the final section of this paper, I would like to say more than I did in that book about why I think the Platonic text supports the idea that all personal goods involve some particular virtue.[8] For the present, though, I need to explain why such elevationism may be a plausible view to take about the relation between well-being and virtue. If it turns out to be so, it will also turn out that satisficing moderation should be thought of not as taking place with respect to independently conceived good things, but as a virtue (one among several) that grounds and defines its own particular element or aspect of human welfare or good lives.

The idea that human or personal goods involve distinctive virtues seems plausible initially in regard to *certain sorts* of goods. Most non-hedonists think that love and friendship are among life's greatest non-instrumental goods, but it is arguable that one necessarily lacks love and friendship and what is good about having them in our lives if one is incapable of genuinely caring about and being morally decent toward those one is said to love or be friends with. Relations of enmity or of mutual "using" intuitively don't seem to add something distinctive and distinctively good to our lives, though they can result in or even involve pleasure and other presumed goods. So I am inclined to think that what (the goods of) friendship and love add to our lives is partly constituted by the moral virtuousness that is necessary to and involved in that happening.[9]

Next, consider the good of achieving or accomplishing something. Nonhedonists, especially advocates of "objective list" approaches, frequently mention this as a distinctive good, not reducible to the pleasure or desire-satisfaction to be obtained from achieving things; but once again this good may require its own distinctive virtue in order to make a life better. Genuine achievements require the virtue of perseverance, or strength of purpose. Even Mozart, in whom musical invention seems to have arisen spontaneously, had to write down, develop, and orchestrate the tunes that occurred to him in order to produce his actual compositions; and if the insistence on strength of purpose or perseverance is correct, that would also explain why we don't treat the raw talent as in itself a personal good in someone's life. If the talent isn't developed – is left fallow – then it doesn't seem to represent any sort of life good for the individual who has it; and so the case of talents contrasts intuitively with what we think about achievements – about successfully making something out of or with a talent or ability. And that is a reason to think that what allows (or helps allow) achievements to qualify our lives as better has to do with the particular virtue that achievements by their very nature involve.

I believe that other plausible life goods also depend on distinctive, particular virtues, but rather than discuss other examples that intuitively involve one or another virtue, let us turn to one well-accepted instance of personal good that seems to defy such analysis, namely, pleasure or enjoyment. If this kind of intrinsic or non-instrumental life good lacks any essential relation to any virtue, then assuming we don't want to go to the Stoic extreme of denying that appetitive pleasure is any part of our well-being, monistic elevationism will be in deep trouble; for there will be one instance of human good whose status as such can't be explained in terms that refer to any virtue. However, in the next section I hope to explain why I think that the good we derive from pleasure cannot be properly understood apart from a particular virtue. If that turns out to be correct or even just not obviously incorrect, then virtue-ethical elevationism may be more promising than might first appear, and satisficing or moderation may turn out to be an essential ingredient in or requirement of appetitive and related life goods.

Satisficing and the Constitution of Appetitive Goods

I want to argue now that individuals totally lacking in the virtue of moderation – those insatiably immoderate in their desires, those unwilling ever to satisfice with respect to appetitive pleasures – gain no personal good from the pleasures they frenetically or restlessly pursue and obtain. Moderate individuals who are enjoying food or drink will at a certain point decide that they have had enough enjoyment and stop pursuing, perhaps even turn down, further gustatory or appetitive enjoyment. But totally insatiable people will never feel that they have had enough and will remain thoroughly unsatisfied no matter how much they have had or enjoyed, and it is not counterintuitive to suppose that such individuals gain nothing good (at least non-instrumentally) from their pursuit of pleasure.[10]

We tend to feel sorry for people who are never even partially satisfied with what they have or have obtained, and in feeling thus, I don't think we are necessarily assuming that the insatiable pursuit of gustatory or sexual enjoyment is automatically frustrating and painful. Rather, it seems somewhat plausible to suppose that we feel sorry for such people because their frenetic pleasure and desire for pleasure are never "rounded off" by any sense of *satisfaction* with what they have or have had. When people gain something good for themselves from pleasure, it is, I am suggesting, because the pleasure is part of a "package" containing both pleasure and satisfaction with that pleasure, and my tentative conclusion then is that appetitive goods require virtuous or rational moderation and satisficing in order genuinely to constitute good things in our lives.

Moreover, I am assuming that there is nothing unintuitive about the supposition that some substantial degree of satisfaction with pleasure is necessary for an appetitive or any other pleasure-related good to occur in one's life. I am assuming, in effect, that the pleasure or enjoyment we take from an activity in some sense *anticipates* some measure of satisfaction, and that where the satisfaction – the sense of having had good enough and fine – never comes, the pleasure seems empty, the activity not (intrinsically) worth it. There is something pitiable about insatiability that reminds us of Sisyphus and also of Tantalus.[11] For surely we can say that insatiable, nonsatisficing individuals wish to have or obtain something good in their lives; yet, on the view that I am suggesting, personal good seems always to recede from such individuals as they seek to approach and attain it. So the appetitively insatiable may not only lack a virtue, but, in addition to and as a result of the lack of virtue, act self-defeatingly in regard to their own good.

But why not say, rather, that insatiable individuals do get something good out of their restless and insatiable pursuit of more and more pleasure, namely, whatever pleasure they obtain along the way? Is this really so contrary to common sense? I think not; but neither, as I have been saying, is the claim that appetitively insatiable individuals *get nothing good* from their appetitive pursuit. I don't think common sense is really decisive on this issue, and so what we say may hang on theoretical considerations. If we think that monist elevationism concerning the connection between well-being and virtue is otherwise promising, that may be a reason to accept the idea that appetitive good requires some measure of moderation;

and if we do accept this, then, of course, we have to view the virtue of satisficing moderation as involved in or required by certain goods, rather than as existing in relation to goods understood entirely independent of the moderate or satisficing attitude.[12] We replace an assumption of teleology with something purely virtue-ethical in our understanding of what rational satisficing is all about.[13]

But I can hardly claim to have made a complete defense of monistic elevationism. I have sketched it briefly and indicated some of its scope and unifying power, as well as its implications for our view of appetitive goods. If such elevationism is true, then (mere) pleasure and enjoyment may be independent of our ability to be satisfied with and satisfice with respect to them; but whether, in relation to such pleasure, one's life is even momentarily *better* is an issue that is not similarly independent of one's own attitudes or motivations. The emphasis overall is on how virtue helps to constitute human good(s), and the element of teleology that optimizing and (earlier versions of) satisficing conceptions of rational choice have assumed goes out the window. However, at this point, I would like to say something about why I think some of these ideas were anticipated (or at least adumbrated) by Plato.

Plato and Satisficing

Plato notably holds that all good things possess or exemplify a common property or pattern, and Aristotle famously criticizes this fundamental view in *Nichomachean Ethics*. But Plato makes a somewhat more specific claim about the things that are good in a rather neglected passage in the *Gorgias* (S. 506), where he says that "all good things whatever are good when some virtue is present in us or them." (I use the Jowett translation here and in the quotations that follow.) Leaving aside judgments about functional goodness – but remembering that good knives and good doctors are commonly spoken of as having their "virtues" – and focusing solely upon judgments about intrinsic (non-instrumental) personal good or well-being, Plato's claim implies the elevationist conclusion that all personal good or well-being requires an element of virtue, whether as part of itself or as necessarily accompanying it.[14]

However, as I mentioned earlier, the elevationist idea that various virtues serve to constitute or ground all personal good(s) faces its greatest challenge in the area of appetitive goods. If all elements of human well-being require distinctive virtues and if, more generally, human well-being is to be explained in terms of virtue rather than vice versa, one has to be able to point to a virtue distinctively required by or involved in all appetitive goods; and it is at least initially not obvious what that distinctive virtue might be.

But we have now seen (or at least defended the view) that all appetitive goodness requires a measure of *satisfaction with* appetitive pleasure or enjoyment – requires that one have some degree of moderation and have a satisficing attitude (or motivational structures) with respect to such pleasure and enjoyment. In addition, though, we think of moderation and a satisficing attitude as exemplifying a form – one form – of virtue. Those who can control their strong appetites have the virtue of self-control and may be said to possess the virtue of instrumental moderation. But we also think better of those whose appetites aren't limitless and insatiable than of those whose appetites *are* like that, and this has something to do with the fact that the insatiable pursuer of sexual and gustatory pleasure seems pathetically needy and dependent on such things. So intrinsic moderation or satisficing also seem to us a virtue, and Plato's view in the *Gorgias* that all goods require (their) virtues is thus borne out in what would naturally seem to many to be its most problematic instance.[15]

However, what would really show Plato to have anticipated the elevationism and the nonteleological view of satisficing I want to defend would be evidence that Plato regarded appetitive good in particular as requiring a virtue like moderation. It is one thing for Plato to make a general statement, as he does in the *Gorgias*, connecting all good with virtue. It is another for him to have realized the implications of that general claim for our understanding of appetitive goods and to have indicated the connection between such good and a virtue like moderation in such a way that this particular instance of his generalization doesn't seem like a counterexample to it. I want to claim now that Plato does in fact take such an additional step – though, as we shall also see, he does so somewhat obscurely and in somewhat metaphorical language.

I think we can see this best by looking at Plato's *Philebus*.[16] The elevationism I have briefly defended in regard to appetitive goods doesn't see all pleasure as automatically constituting or yielding personal good (to this extent it agrees with Stoicism and disagrees with hedonism). For appetitive good to occur, pleasure or enjoyment has to be rounded off by (accompanied by) a degree of *satisfaction with it.*[17] Thus, in my view, there have to be two elements in or accompanying any appetitive good: pleasure and satisfaction with the pleasure. And when we look at the *Philebus*, I think we see Plato working on (or struggling with) the idea that appetitive good has to be constituted out of two elements. But in order to make this plausible, we need to take a look at some of the more general themes of that dialogue (I am going to be brief and rather selective).

The *Philebus* raises some general issues about how things are constituted – what makes them be what they are – in terms of a contrast between the infinite and the finite. Everything in the world and even the world itself can be seen as a mixture or coming together of finite with infinite, and Plato illustrates this idea with respect to music, language, and a number of other areas. Both linguistic and musical sound are, he says, infinite in their potential, but something definite (and good) is achieved through language and music only if infinity is ordered or circumscribed in finite ways (S. 17).

Plato also discusses pleasure in relation to the issue of finite versus infinite. He says that "pleasure is infinite and belongs to the class which neither has, nor ever will have in itself, a beginning, middle, or end of its own" (S. 31). He seems to think that pleasure is not in itself good (S. 32, 66), and the issue of when and how pleasure is or becomes good then naturally arises. Plato's answer seems to be that pleasure can be good only if it is ordered or constrained by measure or harmony that partakes of the finite rather than of the infinite. The infinite, he thinks, cannot make pleasure good (after all, pleasure is by its nature infinite, but not all pleasure is good), so it can be or become good in relation to the infinite only by being *limited* (see S. 28).

Now Plato does talk at various points in the *Philebus* about the (for him) problematic status of "mixed" pleasures, pleasures admixed with pain. But his view that not all pleasure is good and that it is or becomes good only by being limited or subject to measure in some way isn't, I think, (exclusively) based on the problem of mixed pleasures. What he says about the finite versus the infinite suggests at least to me that he holds the logically independent thesis that pleasure is good only when it is taken *in measure* and only when there are *limits* to one's desire or appetite for pleasure. And because Plato takes measure in the soul to be a constitutive element of the psychic harmony that constitutes virtue (see, e.g., S. 64–5), he is saying that we gain something really (if merely temporarily) good from pleasure only if our desire is measured, limited, non-insatiable, moderate, and *virtuous* (see especially S. 52).

In that case, Plato seems to accept the idea that appetitive goods require virtue in the soul that enjoys them, and given the general claim he makes in the *Gorgias* and the fact that the virtue requirement is much more obvious with respect to non-appetitive good than with respect to appetitive ones, he seems to be committed to elevationism as a general thesis about the relation between virtue and human well-being. Plato says that "from a[n] ... admixture of the finite and the infinite come the seasons, and all the delights of life ..." (S. 26); and because Plato, on the present interpretation, so thoroughly anticipates what I have said in defense of elevationism (here and elsewhere), I am inclined to call my own view "Platonic elevationism."

This would also help to distinguish the less bold form of elevationism I wish to espouse from the forms embodied in Stoicism and Aristotle, with their (to my mind) less palatable implications. The Stoic idea that there are no appetitive *goods* (though certain appetitive pleasures may belong to what the Stoics called the class of the "preferred") seems a nonstarter. Aristotle's elevationism (to the extent that it is plausible to interpret him as holding such a view) entails that the obtaining of good must be compatible with *virtue as a whole*, and for reasons I have defended in the book referenced earlier, this view has the implausible implications that vicious people gain nothing good from their immoralities and that what we suffer in the name of virtue doesn't make us worse off. So if we are to accept or develop elevationism, I think it should be in a form that doesn't require all of virtue, but only single (but specific) virtues, in order for various personal goods to exist in someone's life. And that is what Platonic elevationism amounts to.

The Platonic roots have helped to convince me that the picture of satisficing that emerges from our weaker form of elevationism is worth pursuing. But if we accept such elevationism, then we must renounce teleological conceptions of satisficing in favor of a more virtue-ethical approach to satisficing.[18] On the other hand, if we have or turned out to have objections to (such) virtue ethics, that might encourage us to hold on to the view of non-instrumental satisficing and moderation that I assumed or presupposed in first writing about it, a view of satisficing that sees it as occurring with respect to independent goods that we may or may not strive for or care about. Either way, the picture, at least for the present, is more complicated than I originally thought it was.

Notes

1. Herbert Simon, who introduced the term "satisfice" into the literature of economics (it is a Scotticism for "satisfy"), is somewhat unclear about whether satisficing can be rational for other than instrumental (including informational constraints on the ability to maximize) reasons. For example, in his "Theories of Decision Making in Economics and Behavioral Science," *American Economic Review* 49 (1959): 253–83, Simon points out that quite

independently of the costs of gaining further information or effecting new policies, an entrepreneur or firm may simply seek a satisfactory return on investments or share of the market or level of sales rather than attempt to maximize or optimize under any other these headings. This suggests that it might be intrinsically rational not to seek, and to be satisfied with some "aspiration level" of results less than, the achievable best; but in the same article Simon also says that "when a firm has alternatives open to it that are at or above its aspiration level, it will choose the best of those known to be available." Defenders of intrinsically rational satisficing would (some of them) question this kind of assumption. See, e.g., my *Beyond Optimizing* (Cambridge, Mass.: Harvard University Press, 1989).

2. I have used the qualifier "to the extent that" here, because Rawls and others include a further condition in their understanding or definition of teleological theories. Such theories see the good as prior to the right and *also* specify the right in terms of what maximizes the good. (See John Rawls, *A Theory of Justice* [Cambridge, Mass.: Harvard University Press, 1971], 24.) This definition is too narrow, if satisficing, or nonmaximalist but optimizing, forms of consequentialism make sense, and, assuming that they do, we can better define teleological theories as theories which claim that what produces better results than some alternative is always morally better than that alternative. But even this fails to do justice to supposedly teleological forms of virtue ethics like Aristotelian ethics. (On this point, see my article "Teleology" in the second edition of L. Becker and C. Becker, eds. *The Encyclopedia of Ethics.*)

3. See the *Critique of Practical Reason*, Part I, Book I, sect. ii.

4. See my *Morals from Motives* (New York: Oxford University Press, 2001), ch. 6.

5. Incidentally, in the section where Kant defends dualism, he also makes it clear that he regards Stoicism and Epicureanism – he didn't know about utilitarianism – as asserting totally opposite views of the relationship between well-being and virtue. See Kant, loc. cit.

6. That seems to be James Martineau's view, for example; see his *Types of Ethical Theory* (New York: Oxford University Press, 1886). Of course, Martineau's ethics differs from Kant's because of its distinctive virtue-ethical conception of right action as explainable in terms of good motives. But some people have argued that Kant too is some kind of virtue ethicist.

7. For a discussion of whether Aristotle is best interpreted as holding an elevationist view and of some implausible implications of that view, see my *Morals from Motives*, ch. 6.

8. See *Morals from Motives.*

9. Here and in what immediately follows I am borrowing from and greatly abbreviating the argument of *Morals from Motives*; see especially chs. 6–8.

10. Similar arguments may be applicable to power too, but let us keep things simple.

11. Everyone knows about Sisyphus, but Tantalus, according to mythology, was condemned by the gods to stand under luscious grapes that always eluded his reach and in water that always receded when he tried to drink it.

12. Of course, someone might claim that nothing *counts as pleasure* unless the individual who has it is in some degree satisfied with it. But this assumption

clearly makes it easier for monistic elevationism to hold that appetitive goods require some degree of virtue, and it is in any event questionable. The French use the term "alumette" (literally "match") to refer to hors d'oeuvres that are supposed to inflame one's appetite, and this usage more than suggests that such appetizers are pleasurable yet the very opposite of satisfying.

13. At this point, and for simplicity's sake, I am relying on the intuitive assumption that insatiability and an inability to satisfice are anti-virtuous or irrational. I am also assuming that this anti-virtuousness or irrationality doesn't have to be explained by appealing to the idea of what is good (e.g. by reference to the traits' bad consequences), which would lead our present approach in a (vicious) circle. I discuss these issues at great length in *Morals and Motives*, chs. 6–8.

14. The issue of whether various goods actually contain virtue(s) as metaphysical parts of themselves is discussed (but not resolved) in *Morals from Motives*, ch. 6.

15. In *Morals from Motives*, ch. 7, I say more about why moderation or non-insatiability should count as a *rational* virtue.

16. Let me just say in advance, though, that I haven't found any other commentators who interpret *Philebus* in the way I am going to suggest. But I can't claim to have read all the commentaries there are on the *Philebus*.

17. I don't want to get into the issue of *how* satisfied one has to be with what one has enjoyed in order for an appetitive good to occur.

18. In "Moderation, Rationality, and Virtue" (in *The Tanner Lectures on Human Values*, vol. 8 [Salt Lake City: University of Utah Press, 1988]) and subsequently in *Beyond Optimizing*, I assumed the teleological view that rational satisficing occurs with respect to independent goods but didn't assume teleology as a total view of rationality, because I rejected the essential idea (see note 2) that what produces results that are better for one, relative to alternatives, is always more rational (to choose). Teleology, whether about morality or about rationality, contains (at least) two elements, and the one just mentioned was rejected on a number of different grounds in the two works cited previously in the present note. In fact, in *Beyond Optimizing* I even suggested that there may be restrictions on optimizing analogous with the deontological restrictions of commonsense morality, that there might be times when it was rationally unacceptable (apart from effects on others) to do what would have best (or tied-best) results for one. (One potential example concerns a person who has always wanted and long planned to see the pyramids, who is told, when he finally gets to Egypt, that he doesn't have time to see both the pyramids and Luxor, and who capriciously decides to see Luxor instead because "it would be just as much fun as seeing the pyramids.") A deontology of rational choice doesn't require us to renounce the idea that goods are independent; it requires us only to say that there are times when it is less than rational to take more of such goods than fewer.

2

Satisficing as a Humanly Rational Strategy

David Schmidtz

1. Two Kinds of Strategies

Suppose I need to decide whether to go off to fight for a cause in which I deeply believe, or stay home with a family that needs me and that I deeply love. What should I do? My friends say I should determine the possible outcomes of the two proposed courses of action, assign probabilities and numerical utilities to each possibility, multiply through, and then choose whichever alternative has the highest number.

My friends are wrong. Their proposal would be plausible in games of chance where information on probabilities and monetarily denominated utilities is readily available. In the present case, however, I can only guess at the possible outcomes of either course of action. Neither do I know their probabilities. Nor do I know how to gauge their utilities. The strategy of maximizing expected utility is out of the question, for employing it requires information I do not have.

Nevertheless, my friends have not given up trying to help, so they point out that I could simulate the process of maximizing expected utility by assuming a set of possible outcomes, estimating their probabilities, and then making educated guesses about how much utility they would have. I could indeed do this, but I decide not to, for it occurs to me that I have no reason to trust the formula for maximizing expected utility when I have nothing but question marks to plug into it. Better strategies are available, and explaining what they are is the purpose of this chapter.

This section distinguishes between optimizing and satisficing strategies, and between moderate and immoderate preferences. The following three sections discuss, in turn, when satisficing strategies are rational, when they are not, and when cultivating moderate preferences is rational. Later sections offer a way of characterizing rational choice in situations where an agent's alternatives are incommensurable.

In the simplest context, one has a set of alternatives clearly ranked in terms of their utility as means to one's ends. If one is an *optimizer*, one chooses an alternative that ranks at least as high as any other. In contrast, if one is a *satisficer*, one settles for any alternative one considers satisfactory. In this static context, though, it is hard to see the point of choosing a suboptimal alternative, even if it is satisfactory.

In a more dynamic and more typical context, we are not *presented* with a set of nicely ranked alternatives. Instead, we *look* for them, judging their utility as we go. In this context, optimizing involves terminating one's search for alternatives upon concluding that one has found the best available alternative. However, although optimizing involves select-ing what one judges is best, it need not involve judging what is best "all things considered," because sophisticated optimizers recognize that con-sidering all things is not always worth the cost. There may be constraints (temporal, financial, and so on) on how much searching they can afford to do. A person who stops the search upon concluding that prolonging the search is not worth the cost is also employing an optimizing strategy, albeit one of a more subtle variety.[1]

Satisficing, in contrast, involves terminating the search for alternatives upon concluding that one has identified a satisfactory alternative. What distinguishes satisficing from optimizing in the dynamic context is that the two strategies employ different *stopping rules*.[2] Thus, if options emerge serially, a subtle optimizer might choose a known option in preference to the alternative – namely, searching for something better with no guar-antee of ever finding it. The difference between satisficing and this more subtle kind of optimizing has to do with what the two strategies take into account in reaching a stopping point. At any point in the search, we may let the expected utility of stopping the search equal U, the utility of the best option we have turned up so far. The expected utility of continued search equals the probability of finding a better option, $P(fbo)$, multiplied by the utility of finding a better option, $U(fbo)$, minus the cost of further search, $C(fs)$. At some point, the satisficer stops because he believes U is good enough. In contrast, the subtle optimizer stops because she believes that $P(fbo)U(fbo) - C(fs)$ is less than zero. Even if the two stopping rules happen to converge on the same stopping point, they do so for different reasons and require different information.[3]

Unlike the optimizer, who stops searching when she either has considered all her options or has run up against things like time constraints, the satisficer stops the search upon identifying an alternative as good enough.[4] For example, suppose you enter a cafeteria seeking a nutritionally balanced and reasonably tasty meal. You then proceed down the cafeteria line surveying the alternatives. If you are satisficing, you take the first meal you deem nutritionally and aesthetically adequate. If you are optimizing, you continue down the line surveying alternatives until you reach the end of the line or run out of time. You then take the meal you consider optimal, either in comparison to the other known options or in comparison to the alternative of further search. A satisfactory meal may or may not be optimal. Likewise, as cafeteria patrons know only too well, the best available meal may or may not be satisfactory. Of course, if you switch from one stopping rule to the other, you might end up choosing the same meal, but you'll be choosing it for a different reason. Therefore, neither rule is reducible to the other. (You could employ both stopping rules simultaneously, of course, resolving to stop as soon as you find a satisfactory alternative or run out of time or have considered all available alternatives – whichever comes first.) Nor can satisficing be equated with the more subtle kind of optimizing that takes the cost of searching for more-than-satisfactory alternatives into account. Satisficers select the satisfactory alternative because it is satisfactory, not because they calculate that stopping the search at that point would maximize utility. (Of course, what satisficers do may be co-extensive with what is prescribed by subtle optimizing or, for that matter, with what is prescribed by an infinite number of conceivable stopping rules, but I think that probably is irrelevant, at least for my purposes. My question is what rule an agent is using, not what rules are co-extensive with the rule that the agent is using.)

With this characterization of satisficing in mind, we can now clarify the difference between satisficing and *moderation*. Satisficing contrasts with optimizing. Being moderate, however, contrasts not with optimizing but with being immoderate. Being an optimizer does not entail being immoderate, and being a satisficer does not entail that one would be satisfied with a moderate bundle of goods. A person could be both moderate and an optimizer, for the maximally satisfying bundle of goods for a given person may well be of moderate size. Likewise, a person could be both a satisficer and immoderate, for a given satisficer may have wildly immoderate ideas about what counts as satisfactory. Consider a person whose goal in life is to be a millionaire (not a billionaire, mind you, just a millionaire) by the age of thirty.

2. When Satisficing Is Rational

There is an apparent incongruence between the theory and practice of rational choice. Theory models rational choice as optimizing choice, yet in practice satisficing is ubiquitous. We could explain the incongruence away by saying that when people think they are looking for something satisfactory, what they are really looking for is something optimal. But satisficing can be reconstructed as a subtle kind of optimizing strategy only on pain of attributing to people calculations they often do not perform (and do not have the information to perform) and intentions they often do not have. This section tries to explain satisficing in terms of thought processes we can recognize in ourselves. (Explaining tokens of satisficing strategy in terms of optimizing strategies with which they are co-extensive in the particular case is, of course, possible, and indeed easy, but it seems also to be fundamentally boring. Such explanations are just-so stories that do not actually explain anything but are insisted upon for no apparent reason other than to cling to a simple but practically nonfunctional theory.) Satisficing will emerge as a real alternative to optimizing, and thus as a strategy that can be evaluated, criticized, and sometimes redeemed as rational.

We begin with the observation that people have a multiplicity of goals. For example, a person can desire to be healthy, to have a successful career, to be a good parent, and so forth. Some goals are broad and others narrow, relatively speaking. Further, a given goal might be encompassed by another in the sense that the narrower goal's point – the reason for its being a goal – is that it is part of what one does in pursuit of a larger goal. For example, Kate might want to upgrade her wardrobe because she cares about her appearance because she wants a promotion because she cares about her career. Suppose she believes that achieving her various goals is instrumental to or constitutive of achieving a broader goal of making her life as a whole go well. To mark the difference in breadth between Kate's concern for her life as a whole and her concern for particular aspects of her life (such as her health or her career), let us say that Kate seeks a *local* optimum when she seeks to make a certain aspect of her life go as well as possible. Kate seeks a *global* optimum when she seeks to make her life as a whole go as well as possible.[5]

Optima can be defined as such only within the context of the constraints under which goals are pursued. (Thus, when economists speak of maximizing utility, it goes without saying that they are talking about maximizing utility subject to a budget constraint.) We pursue goals subject to the limits of our knowledge, time, energy, ability, income, and so on. More intriguing, however, is that we typically operate under additional constraints that we have deliberately imposed upon ourselves, as if the constraints imposed on us by external circumstances were too loose. For example, if Tom spends an evening at a casino, he is externally constrained (by his savings and his borrowing power) to spend no more than, say, $50,000. What actually defines his set of options over the course of the evening, though, if all goes well, is the hundred-dollar budget constraint that Tom *chose* to impose on himself.[6]

To give another example, in fleshing out the task of buying a house, we need to make some prior decisions. We decide how long to look, how much money to spend, what neighborhoods to consider. We knock only on doors of houses displaying "for sale" signs rather than on every door in the neighborhood. To some extent, these constraints are imposed on us by mundane external factors, but they also have a striking normative aspect, for they are in part rules of conduct we impose on ourselves; we take it upon ourselves to make our constraints more precise and more limiting so as to make our choice set more definite. Local optimizing would often be neurotic and even stupid if local goals were not pursued within compartments partly defined by self-imposed constraints. The constraints we impose on our narrower pursuits can keep narrower pursuits from ruining the larger plans of which they are part.[7]

If we look at life as a whole, we see that life as a whole will go better if we spend most of it pursuing goals that are narrower than the goal of making life as a whole go better. That is why it is rational to formulate and pursue local goals. But it also is rational to prevent narrower pursuits from consuming more resources than is warranted by the importance (from the global perspective) of achieving those narrower goals. Accordingly, when we pursue narrower goals, we pursue them under self-imposed constraints.

Although the constraints we impose on ourselves are imposed from a more encompassing perspective, it is only within the narrower perspective that we become subject to self-imposed constraints. (Of course, we are subject from any perspective to external constraints, limited incomes, and such.) Self-imposed constraints can be applied only *to* narrower pursuits and can be applied only *from* the perspective of a more encompassing pursuit. In more familiar terms, the point is that, because we have broader objectives, there are limits to what we will do for the sake of our wardrobe, or for the sake of a promotion, or for the sake of a career.

Having distinguished between local and global optimization, we can now explain when satisficing is rational. Michael Slote believes that the optimizing tendency can be self-defeating. He says, "A person bent on eking out the most good he can in any given situation will take pains and suffer anxieties that a more casual individual will avoid. . . ." He asks us to consider "how much more planful and self-conscious the continual optimizer must be in comparison with the satisficer who does not always aim for the best and who sometimes rejects the best or better for the good enough."[8] In short, that we have an opportunity to pursue the good is not by itself a compelling reason to pursue the good. Surely, Slote has an important point. Just as surely, however, his point applies to local optimizing rather than to optimizing as such. From the global perspective, seeking local optima can be a waste of time. Global optimizers seek local optima only when doing so serves their purposes. For that reason, satisficing is a big part of a global optimizer's daily routine. A compulsive seeking of local optima is associated with being immoderate, perhaps, but not with being a global optimizer. Effort can have diminishing returns, so a global optimizer will be careful not to try too hard. Local optimizing often gives way to satisficing for the sake of global optimality.

From the global optimizer's point of view, the process of buying a house provides a good example of how satisficing can be rational. When we choose a house, we might proceed by seeking the best available house within certain constraints – within a one-month time limit, for example. We impose such a limit because we have goals other than living in a nice house. Looking for a house competes with our other goals for our time and energy. Or we might look for a satisfactory house and cease looking when we find one. Most of the people I have asked say they would optimize within constraints but would not deem satisficing irrational. Like local optimizing, satisficing can serve our larger plans by setting limits on how much effort we put into seeking a house at the expense of other goals that become more important at some point, given the diminishing returns of remaining on the housing market. An optimizing strategy places limits on how much we are willing to invest in seeking alternatives. A satisficing strategy places limits on how much we insist on finding before we quit that search and turn our attention to other matters.[9]

The two strategies need not be inflexible. People sometimes have reason to switch or revise strategies as new information comes in. If we seek a satisfactory house in an unfamiliar neighborhood and are shocked to find one within five minutes, we may stop the search, acknowledging the stopping rule we previously imposed on that activity. On the other hand, we may conclude that, having formulated our aspiration level under unrealistically pessimistic assumptions, we should resume our search with a satisficing strategy revised to reflect a higher aspiration level. Or we may switch to a local optimizing strategy, spending another day or two looking at houses and then taking the best we have found so far. Or we may do both, looking until we either reach our new aspiration level or reach our time limit. In this way, the two strategies often are interactive.

Likewise, suppose we started out planning to seek the best house we could find within a one-month time limit but have so far been terribly disappointed with our options. In this case, when after two weeks we finally find a house that meets our plummeting aspiration level, we may find ourselves embracing a sadder but wiser aspiration level as a stopping rule, abandoning our original plan to seek a local optimum relative to a one-month time constraint.

Typically, the usefulness of satisficing as a stopping rule will be a function of the concreteness of our local goals. If we do not know exactly what we are looking for, then we usually are better off locally optimizing – that is, setting a time limit and then taking what we like best within that limit. But if we know exactly what we are looking for, then it is rational to stop searching as soon as we find it.[10] So, having detailed information about our *goals* weighs in favor of using that information in formulating aspiration levels as stopping rules. Conversely, the more we know about our *set of alternatives*, the easier it is to identify which alternative has the highest utility, which weighs in favor of seeking local optima.

The stakes involved are also pertinent – indeed crucial. The less we care about the gap between satisfactory and optimal toothpaste, for example, the more reason we have to satisfice – to look for a satisfactory brand and stop searching when we find it. Note the alternative: Instead of satisficing, we could optimize by searching among different brands of toothpaste until we find the precise point at which further search is not worth its cost. But there is a reason why we never do this, namely that an optimal stopping point is itself something for which we would have to search, and locating it would require information (about the probability of finding a better brand of toothpaste, for example) that is not worth gathering, given the stakes involved in the search for toothpaste. Against this, one might object to my assumption that we need precision in the search for an optimal stopping point. Why not seek to learn *roughly* when looking for better toothpaste is not worth the cost? In the search for a stopping point that we might graft onto the original search for toothpaste, it can be more rational to seek to be tolerably close to an optimum than to seek to be at an optimum.

But that is my point: There are cases where we do not care enough about the gap between the satisfactory and the optimal to make it rational to search for the optimal. Searching for the optimal toothpaste can be a waste of time, but so can searching for the optimal moment to quit looking for toothpaste. One way or another, satisficing enters the picture. There will be times when even the most sophisticated optimizing strategies will be inappropriate, for they require information that we may not have and that may not be worth acquiring. And a less sophisticated "all things considered" strategy will nearly always be inappropriate. Rational choice involves considering only those things that seem worthy of consideration, which is to say it involves satisficing, that is, having a stopping rule that limits how comprehensive a body of information we insist on gathering before stopping the search and turning our attention to other matters.

There is also something to be said for having a moderate disposition – a disposition that allows one to be content with merely satisfactory states of affairs. Consider that starting a search too soon can be every bit as wasteful as stopping a search too late. Searching for a house is costly. It is costly partly because people have other goals; the time and energy you spend searching for a house could have been spent on other things. Even if you find a better house than you already have, the process of moving will also be costly. Moreover, it takes time living in and enjoying a house in order to recoup these costs. If you move every month, you will always be paying the costs and never enjoying the benefits of better housing. Moving into a house is part and parcel of a decision to stay a while, for it is only in staying that you collect on the investment of time and energy you made in moving. The general lesson is that costly transitions to preferred states of affairs require intervening periods of stability so that transition costs can be recovered and thus rationally justified. The stability of the intervening periods requires a disposition to be content for a while with what one has – to find something one likes and then stop searching.

Further, even if transition costs are relatively minor, there still can come a point when we should abandon the search for, say, a better job or a better spouse, not because such goals are unattainable or even because the transition costs are too high but rather because such goals eventually can become inappropriate. At some point, we have to start collecting the rewards that come only when we make a genuine commitment – when we stop looking for something or someone better. We need to be able to satisfice within various local compartments (those defining our searches for spouses, jobs, and so on) in order to make our lives as a whole go well.[11]

3. When Satisficing Is Not Rational

Slote says that "choosing what is best for oneself may well be neither a necessary nor a sufficient condition of acting rationally, even in situations where only the agent's good is at stake."[12] For example, a person who is moving and must sell his house might seek "not to maximize his profit on the house, not to get the best price for it he is likely to receive within some appropriate time period, but simply to obtain what he takes to be a good or satisfactory price."[13] When the seller receives a suitable offer, he may rationally accept it immediately, even though there would be no cost or risk in waiting a few days to see if a higher offer materializes. "His early agreement may not be due to undue anxiety about the firmness of the buyer's offer, or to a feeling that monetary transactions are unpleasant and to be got over as quickly as possible. He may simply be satisficing in the strong sense of the term. He may be moderate or modest in what he wants or needs."[14]

Slote does not offer an analysis of rationality. Nor do I want this chapter's argument to rest on any particular analysis of rationality. I do, however, offer this as a necessary condition of rationality: One's choice is rational only if one does not recognize clearly better reasons for choosing any of one's forgone alternatives. Further, it begs none of the questions that concern us here. It does not entail that rational choice be optimizing choice. Rather, it allows that one could rationally choose an alternative because it is satisfactory, terminating the search of one's choice set at that point.[15] Moreover, it also allows that if one has two satisfactory alternatives, one could choose the more moderate of the two on the grounds that it satisfies a preference one happens to have for moderation.

On the other hand, although a suboptimal option may be good enough to be worthy of choice in a given case, that does not mean it is worthy of being chosen in preference to something that is clearly better. If one has two choices and one alternative is satisfactory but the other is not, then the satisfactory choice is rational because it is *better*. But suppose one has two choices and both are satisfactory. (For example, suppose your house is for sale, and you simultaneously get two satisfactory offers, one for $200,000 and another for $210,000, and you prefer the larger offer.) In this case, one does not give a rationale for choosing the inferior alternative merely by pointing out that the inferior alternative is satisfactory. The inferior option is satisfactory, but because this is not a difference, it cannot make a difference either. By hypothesis, the superior option is also satisfactory.

Why, then, should we choose the superior option? Presumably because it is better. Whatever it is in virtue of which we deem that option superior is also a reason for us to choose it.[16] Oddly, Slote denies this. It can be rational to choose the inferior option, Slote insists. Nor do we need a reason to choose the inferior option, Slote argues, because rationality does not always require people to have a reason for choosing one alternative over another.[17] For example, Kate might rationally grab a blouse out of her closet in the morning without being able to explain why she chose that one over the similar blouses hanging beside it. To call her irrational simply because she cannot explain her choice would be a mistake.

This seems right, as far as it goes; not all choices have to be or can be explained. To deem a choice rational, however, is to imply there is an explanation of a certain kind. A person can be rational without being aware of reasons for everything she does, but the things she does for no reason are not rational, and we do not show them to be rational merely by pointing out that they were done by a rational *person*. The person who simply grabs a blouse may be choosing, perhaps rationally, to forgo the opportunity to rationally choose which of her several blouses she ends up wearing. If Kate is running late for the train, then under the circumstances anything that counts as a blouse will also count as satisfactory, so she leaves to impulse the selection from her set of blouses. (In this case, the process of searching among alternative blouses virtually vanishes – there is hardly any choice at all. If she instead gives herself a few seconds to make sure she avoids the blouses with valentine or hammer-and-sickle patterns on them, then she will be choosing within a very small but still real local compartment.)

There may be a blouse in her closet that, given time, would emerge as best. Kate judges, however, that it is not worth her time to wait for this to happen. She is not literally compelled to simply pick something, but it serves her broader ends to forget about seeking the optimal blouse and instead just grab something out of the closet. If Kate is running late for the train, she has reason to simply grab a blouse in preference to the clearly inferior alternative of wasting precious time seeking the optimal blouse. Initially adopting an end and creating a compartment within which to pursue it is itself a goal-directed activity and, from the standpoint of the global optimizer, not one to be engaged in frivolously. Therefore, we can endorse her *method* of selecting a blouse even though we anticipate having no particular reason to endorse her actual selection.

On the other hand, *deliberately* choosing the worse over the better would be irrational, and we do not give ourselves reason to soften this verdict merely by reminding ourselves that rational people sometimes leave their choices to impulse. Rational choice theory can tell us a story about why Kate finds herself going to work in a green blouse with orange polka dots, but the story will require an implicit or explicit distinction between more and less encompassing perspectives. Without the distinction, an optimization story would be glaringly false, for she does not in fact choose the optimal blouse, and a satisficing story would have neither explanatory nor justificatory power, for the point of choosing a merely satisfactory blouse when better ones were available would remain a mystery. To see the point of what she does at the local level, we have to step back and look at her actions from a broader perspective. From a broader perspective, Kate may have good reason to simply grab a blouse out of the closet, knowing it will be satisfactory even if it is not her favorite. However, it cannot be rational to choose something because it is satisfactory while at the same time having a clearly better option already in hand.

4. When Moderation Is Rational

We saw that, when deciding between two satisfactory alternatives, it does not help to point out that one of them is satisfactory. We could, however, choose on the grounds that one of them is more moderate. Consider an example of Slote's. He says it "makes sense" for someone to desire "to be a really fine lawyer like her mother, but not desire to be as good a lawyer as she can possibly be. This limitation of ambition or aspiration may not stem from a belief that too much devotion to the law would damage other, more important parts of one's life. In certain moderate individuals, there are limits to aspiration and desire that cannot be explained in optimizing terms. . . . "[18]

I agree that common sense can recognize moderate aspirations as rational, but to note this fact in an off-the-cuff way is hardly to provide an explanation of moderate aspirations. Our commonsense recognition is precisely what has to be explained. If all we have is an intuition that an act makes sense, but we cannot say what the act makes sense *in terms of,* then we would be jumping to conclusions if we said we were approving of the act as rational. In contrast, if we explain a show of moderation in terms of its conduciveness to overall satisfaction, then we have explained it as rational. We have not merely claimed it makes sense; rather, we have actually made sense of it. We have shown that we had reason to choose as we did, while not having better reasons to choose differently.

How, then, might we explain having moderate career goals? First, there is the issue of tradeoffs mentioned by Slote. We might cultivate an ability to be content with moderate career goals, not because we prefer moderate success to great success but because we care about things other than success. Thus, one reason to cultivate modest desires for wealth is that doing so might improve our ability to adhere to a satisficing strategy with respect to income, thus freeing us to devote time to family, health, hobbies, and so on.

There are also ways in which moderation can have instrumental value that do not depend on the need to make tradeoffs. There can be reasons for striving to be as good a lawyer as one's mother even if one wants to be as good a lawyer as possible. For example, a person might aim at being as good as her mother as a stepping stone to becoming the best lawyer she can be. The modesty that enables a person to concentrate on successfully making smaller steps may eventually put her within reach of loftier goals. There is also value in concreteness. A person may have no idea how to go about becoming the best possible lawyer but may have a much clearer idea about how to become as good as her mother because the more modest goal is more concrete. Further, even given two equally concrete goals, an optimizer might very well choose the lesser on the grounds that only the lesser goal is realistic. Thus, one might become a better lawyer by emulating one's highly competent mother than by wasting one's time in a fruitless attempt to emulate her superstar partner.

Finally, we can at least conceive of moderation's being a preference in itself – not just a quality of a desire but itself the thing desired.[19] One might explain the cultivation of such a preference on the grounds that moderation is less distracting than extravagance, with the consequence that the moderate life is the more satisfyingly thoughtful and introspective life. In various ways, then, moderation can have instrumental or even constitutive value from the global perspective. Insofar as moderate preferences can be deliberately cultivated, their cultivation is subject to rational critique and can thus be defended as rational.

5. When Seeking Optima Is Not Rational

To seek optima strikes us as generally a pretty reasonable strategy, but it is not necessarily so. Section 2 noted that local optimizing can be a waste of time from a global perspective, but this is not the only circumstance that can make it inappropriate to seek optima. For one thing, a set of alternatives need not contain a well-defined optimal choice at all, let alone one that can be easily identified. To borrow a fanciful example from John Pollock,[20] suppose you are immortal and are also fortunate to have in your possession a bottle of EverBetter Wine. This wine improves with age. In fact, it improves so steadily and so rapidly that no matter how long you wait before drinking it, you would be better off, all things considered, waiting one more day. The question is, when should you drink the wine?

A rational *person* presumably would simply drink the wine at some point (perhaps after artificially constraining himself to drink the wine by year's end, and then picking New Year's Eve as the obvious choice within that time frame), but the person would not be able to defend any particular day as an optimal choice. Indeed, it is part of the story that no matter what day the immortal chooses, waiting one more day would have been better. There are no constraints with respect to which he can regard any particular day as the optimal choice, unless he imposes those constraints on himself.

There is something rational about choosing New Year's Eve, but the rationality lies in something other than how that day compares with the alternatives. Although the immortal could not defend choosing New Year's Eve in preference to waiting one more day, the choice is defensible in the sense that he did not have a better alternative to picking *something or other*. Indeed, picking something or other was optimal, because it was better than the only alternative, namely sitting on the fence forever. The distinction between local and global optimizing thus allows us to explain without paradox the sense in which choosing New Year's Eve was rational. Picking something or other – and thus closing the compartment within which he seeks to set a date for drinking the wine – was rational from the global perspective despite the fact that from within that compartment, it was not possible to have a rationale for the choice of any particular day.[21]

The EverBetter Wine story is fantasy, of course, but it shows that we can at least imagine cases in which a set of alternatives has features making it inappropriate to seek the set's optimal member. Seeking optima may serve our ends, but if this is so, it is not a necessary truth but rather a contingent truth about the world and the kind of choice sets we find within it. In the EverBetter Wine case, the set of alternatives has no optimal member. Consider a more realistic story with a somewhat similar structure. Suppose a house comes up for sale in January. Out of curiosity, you take a look and find that you prefer it to the house you now own. When you look into the cost of selling your house and buying the new one, you find that the only cost you care about in the end is the cost and inconvenience of actually moving your belongings and settling into the new house. Suppose this cost, all things considered, amounts to $1,000. Moreover, it is clear to you that such moving costs will be amply repaid over time. You can see that the stream of revenue or utility from the new house will be worth $100 per month more than what you will receive if you stay where you are. Thus, the cost of the move will be repaid in ten months. This is hardly a wild fantasy, and so far buying the house is intuitively reasonable. We see the point.

Now, to make the story more improbable, suppose you change houses in January and, four months later, it happens again. You find another house for sale. The move will cost another thousand dollars, but the new house will be worth $100 per month more than the one you now own. However, if you choose to move in May, that choice will make your January move retroactively suboptimal, a net loss of around $600. Should you move?

Perhaps opportunities to move to ever better houses will surface again and again. You do not know.[22] But you do know this: For any move to be optimal, something must subsequently make you stay put long enough to recover the cost of that particular move. The fact is, if you keep waiting for and expecting the day when the world stops presenting you with such opportunities, and if that day never comes, then sooner or later (in order to live a good life) you will have to begin turning your back on them. As in the EverBetter Wine story, there is no particular point at which it is especially rational to stop moving. Indeed, whenever you finally reject an opportunity to move, it will be true that if you moved one more time before stopping, you eventually would be better off. Nevertheless, you have come to see that there is a point in committing yourself to being satisfied for a time with the house you have. Recall that optima are defined with respect to constraints. If you resolve in May that, once you choose, you will not look at another house for at least ten months, then choosing to move is optimal with respect to that self-imposed constraint. Your January move will then have been a waste of money, but your move in May will be worthwhile, provided that your self-imposed constraint remains firm.

Satisficing strategies strike us as reasonable in part because of contingent facts about ourselves and our world. For creatures as limited as we, satisficing often makes a lot of sense. Perhaps less obvious is that the intuitive reasonableness of optimizing is no less contingent. Seizing on opportunities to make optimal moves serves a purpose partly because the real world is such that we can take for granted that there will be time between moves to enjoy our improved situation. In the real world, opportunities to improve our situation do not come along so rapidly that we find ourselves stepping higher and higher without having time to enjoy the steps along the way. The real world limits our access to opportunities to improve our situation, and if such limits did not exist, *we would have to invent them.* We would have to give ourselves time to enjoy our situation even if that meant rejecting opportunities to improve it.

This section argued that seeking optima is only contingently rational. The argument went beyond the idea that different local goals can come into conflict. To be sure, there can be conflicts between the pursuit of local optima and the attainment of global optima, and such occasions give us reason not to pursue local optima. This section, though, articulated a different kind of reason not to pursue local optima, because the conflict discussed in this section could occur even if one had no goals beyond, for example, living in the best possible house. The nature of the conflict is that, ironically, seeking to live in the best possible house could leave us with no time to actually live in the best possible house.

6. Tradeoffs Among Incommensurable Values

As explained in previous sections, moderate preferences and satisficing strategies can be of instrumental value from the global perspective. Section 4 closed by speculating that moderate preferences might even be considered essential constituents of the good life and thus have more than merely instrumental value. Satisficing strategies, however, can be of instrumental value only. This is because to satisfice is to give up the possibility of attaining a preferable outcome, and giving this up has to be explained in terms of the strategic reasons one has for giving it up. Local optimizing must likewise be explained, for it too consists of giving something up, namely the opportunity to invest one's efforts in some other compartment.

Global optimizing, however, is not open to question and subject to tradeoffs in the ways that local optimizing and satisficing are. Local goals can compete with one another, but no goals compete with optimizing at the global level, at least not in the arena of rationality. A global optimum is not one among several competing goals; rather, in encompassing our lives as a whole, it also encompasses our competing goals. It represents the best way to resolve the competition from the standpoint of life as a whole. Local optimizing can be a waste of time from the global perspective, but global optimizing cannot.

What, then, is the nature of the global perspective? Do we ever actually assume the global viewpoint, or is this merely a theoretical postulate? I do not want to downplay the risks of resting a lot of normative weight on the imaginary verdicts of imaginary perspectives. However, there are occasions when we apparently can and do assume the global viewpoint – namely, when we do what we call "stepping back to look at the big picture." We do step back to ask ourselves if the things we do to advance our careers, for example, are really worth doing. We do not spend all our waking hours looking at the big picture, of course. Nor should we, for when we look at the big picture, one thing we see is that it is possible to spend too much time looking at the big picture. Reflection is a part of the good life, but it is only a part. Part of attaining a global optimum involves being able to lose ourselves for a time in our local pursuits.

In the previous section, we saw that, at least in fantasy cases, there can be rational choice regarding a set of alternatives even when the set has no optimal members. The lesson applies to more realistic situations as well. In particular, as Isaac Levi notes, a person torn between ideals of pacifism and patriotism need not feel that his eventual choice is best, all things considered. Rather, he may feel that his eventual choice is best according to one of his ideals and worst according to another. What we have in such a case is what Levi[23] calls "decisionmaking under unresolved conflict of values." If you have several goals, none of which is subordinate to any other, and you find yourself in a situation where these goals are in conflict, the globally optimal tradeoff may not exist. And such situations (involving concerns for one's loved ones and for one's ideals, for example) may be rather common.

Yet, even in situations where there is no such thing as a global optimum, we can still take a global perspective. We can still look at our lives as a whole even if nothing presents itself as optimal from that perspective. Indeed, conflict of values is precisely that from which broader perspectives emerge. We confront the big picture precisely when we stop to consider that there is more to life than pursuing a career or buying a house or raising children. It is from broader perspectives that we attempt to resolve conflicts of values, with or without an algorithm for resolving them in an optimal fashion.[24]

One might think unresolved conflict is a sign of poorly chosen values. Why should would-be global optimizers risk adopting goals that could leave them having to make decisions under unresolved conflict? One reason is that some of our goals realize their full value in our lives only when they develop a certain autonomy, when we pursue them not as means of making our lives go well but as ends in themselves. We begin to tap the capacity of our ideals, our spouses, and our children to enrich our lives only when we acknowledge them as having value far beyond their capacity to enrich our lives. (Cherishing them becomes more than an instrumental means of making life go well; it becomes constitutive of life going well.) And goals we come to cherish as ends in themselves inherently tend to become incommensurable.[25] We may, for instance, find ourselves in a position where we cannot fight for a cause in which we deeply believe without compromising the care that our loved ones need from us and that we wholeheartedly want them to have. Nevertheless, this is the price of the richness and complexity of a life well lived. To have both ideals and loved ones is to run the risk of having to make decisions under unresolved conflicts of value.

Because some of our values are incommensurable, we sometimes have no method by which to identify optimal tradeoffs among conflicting local goals. In such cases, the goal of making life as a whole go as well as possible remains meaningful, although there may not be any course of action that unequivocally counts as pursuing it. Even if would-be global optimizers cannot identify optimal options, they can still reject alternatives that fail to further any of their goals. In particular, if no better way of resolving the conflict emerges, simply picking something or other will emerge as optimal compared with the alternative of remaining on the fence, for we eventually reject fence sitting on the grounds that it fails to further any of our goals.

To some (although not to me), this will seem a grim picture of rational choice at the global level, but there are two points to keep in mind. First, when faced with a situation in which we must simply pick something, we are likely to have regrets about paths not taken, but we naturally adapt to the paths we take, and normally regret fades as we grow into our choice. Thus, an alternative somewhat arbitrarily picked from a set within which no optimum exists can eventually come to be viewed as optimal from the perspectives of people we are yet to become, even if it could not have been considered optimal at the moment of choice. Second, this discussion of underdetermined rational choice concerns a worst-case scenario. Global optimizers carry out the highest-ranked life plan when they have one. Often, however, there is no highest-ranked plan for life as a whole and thus no well-defined global optimum; there is only a need to cope with competing and sometimes incommensurable local goals. In the worst case, no course of action unambiguously qualifies as making life as a whole go as well as possible, except insofar as it is unambiguously better to move in some direction rather than none. But this gives us enough to avoid paralysis even in the worst case. By hypothesis, simply picking emerges as the best the agent can do, and thus to pick something is to optimize with respect to the choice of whether to spend more time sitting on the fence.

It would be natural to say rational choice is choice "all things considered." The trouble is that we often find ourselves not knowing what to consider, and it would be bad advice to tell us to consider all things. We can consider all things within a limited range, perhaps, but the limits of that range will themselves tend to be matters of choice in large part. We start out knowing that in some sense we want each aspect of our lives to go as well as possible, yet we realize that our resources are limited and that our various pursuits must make room for one another. When looking at our lives as a whole, what is most clear is that rationally managing a whole life involves managing tradeoffs among life's various activities. If the benefits that will accrue from our various pursuits are known and commensurable, then managing the tradeoffs is easy, at least theoretically; we simply maximize the sum of benefits. However, in many of the everyday cases discussed in this chapter, the benefits are neither known nor commensurable with other benefits. Even so, we can effectively manage tradeoffs among particular pursuits by setting limits on how much of our lives we spend on particular pursuits. We can also set limits on how much benefit we insist on getting from particular pursuits. To impose the latter kind of stopping rule on a particular pursuit is to embrace what I have called a satisficing strategy.

Both kinds of constraint play a role in rational choice. Why? Because if we recognized only temporal limits, say, then we would automatically spend our full allotment of time in a given compartment even when we already had an acceptable option in hand. But if we also have strategically limited aspiration within that compartment, then finding an acceptable option will trigger a second kind of stopping rule. The second stopping rule closes the compartment and diverts the unused portion of the compartment's time allotment to other compartments where our need to find an acceptable option has not yet been met. Cultivating moderate preferences may also be advantageous in a supplementary way insofar as moderate preferences may help us adhere to the kind of limit we impose on a pursuit when we embrace a satisficing strategy.

Against the idea that our most important goals tend to become incommensurable with one another, one might suppose our global end is simply to flourish or to be happy – and that our local goals therefore *must* be commensurable in such terms. This would be a tidy climax to an otherwise rather untidy story about rational choice under unresolved conflict of values, but the tidiness would be superficial. One hardly gives people an algorithm for resolving conflicts when one advises them to be happy. What makes such advice vacuous is that flourishing and being happy cannot be concrete goals at the global level in the way finding a house can be at the local level. Of course we *want* to flourish, but we *aim* to flourish only in an especially metaphorical sense. The fact is, we flourish not by aiming at flourishing but by successfully pursuing other things, things worth pursuing for their own sake.

Likewise, happiness can be a standard by which a life as a whole is judged, perhaps, but it cannot be a goal at which a life as a whole is aimed. We do not become happy by pursuing things there would otherwise be no point in pursuing. Rather, there must be a point in striving for a certain goal before striving for it can come to have any potential to make us happy. To aim at happiness is to aim at a property that can emerge only in the course of aiming at something else.[26] So, the point about happiness and flourishing leaves us where we started, having to choose among things we value for their own sake, hoping we will be happy with our choice.

We might add that happiness derives from a variety of local sources, and the different elements of a person's happiness are not interchangeable. Our various local pleasures are not fungible; different dollar bills are all the same, functionally speaking, but different pleasures are not all the same and are not experienced as interchangeable units of the same kind of stuff. We can find happiness in our careers or in our marriages, but the vacuum left by a shattered career cannot be filled by domestic bliss.[27]

7. An Infinite Regress of Perspectives?

The global perspective is the perspective encompassing our lives as a whole. Decision making at this level disciplines the amount of time we devote to particular local compartments. It seems we are capable of taking a perspective this broad even in worst-case scenarios where there is no well-defined global optimum. But even if we suppose we can take a perspective encompassing our whole lives, why should we suppose this is the broadest perspective we can take?

Perhaps there can be broader perspectives than what I call the global perspective. Indeed, in *Rational Choice and Moral Agency*, I argue that we do have access to a larger perspective, that there are aspects of morality that we cannot appreciate except from a larger perspective, and that it can be rational to try to achieve this perspective. On the other hand, it would be unrealistic to suppose there is an infinite regress of levels. There is no need to prove that an infinite regress is impossible. However, because the idea of an infinite regress is unrealistic, it *is* important to show that my theory does not *presuppose* an infinite regress.

The threat of infinite regress arises in the following way. I said we cannot spend all our time looking at life as a whole; we must be able to lose ourselves (or perhaps I should say, find ourselves) in our local pursuits. How much time, then, should we spend pondering conflicting values? How much time should we spend looking at life as a whole? From what perspective do we choose to limit the amount of time we spend looking at our lives from the global perspective? To answer these questions, maybe we need a "superglobal" perspective. After all, how could we decide how much time to spend at a given level unless we did so from a still more encompassing perspective?[28] It seems that my theory can explain the time we allot to a given perspective only by supposing that we retreat to a broader one, ad infinitum.

But the theory presumes no such retreat. There are simpler, more realistic ways to explain the amount of time we spend looking at life as a whole.[29] First, there are things, like sleeping, that we do as the need arises; because we do not *decide* how much time to spend sleeping, we do not decide from a broader perspective, either. Indeed, we might be better off sleeping as we feel the need rather than trying to set aside a calculated amount of time for sleep. Perhaps the same holds true of the activity of looking at life as a whole. Insofar as our purpose in looking at life as a whole is to resolve conflicts arising between various aspects of our lives, so that life as a whole may go well, there will come a time when taking a global perspective has served its purpose. At that time, the compartment in our lives reserved for the activity of resolving local conflicts naturally closes until subsequent conflict forces it open again. There is no residual conflict awaiting resolution at a higher level.

Thus, the question of how much time to spend in contemplation need not itself require contemplation. Rather, we take whatever time it takes to genuinely resolve a conflict, or else we reach a point where we must simply pick something. More generally, we stop contemplating when we judge that pursuing our local goals has come into conflict with – and has become more important than – the activity of thinking about how to juggle them. (For example, we would not dwell on the big picture if we were starving. Conflicts are rarely so important that contemplating them could preempt securing our immediate survival.) In this scenario, we are driven *to* the global level by local conflict and eventually are driven *from* that level by a need to get on with our lives. The question of how much time to spend looking at life as a whole resolves itself. (In passing, we also can be driven to a global perspective by the *resolution* of conflicts. Thus, when we finish a major project that had forced other pursuits to take a back seat, we often take time to evaluate self-imposed constraints and decide how to divide our extra time among previously neglected projects. And what then drives us *from* that global perspective is the eventual resolution of a local conflict between savoring the big picture – a satisfying activity indeed when one is just finishing a major project – and the need, say, to start making dinner.)

We also can imagine a second kind of scenario in which the question does not resolve itself but is instead answered by deliberate calculation, in the same way that we could imagine deliberately calculating how much time to spend sleeping. Could we make a conscious decision of this kind without taking a superglobal perspective? Yes, we could. (I am not saying we typically do, but we could.) Consider that contemplation is an activity that must find its place in our lives along with other activities. For example, I might spend the month of July in a rented cabin, not doing anything to pursue my career, but just thinking about why I ever wanted to be a philosopher and about whether my original reasons still hold. This compartment in my life is reserved for contemplating my career. It is separate from the compartment or compartments within which I actually pursue my career. I also have a compartment, similar in many respects, within which I contemplate life as a whole. But although the *subject* I contemplate is the whole of my life, the contemplation itself is not. The contemplation is only one of many activities about which I care.

Now, if I need to decide how much time to reserve for contemplating life as a whole, I take a global perspective, trying to gauge how important such contemplation is to my life as a whole. Notice, then, what is unique about the compartment I reserve for the activity of contemplating my life as a whole. The compartment is unique because its boundaries are set by the activity that takes place within it. In the course of contemplating life from the global perspective, I decide how much time to reserve for any given activity, including contemplation in general and contemplating life as a whole in particular. In this scenario, as in the previous one, no boundary-setting issue is left to await resolution at a higher level.

We have outlined two possibilities. In one case, we use whatever time it takes to resolve conflicts, subject to preemption by activities that in the short run are more important than conflict resolution. In this case, no decision is required. The discipline is automatic. In the second case, we discipline the compartment from within, as our contemplation of trade-offs leads us to conclude that we should reserve time for contemplation along with our other local activities. Therefore, we do not need a super-global perspective to decide how much time to reserve for the activity of taking the global perspective. Such decisions are precisely the kind we make from the global perspective itself, if we need to make them at all. Unless we introduce something that competes with the goal of making life as a whole go as well as possible (such as, perhaps, the recognition of moral obligations), there is no reason to step back from a global perspective to something even broader.

8. Conclusion

This chapter sets out part of a normative ideal of rational choice suitable for the kind of beings we happen to be, beings who would only hurt ourselves if we tried to maximize our overall utility in every waking activity. It defines satisficing and local optimizing as strategies for pursuing goals within constraints that are in part self-imposed. Satisficing emerges not as an alternative to optimizing as a model of rationality but rather as an alternative to local optimizing as a strategy for pursuing global optima.

Under normal conditions, we employ a combination of heuristics, such as (1) compartmentalizing our pursuits so as to narrow the scope of any particular optimization problem to the point where our limited knowledge becomes sufficient to identify an optimal solution, (2) accepting self-imposed constraints for the same reason as well as to keep particular pursuits from preempting more important ones, and (3) satisficing, which has the often salutary effect of closing compartments as soon as they serve the purpose for which they were created. Under normal conditions, where we lack the information we need to assign probabilities and utilities, this combination of strategies is more effective at making our lives as a whole go well than the alternative of plugging guesswork into a formula for maximizing expected utility. Thus, it is no wonder we so rarely make any attempt to calculate expected utilities, for the truth is that we usually have better things to do.

When goals are in conflict, there may not be any well-defined sense in which one way of resolving the conflict is, from the viewpoint of one's life as a whole, better than the alternatives. Of course, we do well to cultivate moderate preferences so as to reduce the frequency and severity of conflicts of value. But at the same time, there are limits to what one should do to avoid situations of underdetermined choice, for the risk of finding oneself in such situations is one we assume in the process of becoming rationally committed to particular ends as ends in themselves. A life with no regrets (about decisions made under unresolved conflict) is preferable all other things equal, but if the lack of regret is purchased at a cost of not having goals that can come into unresolvable conflict, the price is too high. A person who adopts a number of goals as ends in themselves risks finding himself in situations where global optima do not exist, but there are reasons why a global optimizer would take that risk.

Admittedly, these conclusions about rational strategy are not particularly neat and tidy, certainly not in comparison with the simple maximization model. But tidying up the conclusions at the expense of realism would be a mistake, for the conclusions are meant to be about us, not about mathematically tractable caricatures of us. Rational choice theory developed along the lines indicated here has more power than simple maximization models to explain the ways in which we actually live, but it does not thereby become merely a self-congratulating description of how we live. Rather, it remains (or becomes) a tool for evaluating and criticizing the ways in which we actually live. It sets out a normative ideal of rational choice that it would be natural and healthy for us to try to live up to.

Postscript: The Difference Between Satisficing and Local Optimizing

I distinguished between satisficing and local optimizing as stopping rules. Some readers may find it helpful to consider a graphical representation of that distinction. We might represent a choice among alternatives in two-dimensional Cartesian space with Utility on the y-axis and our set of alternatives arrayed along the x-axis. If we know the shape of the utility curve, we simply pick the highest point. No controversy arises. See Figure 2-1. Much of this chapter concerns what to do when we are looking at a blank; that is, we may suppose there is some curve or other, but often we do not know what it looks like. See Figure 2-2.

Further, suppose we look at our lives from a global perspective, wanting life as a whole to go well. What do we see? We do not see one big graph, blank or otherwise. Rather, we see a collection of little graphs, some of which are more or less blank. The question then arises: Within a particular compartment, how do we make decisions when we do not know the utility

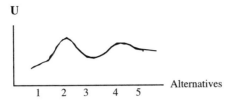

FIGURE 2-1. Searching among alternatives with known utilities

function's shape? The answer is that we search the set of alternatives. We see how much utility a_1 has. We see how much a_2 has, and so on. And because other decisions (searches) are also calling for our limited resources, we pick something at some point.

At what point do we rationally stop searching and pick something? The answer is that we impose two kinds of constraints on our search of the particular local utility space. We impose vertical constraints on how many alternatives we will consider (or if we defined the x-axis differently, constraints on how much time or money or whatever resources we invest in the search). In other words, we operate with limited *inputs*. Or we impose horizontal constraints on how much utility we insist on getting before we stop searching. In other words, we operate with limited aspirations, limits on aimed-at *output*. Or we do both. Then, when we run up against either kind of limit, we stop searching in that local utility space, pick something, and turn our attention to some other local utility space. See Figure 2-3.

In Figure 2-3, the horizontal line represents the point at which $U = U^*$, where U^* is the level of U with which the agent will be satisfied. As mentioned earlier, we can let the expected utility of continued search equal the probability of finding a better option, $P(fbo)$, multiplied by the utility of finding a better option, $U(fbo)$, minus the cost of further search, $C(fs)$. In that case, the vertical line in Figure 2-3 represents the point along the x-axis at which, the agent judges, it becomes true that $P(fbo)U(fbo) - C(fs) = 0$, where $P(fbo)U(fbo)$ is the expected utility of further search and $C(fs)$ is the cost of further search.

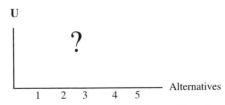

FIGURE 2-2. Searching among alternatives with unknown utilities

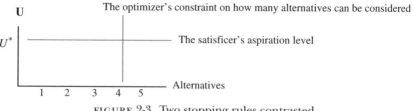

FIGURE 2-3. Two stopping rules contrasted

In Figure 2-3, vertical constraints are constraints on inputs and define the search as local optimizing, taking the best alternative we discover prior to hitting that constraint. Horizontal constraints are constraints on aimed-at output and define the search as satisficing, taking the first alternative we find with that high a utility. The two strategies can be employed simultaneously, of course. The gist of my argument is: (1) This is how we actually live and (2) a global optimizer would have no reason for wanting to do things differently.

The vertical constraints partition our various activities in terms of how much of our total resources are allotted to those activities. Note that we do not need to be able to prioritize our activities in order to ration our resources among them. If necessary, we can arbitrarily set vertical constraints on how much (time, money, and so on) we are willing to spend within a particular compartment. As illustrated by the story about imposing time constraints on our search for optimal toothpaste, we tend to be satisficers when gathering information about where to set vertical constraints. The less we know about what our different endeavors mean to us, relatively speaking, the more arbitrariness there will be when we set the vertical constraints that delimit the different compartments. By the same token, the more comparability we have in terms of the relative importance of our different activities, the less arbitrary will be the boundaries we draw between them.

Notes

This paper is a revised version of "Rationality within Reason," originally published in *Journal of Philosophy* 89 (1992): 445–66. I thank the *Journal* for permission to reprint. I also thank Princeton University Press for permission to use material in this chapter's postscript that originally appeared in David Schmidtz, *Rational Choice and Moral Agency* (Princeton, N.J.: Princeton University Press, 1995). Finally, I thank Michael Byron for encouraging me to revisit this material.

1. Michael Stocker, *Plural and Conflicting Values*. New York: Oxford University Press, 1990, pp. 311–16. Stocker argues that optimizing, even in this subtle sense, is both morally and rationally problematic.
2. Michael Slote, *Beyond Optimizing: A Study of Rational Choice*. Cambridge, Mass.: Harvard University Press, 1989, p. 5; Herbert A. Simon, "A Behavioral Model of Rational Choice." *Quarterly Journal of Economics* 69 (1955): 99–118; Herbert A. Simon, *Models of Thought*. New Haven, Conn.: Yale University Press, 1979, p. 3; James G. March, "Bounded Rationality, Ambiguity, and the Engineering of Choice. In J. G. March, ed., *Decisions and Organizations*. Oxford: Basil Blackwell, 1988, p. 270. I borrowed the term 'satisficing' from Slote, but my characterization of satisficing differs from his. My understanding is closer to that of Herbert Simon. Simon's idea is that, given our limited capacity to acquire and process information, we economize on that limited capacity by setting a concrete goal and then reasoning back to conclusions about what course of action would achieve that goal. This is what Simon means by satisficing. The notion of satisficing as a stopping rule is implied, and it later becomes explicit. Simon treats satisficing as a surrogate for optimizing under particular information constraints and, so far as I know, treats our limited information as an external constraint. I think such constraints are often more accurately viewed as being partly self-imposed. Within the context of constraints that are in part self-imposed, the distinction between satisficing and optimizing becomes more interesting, as explained in Section 2.
3. When pressed to justify stopping a search upon finding a satisfactory alternative, people may say that further search would not have been worth the cost. Does that mean they were optimizing after all? Only if the cost of further search was what in fact made them stop. If the circumstance that actually stops a search is the finding of a satisfactory alternative, then it is a case of satisficing, no matter what might be said, after the fact, in defense of the choice. One can defend two acts in the same way without implying that the two acts are the same kind of act. For more discussion of how the two stopping rules differ and of how they might usefully be combined, see the Postscript to this chapter.
4. There may not be any precise way to characterize 'good enough'. Options promising disease, imprisonment, or premature death are typically held in low esteem, however, so the notion has certain objective elements. But what people consider good enough also seems relative to expectations. As expectations rise, the standards by which an option is judged good enough also tend to rise. This fact can be tragic. It can rob people of the ability to appreciate how well their lives are going, all things considered. Of course, it is rational to set *goals* with an eye to what is attainable, raising one's sights as higher goals become attainable. But raising the standard by which we deem our situation satisfactory is harder to fathom. Perhaps people are psychologically incapable of aiming at higher goals without simultaneously reformulating their notions of what is satisfactory. I do not know.
5. Jon Elster, *Ulysses and the Sirens: Studies in Rationality and Irrationality*. New York: Cambridge University Press, 1984, p. 9. I borrowed the terms 'local' and 'global' from Elster, although the way he uses the terms bears no resemblance

to the way they are used here. (He says the definitive difference between locally and globally maximizing machines is that the latter, unlike the former, are capable of *waiting* and *indirect* strategies.)

6. For someone wanting to construct a tractable mathematical model, it might be easier to ignore the felt experience of pursuing local goals under self-imposed constraints and concentrate instead on the global perspective, from which self-imposed constraints appear, more or less, as preferences about how to operate within external constraints. I want to explain satisficing in terms of thought processes we can recognize within ourselves, though. So for my purposes, the fact that we have both broader and narrower perspectives cannot be ignored.

7. David Gauthier, *Morals by Agreement.* Oxford: Clarendon Press, 1986, p. 170. As Jules Coleman has pointed out to me, what Gauthier calls constrained maximization is a particularly interesting kind of local optimizing under self-imposed constraints. Constrained maximizers seek maximum payoffs in Prisoner's Dilemmas subject to this constraint: They will cooperate (and thus pass up the opportunity to unilaterally defect) if the expected payoff of cooperating is higher than the known payoff of *mutual* defection, which it will be if and only if they expect their partners to cooperate.

8. Michael Slote, *Beyond Optimizing: A Study of Rational Choice.* Cambridge, Mass.: Harvard University Press, 1989. p. 40.

9. The Postscript to this chapter uses graphical analysis to illustrate the difference between the two kinds of self-imposed limit.

10. Jay Rosenberg tells me that, before he began looking for a house, he made a list of desirable features, telling himself he would take the first house having 85 percent or more of those features. As it happens, the first house he looked at scored 85 percent. He stopped looking, bought the house, and has lived there ever since.

11. In a draft version of "Satisficing and Optimality," Michael Byron said I did not address in any significant detail the conditions under which satisficing is rational. Commenting on that draft, I alerted Byron to the fact that I had addressed the issue at length, in the foregoing section. The published version of Byron's paper, seemingly trying to accommodate this, said, "Although Schmidtz discusses several cases to illustrate some instances of rational satisficing, he does not seem to extract a systematic account of rational satisficing from these. Schmidtz reminds me that I haven't done much better on this score; yet I am not here proposing an account of rationality." See Michael Byron, "Satisficing and Optimality," *Ethics*, 109 (1998) 67–93, here footnote 18. Suffice it to say, the thrust of my reminder was that I had an account, not that his was only a little better.

12. Slote, *Beyond Optimizing*, p. 11.

13. Slote, *Beyond Optimizing*, p. 9.

14. Slote, *Beyond Optimizing*, p. 18.

15. That is, an optimizer might choose a satisfactory option in preference to searching for better options that might never materialize. Slote, however, says we intuitively recognize the rationality of taking the first satisfactory offer even in abstraction from the real-world risks and anxieties of having to

sell one's house (p. 18). However, if we are going to talk about common sense allowing a seller to immediately accept the firm offer even though the seller has the option of waiting a few days in hope of a higher offer, then we have to stick to conditions under which common sense holds sway. We do indeed have intuitions about what to do in risky situations, but we cannot, as Slote wants to do, simply *stipulate* that our intuitions regarding risky situations have nothing to do with the fact that in the real world such situations are risky. In the real-world housing market, to turn down an entirely satisfactory offer in quest of something better is to court disaster, to tempt fate. This is one reason why it is common sense, and rationally explicable common sense, for a global optimizer to be hesitant about turning down a satisfactory offer. Even from a local perspective, the expected gain from further search may not be worth risking the potential loss.

16. Philip Pettit, "Sacrificing Consequentialism." *Proceedings of the Aristotelian Society* suppl. 58 (1984): 172. Pettit makes the same point.

17. Slote, *Beyond Optimizing*, p. 21.

18. Slote, *Beyond Optimizing*, p. 2.

19. I thank Mark Ravizza for this point.

20. John Pollock, "A Theory of Moral Reasoning," *Ethics*, (1986): 506–523; 517.

21. Edna Ullmann-Margalit and Sidney Morgenbesser, "Picking and Choosing," *Social Research* 44 (1977): 758–759 say one *picks* between A and B when one is indifferent between them and prefers the selection of either A or B to the selection of neither. What I call "picking something or other" presumes the latter but not the former condition, for one could be in a picking situation even if one was not indifferent between one's alternatives. In the EverBetter Wine case, one cannot find even a pair of alternatives over which one is indifferent. Even so, one still is forced to simply pick.

22. If you knew that ever better opportunities would keep coming in a steady stream, the optimal long run strategy would be to make a big move up every ten months, skipping intervening steps.

23. Isacc Levi, *Hard Choices: Decision Making Under Unresolved Conflict*, Cambridge University Press, 1986, 13ff.

24. As Allan Gibbard, *Wise Choices, Apt Feelings*, Cambridge: Harvard University Press, 1990, 321 says, we have ways of coping other than by resolving everything.

25. T. K. Seung and Daniel Bonevac, "Plural Values and Indeterminate Ranking," *Ethics* 102 (1992): 799–813 distinguish between *incommensurate* rankings (in which no alternative comes out best) and *indeterminate* rankings (in which several alternatives come out tied for best). Most of what follows is about incommensurate rankings. In contrast, most of the cases discussed in Ullmann-Margalit and Morgenbesser, "Picking and Choosing," like the case in which a shopper chooses among identical cans of tomato soup, are about indeterminate rankings.

26. As Bernard Williams (in J. J. C. Smart and Bernard Williams, *Utilitarianism: For and Against*, Cambridge University Press, 1973, 113) puts it, one has to want other things for there to be anywhere that happiness can come from.

See also the eleventh of Joseph Butler's *Fifteen Sermons,* Oxford: Clarendon Press, 1874, 139.

27. I thank Nick Sturgeon for a discussion from which this point emerged. See also Chapter 6 of Stocker, *Plural and Conflicting Values* and, of course, Chapter 2 of John Stuart Mill *Utilitarianism,* Indianapolis: Hackett, 1979.

28. Holly Smith, "Deciding How to Decide: Is There a Regress Problem?" in M. Bacharach and S. Hurley, eds. *Foundations of Decision Theory,* New Yrok: Blackwell, 1991, 194–219 worries about the same sort of problem.

29. The simplest way to explain the amount of time spent at the global level would be to say we take whatever time we need to consider *everything*. The trouble is that we do not have time to consider everything that might be relevant to life as a whole, any more than we have time to consider everything that might be relevant to the purchasing of a house. The explanation will have to be more complicated than this; hence the line of thought pursued in the following text.

3

Maxificing: Life on a Budget; or, If You Would Maximize, Then Satisfice!

Jan Narveson

The Issue

In recent times, the view that the doctrine of maximization is *too* something – too demanding, too unrealistic, too stringent, or some such thing – has come into a certain vogue. Not that we are supposed to "minimize," however: The Hegelian synthesis proposed has it that instead, the rational individual "satisfices." Roughly, the idea is that we set a threshold such that the next sample of what we are looking for – call it F – that meets that criterion is to be chosen, even though we may be well aware that somewhere out there, there are bigger and better Fs.

The question has always been what the status of the satisficing template is by comparison with the maximizing one. *Prima facie*, if the rational chooser is confronted, essentially simultaneously, with *two* samples of F, one clearly better than the other, and he must choose between them, then he will choose the better. It seems incomprehensible that he should choose the worse, in the absence of special contexts or reasons. Is the satisficer insisting that he do so?

There is considerable temptation simply to say that one who prefers x to y even when he agrees that y is better is *eo ipso* irrational. If we do say this, it would be, I think, because of the practical commitments of appraisal words like 'better' and 'good.' Is to say that x is good to imply that one *would* choose x, other things being equal? If so, it seems also reasonable to suggest that to say that x is *better than* y is to imply that one would choose x over y, other things being equal. But as we all know, the concept of an "other thing" and especially of the sum of other things, relative to a particular choice, "being equal" is not exactly a model of luminous clarity.

We should immediately take note of the fact that choice contexts, invariably, involve two quite different things. First, there are the virtues and vices, the merits and demerits, relevant to the particular kind of thing we are choosing – socks, cars, jobs, and so on. But second, there is an indefinite background of involvements, previous choices made on all sorts of things, and this background imposes constraints, sometimes sharply defined, more often rather vague. Yes, this would be the *best* pair of socks, but frankly I can't afford them; or, *best* absolutely, yes, but unfortunately Mary hates them; or. . . . And the impingement of these background matters will certainly often tell us to take the worse of two choices, if the respects in which they are "worse" are narrow and specific and, as such, take little account of that welter of background value-involvements.

Occasions of the aforementioned type, then, where we can rationally prefer the worse in these narrowly defined respects are, in truth, legion in human life. We will do x "other things being equal," indeed – but how often does that happy condition obtain? Not, it might be said, often. But if we are to appraise possibilities at all, we must be able to evaluate choices at some degree of abstraction before we can evaluate them in the concrete. For what is the concrete if not a thick congeries of abstract properties or features? Would it be nice to have Dan over for dinner? Well, he's a nice guy (usually), a good conversationalist (with any luck as to topics) – but he has a few annoying habits – and is likely to get a phone call on his pager and have to leave early. . . . Weighing these all up is not easy, but the case is a typical example of classic choice making. What can we do but size things up one by one, somehow put them all together, with plausible estimates of the relative importance of each consideration – and then hope that reality doesn't bring too many nasty surprises?

Hard is it to maximize, then. Or is it? Those who suppose it is may have the following picture in mind. If we want the best F we can get our hands on, we seem to be committed to enormous – possibly unending – research. When do we quit and take *this* one? If there is any answer to that question, have we then given up on maximization? After all, if you choose this one at time t, there is likely going to be a better one accessible at t + n.

The catch is that we may not have the time to wait. And in some cases, there will be what is normally known as a budgetary problem: Sure we'd like a better one – but we just can't afford it.

Life on a Budget

When we think about it, we can see, I believe, that this matter of budget turns out to be the crux of the issue. All of us have budgets: of time, money, energy, or whatever. The budget operates as a constraint on choice: It's what you have to work within.

But why is our budget what it is? In the case where it's a sum of money, for instance, then you or someone has allocated that amount for this purpose. Why not more? Or less? Here the question of maximizing versus satisficing would seem to arise again: Increase the budget for this, and you have less to spend on that. You have to weigh your desire for this against your desire for that, and see what mix you come up with. Surely we'd like the best one.

Maximizing has a natural advantage in that context. When we have some control over budgets, does it even make sense to talk of satisficing? If I decide that $X will be enough, on what other ground could this be, if not that allocating more will cost too much elsewhere? The overall mix, we think, is the best we can do. It is hard to see how it could be rational to prefer a less good mix to a better mix if we can know them to be such.

If we think that that may also not be true, there is the real chance that, again, our overall budget assessment is too narrow. For example, money, as they say, isn't everything – even when it comes to budgets. They say it because it is, simply, true. Suppose that by investigating carefully for another five hours, I can improve my overall mix a bit. But is it worth spending all that time on this problem? Probably not. The marginal cost of more thinking about it exceeds the potential benefits of a better rethink, and that's true even if we can't put a monetary estimate on the relative values involved. The point is, that's maximizing talk, not satisficing talk.

Suppose we are allowed to factor into our deliberations considerations about our budget, along with our appraisals of the objects of choice. What then? Clearly, if we do *not* attend to budgets, maximization of anything is out the window. Rational choosers do not maximize, unqualifiedly, on any definite thing, because if they did, they would find that they cannot actually choose anything at all. There are always more fish in the sea, more attractive friends, better performances of the Hammerklavier Sonata, and so on. Yet once we have a budget constraint, it will be difficult to distinguish maximizing from satisficing.

Here you are at the supermarket, with just so much time and just so much money. Which of the seven different brands of F on the shelf, in their four different-sized packages, do you get? Suppose experience has revealed that Brand Y in size S2 is the one that best suits, given your general budget. Can we, knowing this, rationally choose instead some other package? Again, aside from the always-possible Other Thing that turns out to be Not Equal on this occasion, not obviously. Given no downside at all to choosing the best, we choose it, and if we do not, explanation is needed.

The context of marriage provides an excellent example here, both because it is familiar to most of us (married or unmarried) and because it so clearly illustrates the relevant variables. My father once remarked to me that one of my brothers was "looking for the perfect woman." Not surprisingly, he hadn't found her at last report. What he did instead was to abandon that search and settle for a nice woman who is well suited to his peculiarities – in short, he has satisficed. But didn't he maximize while he was at it? You don't maximize by spending your life looking for the most beautiful woman on earth – unless what you want to do is spend your life looking for the most beautiful woman on Earth, in which case, once again, you can't distinguish between satisficing and maximizing.

My thesis is that in satisficing, we maximize, given our budgets. We choose the best one before the time limit arrives, before our money runs out, before we are exhausted, before we are in despair. . . . Within the limits imposed by our budgets, we do the best we can. We do not, as some characterizations of satisficing seem to suggest, establish a threshold and pick the first one that meets the criterion *even when we can see that a better one is readily available* – that is, even if our budget permits us to wait a little longer, spend a little more, or, in general, expend more of whatever our budget may consist of. But it is also possible that the bit more we can expend isn't worth it.

Aristotle

For purposes of shedding, perhaps, more light on this, and anyway adding tone to this deliberation, let's turn our attention for a moment to the eternally interesting (to scholars, anyway) subject of Aristotle's Ethics. Aristotle is generally held to make the following two claims:

- we all seek to be as happy as possible
- but not just in any old version of happiness; rather, the way to go is to aim at being virtuous.

Virtues are specific "excellences." Now, probably the most important department of virtues for this purpose is *moral* virtue, which has to do with the "intermediate part of the soul" – roughly, our emotional makeups. The way moral virtue works is this: You achieve it by finding and acting on the "mean" in regard to your "passions." And the mean, we are told, is in general to be found between possible extremes, which consist of displaying "too much" or "too little," respectively, of the particular passion in question.

Life gets complicated, however – both in itself and for would-be interpreters of Aristotle – by the fact that we have to do the right thing *in the circumstances* and such:

> For instance, both fear and confidence and appetite and anger and pity and in general pleasure and pain may be felt both too much and too little, and in both cases not well; but to feel them at the right times, with reference to the right objects, towards the right people, with the right motive, and in the right way, is what is both intermediate and best, and this is characteristic of virtue. Similarly with regard to actions also there is excess, defect, and the intermediate.[1]

Aristotle does not supply an algorithm for determining which times are the right times, which objects the right objects, which people the right people, and so on. That may be unfortunate, but it's hardly surprising, and luckily, we don't have to supply it either. All we want to know is whether Aristotle's picture is one that would make sense of a satisficing as opposed to a maximizing model. One reason for doubting this is that it does seem as though Aristotle thinks we should maximize virtue itself. It is not clear just how this is done, but presumably on each and every occasion when we act, there would be some best act that would maximize virtue on that occasion, and we should aim to do that on each and every occasion. The good man "strains every nerve"[2] to achieve virtue. That seems quite maximizing enough.

On the other hand, of course, the formula he does supply is such that on each occasion, we are quite specifically *not* to maximize fulfillment of the passion in question. Now, this may or may not raise the issue we are interested in, but I think we can warp it so that it does. It doesn't raise that issue, or at least not directly, if we say that Aristotle, like Plato, doesn't think that fulfilling a passion is even *prima facie* a good thing anyway. Therefore the issue of why isn't more of it better doesn't arise. OK: But it's more interesting if we suppose that when you desire something, including desiring to *do* something, then what *you* think, anyway, so far as it goes, is that the thing you desire would be a good thing to have or do. Now, if it's a thing to do, there might not be a question of maximizing anyway (though if there's no question of degree, Aristotle's recipe can't even be invoked); but if it's a desire for a quantity of something or other, then it looks more like a desire such that more seems to the desirer to be better.

Plato argued in *The Republic* that desires are inherently infinite, and that that was what was wrong with them. His actual argument is fallacious, for what he argues is that thirst, for instance, is just a desire for drink, not for any particular amount of drink.[3] It certainly doesn't follow from that true premise that any particular case of thirst is actually a desire for an infinite *amount* of drink, and of course no human being ever does desire an infinite amount of drink. On occasion, somebody might be up for a gallon or so, and even he would have a problem.

Now this enables us to make a couple of important points about maximizing and satisficing. Suppose I'm thirsty. It is normal human experience that I begin to drink, and after a bit decide I've had enough. Does this exemplify satisficing as opposed to maximizing? Well, it certainly exemplifies satisficing as regards quantities of *water* (or beer, or whatever). But then, who ever thought that, when it comes to thirst, more *liquid* defines what is *better*? What's more plausible to say is this: We can "slake" thirst. We do this when we drink a quantity such that we are no longer thirsty at that point, and so we quit. Please note: In this case, it seems enormously plausible to say, satisficing *just is* maximizing. Having too little would not maximize, but it wouldn't satisfy either; having too much would also not maximize satisfaction of the desire we had – drinking too much, even of water or soda pop, let alone beer or scotch – is uncomfortable.

If we had a meter for this purpose, measuring the satisfaction that is the object of thirst-on-this-occasion, the meter would peak out when we've had (finite) quantity X; and quantity X + Y, where Y is just discernibly more, would cause the meter to begin *declining.* This is an especially clear case for the thesis that to satisfice is to maximize: In getting just the right amount of F, we do the best thing – we achieve the highest level of virtue.

Plenty of cases fit the broad Aristotelian formula. It's often true of quantities that we do best with an amount that can be either exceeded or fallen short of. But 'best' here does not, as we have seen, mean maximizing *as opposed to* satisficing.

Pleasure

This naturally brings us to the subject of pleasure. Satisfaction has an important ambiguity, as has often been noted. We may say that the desire to have x is satisfied if and only if the agent has x. But still, much though he may have desired x before he got it, he could be dissatisfied with x when it arrives. In various ways, it does not satisfy. (An interesting question, of course, is whether we can respond by insisting that our desire had been inadequately specified: Yes, we wanted a steak, but not one quite like *this.*) Perhaps we can work an effective fiddle to unify the two notions of satisfaction: We are truly satisfied when and only when we get *exactly* what we wanted. If that is to succeed, however, it seems we will have to add that we may not have known quite what it was we wanted. And again, if we are allowed it, this maneuver promises also a resolution of satisficing versus maximizing: Perfect satisfaction is getting exactly what we want, neither more nor less. There's no room for Aristotelian qualifications there.

Except, of course, that whenever what we want is something in particular, then getting it may raise hob with some other interest, and getting exactly what you wanted in the way of F leaves you dissatisfied in respect of G. If a split between satisficing and maximizing is thought to re-arise from that quarter, I would reply that the sense of its doing so is illusory. More of F *isn't* better, and the right amount is so because of its relation to G, H, and so on, and not just in the abstract, but in reality.

This also brings up the subject of pleasure – as the reader may not have realized. Can we have too much pleasure? Aristotle seems to think so, in the previous quotation. Yet it is this same Aristotle who argues that the best life, which is (of course!) that of the philosopher, will also be the most pleasant ("... but the activity of philosophic wisdom is admittedly the pleasantest of virtuous activities...."[4]). Now, that should be an odd thing to say for somebody who has told us that there is a "right amount" of pleasure, and that amount isn't the maximal amount – "pleasure and pain may be felt both too much and too little."

Let's suppose there is a specifically philosophical sort of pleasure, and let's suppose that the best life is that of the philosopher. Could we, then, have "too much" philosophical pleasure? There's still some reason for thinking so: You might get off on the Theory of Universals so much that you failed to eat and ended up starving to death. If that problem arises, it seems a reasonable case for concluding that, yes, even philosophical pleasure can be overdone. *Mutatis mutandis* – at least if you are as square (or as busy? or repressed?) as Aristotle (and most of us) – for, say, sexual pleasure. We will be hard-pressed to find any specific kind of pleasure such that we would expect to be happiest by maximizing *it.* At best we would have to take one or the other of two arguably desperate options.

Either (1) we argue, à la G. E. Moore and Bentham, that there really *is* just exactly one kind of pleasure, that all pleasures are so by virtue of exemplifying that one sort (underneath it all, no doubt), and so that the good life is the one with the maximum of that; or (2) we find some super-complex formula for integrating different kinds of pleasure into the ideally pleasurable life, despite admitting that they are mutually irreducible, even *qua* pleasures.

Now, I think it an interesting question whether we truly wish to affirm that there are good things which are (a) not experiences at all, of any kind, or (b) are experiences all right, but are purely "neutral" ones, neither enjoyable nor the reverse, and (c) such that their goodness can be fully instantiated even if nobody gets any shred of pleasure from contemplating those things, or doing whatever there is to do with them. I am inclined to doubt it, current consensus to the contrary notwithstanding.

Even so, it is obvious that our pleasure, once you get beyond the exceedingly rudimentary, is a function of our perception of the sort of things that give the pleasure to us, and of our attitudes toward them. Consequently, if we look at any particular source of pleasure, an out-and-out hedonist will always be able to agree that it would be possible to have "too much" of *that* kind, on a given occasion or even in general. For more than a certain amount of it may be incompatible with securing pleasures from other sources, and then on either model (a) or model (b), the overall "quantity" of pleasure in our lives will be less than it otherwise could be. Again, maximizing and satisficing converge.

Can we generalize this result? I am inclined to think so. For it seems to me difficult to deny that we are interested in living the on-the-whole *best* life we can. Now, here I want to pay attention, for just a moment, to the subject of morals. There are extremely tricky, extremely important questions about the relation of our own good life to morality. Must the best life be the morally best life? It is hard to say either yes or no, but there is certainly a good deal to be said on behalf of a negative answer. However, I will airily wave my hand at this question and just assume that we have the right answer, whatever it is, and that this answer enables us to factor morality into the other aspects of life in such a way that we can say, without conceptual (though no doubt with plenty of other) problems, that Life X is, absolutely – *all* things considered – better than Life Y. And what I want to know is this: If we could know that (and I agree that we probably can't, or at least that knowing it generally, for *all* x and *all* y, is probably out of the question) – *if*, as I say, we *can* know this, in a particular case, does it really make any sense to say that nevertheless we should choose Y rather than X *on the ground* that X satisfices? I don't see it.

Instead, I suggest, what will happen is that the various components that go into Life X and make it on the whole better than Life Y will be satisficing components. With respect to lots of specific values, the best way to go is to select just some suitable degree of those, without striving to do better along those dimensions. But that will be because to strive to do better will, in the end, be worse.[5]

First- and Second-Order Desires

Grant Brown advances a number of arguments for satisficing, though it is not entirely clear whether he is indeed proposing that it should genuinely, full-fledgedly replace maximizing. But we should discuss it with that possibility in mind, because otherwise the needed rivalry between the views is lacking. "They imply second-order values, which cannot be assimilated on the same level as the values implied by first-order desires. These are just the kind of concerns and values with which the maximizing model is incapable of dealing properly."[6] Well, why not? Here's a model on which it could: Suppose first-order desires are, as it were, out of touch with one another. As far as my desire for oatmeal is concerned, my desire for Shostakovich is nowhere and nothing – but I have all these. So my impartial umpire Second-Order Command Center looks down upon this welter of first-order desires and notes that some of them can be much more substantially fulfilled, given my resources, than others. So it directs me to act on those, and not the others. But it does so by comparing my potential utility income from these diverse sources.

This requires, of course, denial of a claim that many, including Brown, want to make: that all of our desires are, after all, comparable in terms of a convertible "utility income." What about this claim?

Well, first, it is not entailed by the second-order desire model. On my alternative model of that type, although first-order desires are out of touch with one another, the second-order desirer is in touch with all of them. Moreover, it compares them on this linear scale. Brown notes this: "Thus, the hierarchical structure of the autonomous will does not necessarily imply a non-linear structure of value. A maximizing agent could be autonomous in this way, without ceasing to be a maximizing agent."

So suppose it can't. I then want to know what good a second-order desire is. If we don't think that the output of a second-order desire is *better* than what we could do without it, why bother with it? Or is it just *there*, like death and taxes? Brown says,

I suggest that second-order desires need not be restricted to this kind of adjudicating role, the resolving of conflicts between first-order desires. A rational and autonomous satisficing agent also has second-order concerns about how first-order desires are *related* to one another, and how they are to be *pursued*. These second-order concerns are to a degree independent of the values implicit in the agent's first-order desires. They imply second-order values, which cannot be assimilated on the same level as the values implied by first-order desires. These are just the kind of concerns and values with which the maximizing model is incapable of dealing properly.

That is not obvious, though. Brown has just got through noting that such functions can, logically, be performed on a maximizing model. How are we to pursue first-order desires? By seeing how much we gain versus how much we lose by pursuing them. How do we decide how to pursue them? Again, by the method that yields the highest benefits in relation to costs. We must be given reasons why this should not be possible. Are we?

Brown says of the sort of model just sketched, "No doubt this is true of some cases of moderation, but not all. Sometimes agents settle for what is satisfactory simply because they feel they have quite sufficient as it is and do not need or care for more." But if we "don't care for more," that is usually exactly what is meant by saying that the marginal utility of more is zero. *Prima facie*, Brown's counter-case is just anther confirming instance after all.

It has to be agreed that we might simply happen to like only so much of something. But this is no problem: To be a maximizer is not to be in favor of maximizing just any old variable. Take one's waistline, for example. Here there is, I imagine, no presumption that more inches are, even *prima facie*, better – or less, either. What we want is "the right amount," and its rightness is an aesthetic judgment (plus or minus some evolutionary biological explanation, or perhaps nutritional). But then, we will want to get as close to the ideal as possible – maximization rears its head yet again. And it will do so even more when we relate our intuitions about ideal waistlines to our desires for more chocolate sundaes. There again, we might have some balancing ideal. The waistline preference might rule entirely over the chocolate desire – but then, we might find some other compromise. Suppose I can increase my quota of chocolate at the cost of one extra inch. I might decide that this is best, on the whole – why not? And if I do, could we not express this by declaring that the overall utility of this combination is higher than would be either the perfect waistline with too little chocolate, or letting the waistline go to hell and eating tubs of chocolate?

Brown cites Michael Slote's claim that the maximization habit militates against spontaneity. Maybe. But then again: Spontaneity, for most of us, isn't everything. It is, however, something. We can develop a pretty sharp sense of when to stop running our mental computers and just act on our instincts – and when not to! Now, unless Slote is claiming that we should *never* let our computational tendencies interfere with our spontaneous behavior, I am puzzled why he should think there is something basically wrong with maximizing. Say I have a sudden, spontaneous urge to jump out this tenth-story window, just for the hell of it. It seems to me that a quick calculational burst, averting me from pursuing this spontaneous impulse, is an awfully good idea.

Again, Brown agrees with this, I guess: "Spontaneity is one such virtue, which the highly reflective maximizer has lost to an extreme. In order to recover it, the maximizer must become less reflective, less concerned with maximization; he or she must cultivate a disposition *not* always to maximize." That is, Brown agrees that spontaneity isn't everything, but it is something. So the question for each of us is: how much? I don't see why we shouldn't represent a rational answer to that question as a judgment that we will, on the whole, do best if we let spontaneity rule here, there, now, then, and not just there or that place or that time. . . .

Will the judgment that our lives should have so much spontaneity and so much predictable stuff be like the judgment about the ideal waistline? Or will it be like the judgment about what to charge our customers, given what we know about their pockets, habits, and preferences?

Brown's final example is morality, and it is certainly an important example – indeed, the best there could be. He cites Gauthier's moral theory as involving a switch to satisficing and away from maximizing. But that is not textually accurate. Gauthier calls upon us to switch from "straight" maximization to "constrained" maximization not because maximization is wrong: On the contrary, it's because, to put it paradoxically, straight maximizers don't maximize. We do better if we optimize – and we do better in terms of *the very things that the straight maximizer is after.* The straight maximizer invites, by his activities, replies in kind, and will certainly get them later or (more likely) sooner. The result is suboptimal for all.

It seems to me that satisficing makes no intrinsic sense if it is genuinely inconsistent with maximizing *in general.* But my thesis has been that it is not. We satisfice that we may maximize.

Notes

1. Aristotle, *Nicomachean Ethics*, Ross translation, 1106b16–20, in Richard McKeon, ed. *The Basic Works of Aristotle*. New York: Random House, 1941.
2. Aristotle, *Nicomachean Ethics*, 1169a6–10.
3. Plato, *The Republic*, S. 439–439b, tr. Richard W. Sterling and William C. Scott. New York: W. W. Norton, 1985.
4. Aristotle, *Nicomachean Ethics*, 1177a24–25.
5. The debt I owe to David Schmidtz in this paper is obvious to anyone acquainted with his work – to the point that I would be happy to stick him with its faults as well as such virtues as it has. I shall, alas, have to take responsibility for the faults myself; that he should get credit for at least most of its virtues is clear. See, especially, David Schmidtz, *Rational Choice and Moral Agency*, Princeton University Press, 1995, 31–40.
6. Grant Brown, "Satisficing Rationality: In Praise of Folly," *Journal of Value Inquiry* 26 (1992): 261–70.

4

Satisficing and Substantive Values

Thomas Hurka

Satisficing theories, whether of rationality or morality, do not require agents to maximize the good. They demand only that agents bring about outcomes that are, in one or both of two senses, "good enough." In the first sense, an outcome is good enough if it is above some absolute threshold of goodness; this yields a view that I will call absolute-level satisficing. In the second sense, an outcome is good enough if it is reasonably close to the best outcome the agent could bring about; this leads to what I will call comparative satisficing. These two views coincide in their implications for a specific sort of case, in which the situation is now fairly far below the absolute-level threshold and an agent can at best bring it to a point somewhat above that threshold. Here both absolute-level and comparative satisficing say that one need not bring about the best available outcome, though of course one may; one is required only to improve the situation to the absolute threshold. But in other cases the views diverge. If the situation is now far below the absolute threshold and, no matter what, will remain below it, absolute-level satisficing requires agents to do everything they can to improve the situation; here its implications coincide with those of maximizing. But comparative satisficing is less demanding, requiring agents only to make some reasonable percentage of the largest improvement they can. By contrast, if the situation is already above the absolute threshold, absolute-level satisficing does not require agents to do anything at all to improve it, whereas comparative satisficing, which is now more demanding, still requires them to make some reasonable percentage of the best possible improvement.

Because of these differences, a satisficing theory can take any of three forms. It can adopt only absolute-level satisficing, only comparative satisficing, or both. Michael Slote's influential writings make both absolute-level and comparative claims and therefore suggest a theory that relaxes in both possible ways the demands of maximizing.[1]

Whatever its form, a satisficing view can be stated independently of any substantive view about the good. More specifically, it can be stated independently of the choice between subjective and objective views of each person's good. Subjective views identify this good with some subjective state of a person such as pleasure, happiness, or the satisfaction of desires; objective or perfectionist views identify it with states such as knowledge, achievement, and virtue – states that they value independently of how much one wants or enjoys these states. But both views can be combined in the same way with satisficing. Thus, if the good is pleasure, absolute-level satisficing requires agents to ensure that everyone is above some threshold level of pleasure, whereas if the good includes knowledge, the same view requires agents to ensure that everyone has at least some threshold quantity of knowledge.

Formally, then, satisficing views are independent of views about the good. But I believe that, intuitively, these views are more plausible given some views about the good than others. More specifically, there is a form of satisficing that is intuitively attractive given subjective values but is not attractive given objective or perfectionist values; for the latter, maximizing is the intuitively preferable alternative. This is not an unusual phenomenon, because it often happens that formal principles that are plausible given one set of values are not so given another.[2] For an illustration, consider Nietzsche's anti-egalitarian view that society should be organized so as to maximize the excellence of its few most excellent members.[3] Given the perfectionist values Nietzsche assumes, this view is at least intelligible, in that we can understand how someone with those values might care most about the lives in which they are most achieved. But the same view is not intelligible given subjective values. There is, I take it, no appeal whatever in the idea that society should strive to maximize the happiness of its happiest members.

In the case of satisficing, I think its absolute-level form is attractive given subjective values. This is illustrated by numerous examples of Slote's. Imagine that you had a good lunch and are not now hungry, though you are also not sated. You would enjoy a chocolate bar or soft drink if you had one, and such snacks are in fact available close by at no charge.[4] A maximizing view says that you act wrongly if you do not get a chocolate bar or a soft drink, but surely that is implausible. If you are already reasonably content, why must you make yourself more so? The same point applies to bystanders: They too need not get you a chocolate bar or a soft drink. They would be required to make you happier if you were miserable, but not if you are feeling fine. Given subjective values, there is no requirement to improve anyone's condition beyond a reasonable level of pleasure or contentment. By contrast, the comparative form of satisficing does not seem to me plausible for these values. It implies that if a person is in intense pain and you can at no cost relieve all of that pain, you do no wrong if you relieve only some reasonable percentage of the pain, or that if many people are in pain, you again do no wrong if you relieve the pain of only some of them. Because I find these implications unacceptable, I also find comparative satisficing unacceptable. But absolute-level satisficing seems positively attractive given subjective values. If a situation is already reasonably good by subjective standards, there is no moral demand to make it better. Though we are required to do what we can to ensure that people are reasonably happy, we are not required beyond that to make them ecstatic.

Given objective values, however, the same form of satisficing is not attractive. These values generate a duty to develop one's talents, just as an end in itself. But imagine geniuses like Bach or Einstein whose talents are so great that with only a small effort they can reach the satisficing threshold for achievement in their specific fields and also for achievement generally. (If this is not so, the threshold is set so high that it will never come into play for most people.) Then absolute-level satisficing says such people have no duty to expend more than this small effort, which is counterintuitive. Intuitively, the duty to develop one's talents applies no less to those with the greatest talents than to those with the least, so it is unacceptable to say that it vanishes for a Bach or an Einstein. It may be said that in making this judgment we are influenced by the contribution such people can make to other people's achieving objective goods, by giving them beautiful music to listen to or a deeper understanding of the universe. But though these other-regarding reasons for developing one's talents certainly exist, I think we can separate the self-regarding reasons from them. And when we do, I do not think we find these reasons weakest for those whose talents are greatest. If anything, it is more plausible to hold that the self-regarding duty to develop one's talents is stronger for those with more talent, so they do a greater wrong if they fail to fulfill it. (Something like this view is implicit in Nietzsche's emphasis on the excellence of the most excellent.) But even if we do not go this far, the idea that there is an absolute level of perfectionist achievement beyond which there is no duty to pursue further achievement is simply not plausible.

However appealing this form of satisficing is for subjective values, it does not intuitively fit with objective ones. For these values the most attractive view makes the duty to develop one's talents always the maximizing duty to develop them as far as possible.[5]

This contrast is reflected in some of the language we use for the two types of value. The term 'pleasure' is neutral about how far its referent should be pursued, but 'happiness,' 'satisfaction,' and 'contentment' have, to my ears, satisficing connotations. Though each admits of degrees, a person can be simply happy or simply satisfied or simply content, and the use of these terms therefore suggests that what matters morally is only that each person reach that simple state. Joseph Raz recognizes something like this when he says that happiness is a "satiable" value, one whose demands can be completely satisfied.[6] I think Raz is wrong when he suggests that happiness is conceptually satiable, so a person who is happy cannot become more happy in the way that a perfectly round circle cannot become more round. Even if on some conceptions of happiness happy people cannot be made more so by the addition of an extra pleasure like that of an extra ice cream, as Raz points out, these conceptions allow that we would be happier if we felt a more intense satisfaction in our lives as a whole.[7] I think that happiness is a normatively satiable value, so that once people are simply happy there is no moral demand to make them happier. This satisficing view is reflected in popular attitudes to happiness, which often tell us to aim just at simple happiness. Thus, the song lyric says, "Don't worry, be happy," not "Don't worry, be as a happy as you can be."

By contrast, the language we use for objective values often has maximizing connotations. Terms like 'perfection' and 'excellence' suggest that we are to pursue these values to the highest levels or as far as possible, and the same view is again implicit in popular attitudes. The common ideal is for people to develop their talents or potentials not just to some degree but to the full; the longtime recruiting slogan of the U.S. Army was not "Be at least two-thirds of all that you can be," nor is the motto of the Olympics "Reasonably fast, reasonably high, reasonably strong."

The same contrast appears, albeit imperfectly, in philosophical theorizing about these values. Obviously, some philosophers combine subjective values with maximizing; think of the many utilitarians who talk of "the greatest happiness of the greatest number." But I find it striking that all the examples Slote uses to motivate satisficing concern subjective values like the pleasure to be had from an afternoon snack or from the pot of gold a hero can wish for in a fairy tale,[8] whereas Raz says only of happiness that it is satiable. On the other side, perfectionists have consistently associated their values with maximizing. Aristotle says we should "strain every nerve" to develop the best part of us, and that the best government is the one under which each person can act best.[9] Wilhelm von Humboldt defines each person's good as not just some development, but "the highest and most harmonious development of his powers to a complete and consistent whole,"[10] and F. H. Bradley says the best individual "most fully and energetically realizes human nature." To be a good human "in all things and everywhere, to try to do always the best, and to do one's best in it . . . this and nothing short of this is the dictate of morality."[11]

My claims here should not be exaggerated. I am not arguing that only one formal principle is logically possible for each type of value; on the contrary, I have insisted that each of maximizing and satisficing can be formulated independently of any substantive views about the good. Nor am I suggesting that for each of subjective and objective values one formal principle is intuitively compelling and the other completely unacceptable; my thesis is not that strong. I have argued only that, even if each of maximizing and satisficing has some plausibility for each type of value, the balance of intuitive judgments favors a different one of them in each case. Absolute-level satisficing seems to me on balance most attractive for subjective values, whereas maximizing fits best with perfectionist ones. At the least, the intuitive appeal of the two principles is not independent of substantive values but is greater given some values than others.

Notes

1. Michael Slote, *Common-Sense Morality and Consequentialism.* New York: Routledge, 1985, chap. 3; *Beyond Optimizing: A Study of Rational Choice.* Cambridge, Mass.: Harvard University Press, 1989, chaps. 1–2.
2. For an elaboration of this theme, see my "Consequentialism and Content," *American Philosophical Quarterly* 29 (1992): 71–8.
3. See, for example, Friedrich Nietzsche, *Schopenhauer as Educator,* trans. James W. Hillesheim and Malcolm R. Simpson, Washington: Gateway Editions, 1965, 59–60; and *Beyond Good and Evil,* trans. Walter Kaufmann, New York: Vintage, 1966, sec. 258. I discuss Nietzsche's view in *Perfectionism,* Oxford University Press, 1993, 75–9.
4. Slote, *Common-Sense Morality and Consequentialism,* 52.
5. Comparative satisficing is not as counterintuitive for objective values, because it still gives Bach and Einstein some duty to develop their talents. But it still seems to me less attractive than maximizing, which, as I show below, is the view that has always been applied to these values.
6. Joseph Raz, *The Morality of Freedom.* Oxford: Clarendon Press, 1986, 241–3.

76 *Thomas Hurka*

7. For this view of happiness, see, for example, Robert Nozick, *The Examined Life*, New York: Simon and Schuster, 1989, chap. 10; and L. W. Sumner, *Welfare,* *Happiness, and Ethics*, Oxford: Clarendon Press, 1996, chap. 6.
8. Slote, *Common-Sense Morality and Consequentialism*, 43.
9. Aristotle, *Nicomachean Ethics*, trans. W. D. Ross and J. O. Urmson, in Jonathan Barnes, ed. *The Complete Works of Aristotle*, Princeton University Press, 1984, 1177b35 (see also 1169a6–8); and *Politics*, trans. B. Jowett, in Barnes, ed., *The* *Complete Works of Aristotle*, 1324a22–3. In her attempt to enlist Aristotle as a liberal-egalitarian, Martha Nussbaum attributes to him a satisficing view ac- cording to which society's goal is only to bring each citizen up to a threshold of capability for objectively good functioning: "The focus is always on getting more to cross the threshold, rather than further enhancing the condition of those who have already crossed it" ("Aristotelian Social Democracy," in R. Bruce Douglas, Gerald M. Mara, and Henry S. Richardson, eds. *Liberal-* *ism and the Good*, New York: Routledge, 1990, 203–52). But this satisficing interpretation ignores Aristotle's many maximizing remarks, including one Nussbaum herself cites about how, whereas the usefulness of instrumental goods always has a limit, with intrinsic goods more is always better (*Politics*, 1323b7–34).
10. Wilhelm von Humboldt, *The Limits of State Action*, trans. J. W. Burrow, Cambridge University Press, 1969, 16.
11. F. H. Bradley, *Ethical Studies*, 2d ed., Oxford: Clarendon Press, 1927, 215, 228.

5

A New Defense of Satisficing

Michael Weber

Satisficing versus Maximizing

It is widely maintained that self-interested rationality is a matter of maximizing one's own good or well-being.[1] Rationality more generally is also frequently characterized in maximizing terms: The rational thing to do in any decision context is whatever is best in terms of one's interests or will lead to the greatest preference-satisfaction. This orthodoxy is surprising given that we often justify what we do, to ourselves and others, by saying that the option we prefer is not the best but is instead simply adequate, sufficient, or "good enough," whereas a rejected alternative "more than enough," "more than is needed," or simply unnecessary because we are "satisfied," "content," or "fine as we are." The prevalence of such locutions inspires some, most notably Michael Slote, to propose a "satisficing" alternative to the orthodoxy, according to which a person is rational if the preferred option is good enough, where options other than the best are good enough.[2] In the self-interested case, which will be my exclusive concern here, the satisficing claim is that it is rational to prefer an option so long as it is good enough in terms of one's own good or well-being.

Proponents of maximizing conceptions of rational choice must claim that the justifications we give in terms of adequacy or sufficiency are either illegitimate or nonliteral: "Good enough" and other similar locutions are part of legitimate justifications according to the maximizing conception only when they are used elliptically, as a way of indicating that despite appearances the course of action is in fact best.[3] Although I think these ordinary locutions are sometimes used elliptically in justifications, I think

77

they are not always used in this way and that when they are not, such justifications are, at least sometimes, legitimate. In other words, I think satisficing is at least sometimes justified in cases where only the agent's good is at stake. Although my defense will build on what Slote and others have said in defense of satisficing, I will offer here a defense that differs from those previously given.[4]

It is natural to start with an example.[5] You are trying to decide on a restaurant for dinner. Rather than evaluate all the options, you consider a few and choose one because you judge that it is a nice restaurant – good food, atmosphere, and so on. It is, in your estimation, "good enough." Let's agree that this kind of decision is rational. Does this show that satisficing is rational? Proponents of maximizing will claim that it does not, that it is in fact grist for their mill, as there is a plausible account according to which "good enough" here is elliptical for best under the circumstances: The expected costs of further evaluation of options are greater than the expected benefits of finding a superior restaurant. Thus one maximizes overall by employing this satisficing strategy, according to which one stops one's search when an option that is good enough is identified. Satisficing, on this construal, is merely strategic or instrumental.[6]

Strategic or instrumental satisficing is widely regarded as rational. But what Slote defends, and what I too want to defend, is what I'll call genuine satisficing, according to which the rationality of preferring an option that is good enough does not depend on its being a strategy for maximizing. According to genuine satsificing, it can be rational to settle on a restaurant that is good enough quite independent of whether the likely costs of further search outweigh the likely benefits, indeed even if the expected costs of further deliberation do *not* outweigh the expected benefits.

Consider a second example, which might be thought to support genuine satisficing because it is not amenable to the same kind of treatment as the restaurant case: You've just had lunch which included a small dessert when a friend stops by your office and offers you some chocolates. You're not hungry, and you're not really craving sweets either because you had dessert. But you're not stuffed either or sated in your desire for sweets, and you would still enjoy a few chocolates. You turn down the chocolates anyway, because the dessert with lunch was *enough* – you don't *need* any more sweets. I'll assume this is rational. Here there are no costs of search as there were in the previous case – no wasting time evaluating more alternatives. Does this example then support genuine satisficing? Not necessarily, because it too can be accounted for in instrumental terms: There are different costs – you might spoil your dinner, your diet, or your work efficiency – if you take a break to enjoy the chocolates, and these costs might outweigh the benefits.[7]

Because there is a maximizing interpretation in each case, such examples don't settle the matter. There is another drawback to the examples given so far: They involve relatively trivial matters. I therefore want to discuss two more examples, so as to make clear that there really is something significant here about how to live one's life. Imagine that you are selling your house. Rather than set the price above market value, so as to get the best offer possible, you set the price at a level you deem good enough (e.g., good enough to buy the house you're hoping to move to) and take the first offer that meets your price. The case is clearly not trivial. But it no more settles the matter between maximizing and satisficing than the previous examples, because some will think this either irrational or subject to a maximizing interpretation according to which the expected costs – time, anxiety – of a protracted sale outweigh the expected benefits: the additional money one might get.

Finally, consider a college senior ready to embark on a career. She has chosen law and seeks not to be the best lawyer, or even the best lawyer she can be, but simply to be a really fine lawyer like her mother, whom she admires greatly. Again, the case is not trivial. But even if we assume that this is rational, there is a maximizing interpretation: Being the best lawyer she can be would require sacrifices – for example, she would not be able to dedicate herself to family as much, or continue with her activities such as the violin and playing soccer on weekends, or simply to take some time for "leisure," such that the best life for her overall is one in which she limits her professional ambitions. Of course this example could be repeated with respect to any career: One might seek to be a really fine philosopher, even if not the best philosopher, or even the best philosopher one could be.

It seems, then, that any proposed example of genuine satisficing which appears rational can be accounted for in maximizing terms. The case for satisficing, then, cannot be easily won by appeal to cases – that is, by providing a powerful counterexample to maximizing rationality. With enough ingenuity, any proposed counterexample can be redescribed in maximizing terms.[8] This does not mean that these kinds of examples do not lend any support to satisficing, for two reasons. First, some people – and I certainly include myself – have a strong intuition that the choices involved in these kinds of examples are rational independent of the instrumental considerations. Second, I think that sometimes the maximizing accounts stretch plausibility, attributing to the agent an absurd disutility to, for example, further search, or anxiety, or an absurd utility to, for example, "leisure" or "ease," in order to make the choice come out as maximizing.[9] Indeed, maximizers are all too ready to assign values that make the calculus work out in their favor. This doesn't mean that maximizing is in error, though it does make it, in the hands of these practitioners, a dogma.

I am nonetheless dissatisfied with relying on intuitions about cases, or about various utilities and disutilities, in part because they are not widely shared, and thus one appears simply to beg the question. We have to accept the possibility that our intuitions could be mistaken. As Shelly Kagan insists, an adequate justification of a theory "requires an account of the distinctions, goals, restrictions, and the like, which [it embodies]." We must, in other words, explain what lies behind intuitions, what *reasons* there are for accepting the intuition (at least when it is controversial). Unless such reasons can be found, Kagan is right to say that "we have to face the sobering possibility that... our intuition[s] ... [are] in error."[10] It is for this reason that Slote's defense of satisficing is not entirely satisfactory: It turns too much on appeals to controversial intuitions about cases and provides little explanation in their defense. It is not that I think there is some alternative to appealing to intuitions in ethics, or in philosophy in general. Rather, I think that we can seek deeper (shared) intuitions – we can hope to undergird and rationalize our (controversial) intuitions about cases by appealing to intuitions at a more general level, or in a different but relevant realm. The method, then, is simply one of (wide) reflective equilibrium.[11]

Well-Being and Time

In the spirit of wide reflective equilibrium, I want to step outside the narrow debate between maximizers and satisficers. I want to argue, first, that a characteristic of human beings is that they experience their lives from a variety of perspectives, most importantly from a variety of temporal perspectives. These include not only a succession of momentary or present-tense perspectives but also a perspective of tenseless reflection on life as a whole. The way to get a handle on this, I think, is to come to see that the so-called "narrative structure" of a life bears greatly on its quality: A life without a narrative structure is lacking, and some narratives are better than others. The quality of one's life as a whole is organic in that the quality of a person's life as a whole is not simply a sum of the value of its parts, or the individual days, months, and years that make it up.[12]

Consider this example introduced by Slote:

A given man may achieve political power and, once in power, do things of great value, after having been in the political wilderness throughout his early career. He may later die while still "in harness" and fully possessed of his powers, at a decent old age. By contrast, another man may have a meteoric success in youth, attaining the same office as the first man and also achieving much good; but then lose power, while still young, never to regain it.[13]

Slote claims, and I agree, that the first politician's life is superior – a better, more desirable life. What seems to make it better is its narrative structure: It is a better, more desirable life because it displays an upward trend – his success is, in David Velleman's words, the "culmination of a slow ascent," whereas the second politicians' life displays a downward trend – it is a life of decline.[14]

Of course the example establishes that narrative structure makes a difference only if we are clear that the two politicians enjoyed an equal number of equally good years and an equal number of equally bad years: They spent the same time in office and were equally successful, and they spent the same time out of office and were equally unsuccessful. It could be argued that once this is made clear, the intuitions that the first politician's life is superior do not persist.

Experiments by Daniel Kahneman and some of his colleagues, however, seem to indicate that people's preferences are sensitive to structural or narrative features of extended periods of time, even when all else is held constant. In the experiment, subjects undergo two painful episodes. In one, the subject's hand is placed for one minute in water that is fourteen degrees Celsius, which is cold enough to be painful. In the other, the subject's hand is placed in very cold water for one and a half minutes. For the first minute, the water is the same fourteen degrees Celsius; during the last thirty seconds, it is gradually warmed to fifteen degrees Celsius, which is still painful but less so. As a control, some subjects suffer the shorter episode first, whereas others suffer the longer episode first. It is plausible to think that more (total) pain is experienced in the longer test, because it includes the same one minute of fourteen-degree water plus the additional thirty seconds in still very cold water. Nonetheless, a majority of subjects report that if they had to repeat one or the other of the episodes, they would prefer to repeat the longer (more painful) one. Preference, then, takes into account not merely the total quantity of pain but also structural features of the painful episode – in this case, that it gets better, or less bad, at the end.[15]

The normative claim that the value of extended periods of time is organic cannot of course be established by empirical psychology: The fact that people prefer any A to B does not show that A is more valuable than B. The preference could be irrational – a cognitive error of the sort Kahneman and others have detailed. Indeed, a plausible case can be made that there is a cognitive error involved in cases like those discussed so far. As time passes, we all know, memory characteristically fades: We remember better and more vividly the more recent past.[16] The recent past is more salient. For this reason, it might seem, reflective evaluation will be skewed: What is most recent – that which occurred at the end of a time segment – will be better and more vividly recalled and therefore will have a disproportionate effect on the evaluation of the entire time segment. Time segments that have an upward trend, or just end well, will therefore be overvalued because the later, better portions of the segment are especially salient and will count disproportionately toward the evaluation of the entire time segment.

It could be argued, then, that the intuition that the first politician's life is better is mistaken, the result of a cognitive error. When we evaluate each life we imaginatively put ourselves in the place of the person near the end of his life, surveying his life as a whole. It is "deathbed" evaluation. But from the death bed, the good years are recent – salient – for the first politician, whereas they are distant for the second.[17] This leads to an overvaluation of the first politician's life. To see this, try to imagine each life not from the "deathbed perspective" but from a "bird's-eye perspective" – from above, so to speak. From this vantage point, it is not at all clear that the first politician's life is superior – that the trend, be it up or down, bears on the quality of the life as a whole. From the bird's-eye perspective, it seems that an upward trend is no better than a downward trend. And because the bird's-eye perspective eliminates the distortion, it is the proper perspective for the evaluation of one's life as a whole.

Even from the bird's-eye perspective, however, I want to claim, the first politician's life is superior. For the first politician, the success came after his struggles in the political wilderness, so let's assume that they were instrumental to his later success: The long years were spent building grassroots support, gaining valuable experience, and so on. For the second politician, however, the success came before the struggles, and we will assume that the struggles did him no good and were not a part of his political success. What makes the first politician's life superior, then, is not that it displays an upward trend but that the hardship served a purpose – the bad years contributed to the good. This doesn't change the fact that the bad years were bad: Living through them was difficult and painful. However, it does change how they bear on the quality of his life as a whole. What made the first politician's life better, then, is not that it displays an upward trend but that it is the *culmination* of a slow ascent. What matters is not so much that it was an ascent but that it was a culmination – that the hardship was linked to the success.

Imagine, instead, that the first politician's later success was unrelated to his earlier struggles – for example, he simply rode the coattails of a popular presidential candidate. In this case, too, his life would indeed have an upward trend. However, that fact would not contribute to its overall value: The value of the life would not exceed the value of the sum of its parts, or at least not for this reason. What makes the value of a life exceed the value of the sum of its parts has to do with whether the hardships have meaning and are in some significant way related to the success. An upward trend does entail that there is such meaning in the hardships. An upward trend, then, is not sufficient for the kind of meaning that makes the value of a life greater than the sum of the value of its parts.

It is not necessary, either. Consider the life an athlete, a hard-throwing, major league pitcher for instance. He is a star early in his career, but being a "fireballer," he throws out his arm at an early age. In pain, he plays a few more depressing and frustrating years as a mediocre player in the majors, then finishes out his career as a minor league pitching coach. Here is a life of decline. However, the hardships of his later career are the direct result of his early success: Throwing out his arm and suffering the decline he did are the direct result of his hard-throwing style that made him a star. In this sense, the hardships of his life – his later frustrating and depressing years in the majors and as a coach – have meaning, because they are linked to his success, even if they come after the success. His later life, even if it is not so great, at least "makes sense." Compare his life with that of a similarly successful young pitcher who falls into decline and ends up as a coach because of a freak accident. There is something particularly sad in this case: His years as a coach are not redeemed in the way they are for the pitcher who throws out his arm because there is no (meaningful) connection between his current station and his previous life. For the pitcher who throws out his arm, the hardship of his later life has a meaning – the meaning that makes the value of his life greater than the sum of the value of its parts.[18]

What this shows, I think, is two things: First, what might be called the "geometry of life" – whether it trends up or down, the slope of the curves, or anything like that – is not as important as it might have seemed, or as many have emphasized in their treatment of the narrative structure of life. That is not surprising: Life is not reducible to mathematics, despite the hopes of some. Second, there is a difference between the value of an event or time period in one's life when viewed "at the moment" and when viewed in the context of one's whole life. The lives of the two contrasting politicians when in office, and of the two contrasting pitchers when coaching in the minors, are more or less the same: *As lived*, staying in the moment rather than putting it in the context of one's whole life, the experiences are essentially the same, full of the very same satisfactions and disappointments. However, when put in the different contexts of their different lives, the experiences are not the same and make different contributions to the quality of the individuals' lives as a whole.

There are, then, different temporal perspectives on life, some broader than others, and different perspectives reveal different evaluations. This is a version of a point Thomas Nagel has emphasized: We can view things from a variety of perspectives, some of which are narrower or more "subjective" than others, which are wider, more comprehensive, more "objective." When we move to a broader or more objective point of view, he claims, new values or goods come into view: " . . . objectivity allows us to transcend our particular viewpoint and develop an expanded consciousness that takes into account the world more fully . . . this applies to values and attitudes as well as to beliefs and theories."[19] So, I claim, from a narrow temporal point of view – the "momentary point of view" – we see certain goods or values, for example pleasure and pain, that make us better or worse off at the moment and thus contribute to our "momentary well-being." On the other hand, from the wider, tenseless perspective of a whole life, where we consider a life not merely as a series of moments but as a connected set bearing relations to one another, certain goods or values come into view that were invisible from the momentary point of view, for example the value of turning long years of hard work into triumph. Moreover, things that seemed important from the more narrow point of view seem less important from the broader point of view – for example, pain seems very bad in the moment, but less significant when put in the context of one's whole life.

The upshot is that there are two distinct measures of a person's good or well-being, as Velleman has claimed.[20] There is the good experienced at a given moment, which can be summed to generate total momentary good or well-being over a lifetime. Then there is the quality of life as a whole, as viewed from the perspective of one's whole life. These two measures can, and usually will, come apart.

Now you might accept that there are these different perspectives – and correspondingly different conceptions of well-being – but maintain that only the broadest of perspectives has normative legitimacy – and hence only one "true" measure of well-being. This is what utilitarians and consequentialists generally claim: It is only the broader perspective – the impersonal or universal point of view – that counts, and the narrower point of view – the personal point of view – has no standing.[21] But I think this claim is a mistake, both in moral philosophy and in the theory of individual rational choice. I think, like Nagel, that the different perspectives each reveal genuine values. Just as some genuine values are lost to narrower perspectives, as they are accessible only to broader perspectives, some values are lost to broader perspectives, as they are accessible only to narrower perspectives.

An objective standpoint is created by leaving a more subjective, individual . . . perspective behind; but there are things about the world and life and ourselves that cannot be adequately understood from a maximally objective standpoint, however much it may extend our understanding beyond the point from which we started. A great deal is essentially connected to a particular point of view, and the attempt to give a complete account of the world in objective terms detached from these perspectives inevitably leads to false reductions or to outright denial that certain patently real phenomena exist at all.[22]

As Nagel says elsewhere, there are different *sources* of value.[23] So it would be a mistake to think that only the broader perspective of one's whole life is legitimate when it comes to self-interested rationality.[24] It would therefore also be a mistake to recognize only well-being understood as the value of one's life as a whole, that is, viewed from the perspective of one's whole life. "Well-being," then, the concept at the very center of maximizing accounts of self-interested rationality, is not univocal – is not as simple as it might have seemed. Narrower perspectives, and alternative measures of well-being too, must be taken into account, lest genuine values be simply ignored, with the result that action does not reflect the full evaluative circumstances.

There is a problem, however: If value is "fragmented," as Nagel says, it seems impossible for action to reflect the full evaluative circumstances. There may be a plurality of sources of value, and plural conceptions of well-being, but action is nonetheless unitary: We must choose one thing to do, even if it is to do nothing at all. We cannot, then, answer to all the values in play. If there were some all-encompassing perspective that somehow could bring together and commensurate the values of the different perspectives, then there would be no problem. But this is just what is lacking.

Some maintain that without an all-encompassing perspective there is no choice but to resort to picking: There is nothing to do but simply pick one perspective and act according to its dictates, according to what it regards as best. The choice between perspectives – and hence choice in general – is thus fundamentally nonrational. According to this picking model, choice can never fully take into account all the perspectives and hence all the values at stake. This seems to me a dire conclusion. Can it be avoided?

Nagel offers his own solution, which he attributes to Aristotle: Although there is no way to resolve conflicts between different perspectives – no way, for example, to aggregate their results, or establish lexical priorities – there is the faculty of "judgment" which can, in the face of these conflicts, identify a rational choice consonant with all the values in play. This kind of practical judgment, it seems, is like some conceptions of an artistic judgment – an impression one gets when taking it all in. Indeed, Nagel emphasizes that this practical judgment is inarticulate, in the way many people think artistic judgment is: There is no articulable rationale, or justification, for the judgment one makes.

Although Nagel's account of rational choice has the virtue of taking into account the variety of perspectives and thus the full evaluative circumstances, it seems to me that giving up on justification altogether is just as dire as giving up on somehow taking into account the variety of perspectives, leaving it merely a matter of picking between them. A theory which claims that our choices cannot be defended and rational choice is just a matter of "seeing it right" is deeply unsatisfying – and deeply subject to abuse.

Fortunately, to borrow a famous phrase from John Rawls, there is another way to deal with the situation. Consider for a moment moral philosophy. Much of moral philosophy can be illuminated by thinking of it as dealing with the competing claims of the impersonal and the personal points of view. Nagel, as I've noted, and Samuel Scheffler too, complain that consequentialists simply disregard the personal point of view. Scheffler complains that consequentialists don't do justice to the way in which personal "concerns and commitments are *naturally* generated from a person's point of view independent of the weight of those concerns in an impersonal ranking of overall states of affairs."[25] Egoism, of course, makes the opposite mistake, ignoring the legitimacy of the impersonal point of view. Scheffler's solution is to suggest that morality include an agent-centered permission, a limited permission to "devote energy and attention to [one's] projects [and commitments] out of proportion to the weight from an impersonal standpoint of their doing so."[26] In other words, in virtue of the narrower, personal perspective, one has a permission to do what is suboptimal with respect to the broader, impersonal perspective. Scheffler expresses this permission in mathematical terms: One can multiply the value or disvalue of some factor according to the impersonal point of view by some finite number n. So, for instance, if one can save one's drowning spouse or save two strangers, but not both one's spouse and the strangers, the agent-centered permission allows one to save one's spouse, because the impersonal disvalue of one's spouse dying, which we'll assume is the same as the impersonal disvalue of some other person dying, can be multiplied by n, where $n > 2$, so that in the final calculation which determines what is morally acceptable, the disvalue of one's spouse dying is greater than the disvalue of the two strangers dying.

Now it seems to me that this schema is crude: I doubt that any precise mathematical account of the situation can be given. It seems to me, at a minimum, that n is not constant and depends on a variety of contextual factors. But I want to endorse the spirit and not the details of Scheffler's proposal; the idea is that narrower perspectives in some sense condition broader perspectives. In virtue of the narrower perspective, demands of the broader perspective are conditioned, such that one is permitted to do other than what is best from the broader perspective. Note, however, that one must still do what is "good enough" from the broader perspective: Because n is finite – and generally relatively small – one is not permitted to do what is ranked too far down on the impersonal perspective. For instance, one could not save one's spouse if one could otherwise save thousands of drowning victims.

The Defense of Satisficing

Now it should be clear how I propose to defend satisficing. Just as the narrow, personal perspective conditions the broad, impersonal perspective in the moral case, the narrow, momentary perspective conditions the broad, whole life perspective in the case of individual rational choice. So, just as there is an agent-centered moral permission to do other than what is best from the impersonal point of view in virtue of the personal point of view, there is a rational permission to do other than what is best in terms of one's life as a whole in virtue of the momentary point of view. So, for instance, seeking to be a fine lawyer or philosopher rather than the best lawyer or philosopher, or even the best one can be, is rationally acceptable, not because spending less time on lawyering and philosophizing makes a life better by allowing one to spend time with family or in athletic and artistic endeavor, but because pursuing other than the best life as a whole is rationally permitted in virtue of the claims of the momentary perspective.

Let me be perfectly clear that I am saying something different from the maximizer, and that my account deems certain actions rational that the maximizer would deem irrational. The rational permission here does not depend on the claim that spending more time with one's family, or in artistic or athletic endeavor, or in "leisure," ultimately makes for a better life overall. Having lower professional aspirations can be rational, then, even if the benefits, in terms of more time for family or activities such as athletics, artistic creation, or "leisure," do *not* outweigh the costs to one's career – even if it doesn't make for a better life overall.[27] People frequently say that they don't want to work too hard and would like to have an easier life. What I'm suggesting is that this aim is rational, and it need not be understood as a claim that an easier life is a better life overall – a claim that I think requires attaching an absurd value to "leisure."[28] Rather, the point is that despite its not being better, it is rationally acceptable.[29]

The defense of satisficing I've so far provided handles the second two of the four cases with which I began: the case of career aspirations, as I've explained in detail above, and the case of selling one's house. It does not fare so well, however, with the first two examples I introduced, settling on a restaurant and forgoing chocolates after lunch. The rational permissions I've defended are granted with respect to a broader point of view in virtue of a narrower point of view and therefore justify satisficing with respect to the quality of one's life as a whole so as to make the moments of one's life better – to indulge in momentary satisfactions even if they are at the expense of one's life as a whole. Such permissions seem to go in the wrong direction for the restaurant and chocolate examples: They would justify *not* settling on a good enough restaurant or declining the afternoon snack but instead exhaustively searching for the best restaurant and indulging in the afternoon snack even if this is not well advised from the perspective of one's whole life, because it will promote momentary gains.[30] To avoid confusion, it is worth noting that the model I've presented so far does allow rational persons to settle on a restaurant and to forgo the chocolates. However, insofar as these choices are rational, it is because they are maximizing – because the likely costs of the alternatives outweigh the likely benefits. So when I say that the model presented so far does not fare so well with the first two examples, what I'm saying is that it cannot treat them as cases of rational satisficing: It cannot capture the initial intuition that these choices are rational because the options are simply good enough.

I do think, however, that the model I've presented so far can be extended so as to cover examples such as these – to account for them in satisficing terms. My defense of satisficing thus far turns on the claim that in virtue of a narrower perspective it is permissible to do other than what is best in terms of a broader perspective. This seems to me a common line of thought: We can be misled when we think only in terms of the "big picture," in terms of the broad(est) perspective; it is important, also, to consider the smaller and narrower, which qualify the demands of the larger.[31] However, an equally common line of thought is that stepping back and taking up a broader perspective – "putting things in perspective," as we say – can qualify the claims of the narrower perspective. I want now to develop this thought, which will do what my defense of rational permissions thus far could not do, namely explain why it is rational to settle on a restaurant or forgo the chocolates, and not for the maximizing reason that doing so will maximally contribute to the quality of one's life as a whole.

Frequently things don't turn out as we might have hoped – for example, the afternoon picnic is spoiled by rain. This can be upsetting, no doubt. But in such circumstances we often counsel people to put it in perspective: If they think about it in the larger context of their whole life, they will see that it is no big deal, in which case the upset is mitigated. This works because of a general phenomenon: What seems important from a narrow perspective is simply of no significance from a larger or broader perspective. From the momentary point of view, an enjoyable afternoon picnic is important. However, from the broader perspective of one's life as a whole it is not. In a passage already cited, Nagel suggests this idea that just as new values emerge when we take a broader perspective, so too do certain values disappear; certain things are invisible from broader, more objective points of view. "A great deal is essentially connected to a particular point of view, and the attempt to give a complete account of the world in objective terms . . . leads to . . . [the] denial that certain patently real phenomena exist at all."

Consider a different example: being stung by a bee. In the moment, this is a matter of great import: The pain is a matter of great significance, and eliminating it seems of primary importance. However, in the context of one's whole life, being stung by a bee and suffering the minor pain are of little consequence. Perhaps this is just because the pain was relatively minor and short-lived, such that it is insignificant in the way that the loss of one grain of sand on a beach is a loss but is too small to affect the quality of the beach as a whole. But an even stronger thesis seems plausible to me: When considered in the broader context, such pains do not matter at all, and my life as a whole would *not* have been better if I had not been stung. The experience of *significant* pain may count from the perspective of one's life as a whole. However, minor pains seem to fall out. This is supported by the thought that in order to evaluate our life as a whole, we do not need to take stock of the quantity of minor pains we suffered – the bee stings, skinned knees, stubbed toes, and so on.[32] Doing so would be absurd.

So too with pleasures. The pleasure of a nice meal, or a chocolate, can bring great satisfaction in the moment. However, from the perspective of one's life as a whole, whether one enjoyed such a meal or snack is of little or no significance. Indeed, all the minor ups and downs of day-to-day life are of little importance from the perspective of one's life as a whole. What matters most to the quality of one's life are one's long-term projects, which may include commitment to family, career, art, or politics. People often say, seemingly against this, that it is the little things that matter in life, for example, an ice cream cone on a balmy summer afternoon, or running through a sprinkler. It seems to me that this is right in one sense but wrong in another. Such minor pleasures are extremely important to the quality of one's life as a whole *if* they are tied up, as they often are, with more significant, temporally extended features of our life – for example, the ice cream cone is shared with one's parent, or child, or if it involves some other long-term relationship that figures in the narrative of one's life as a whole. However, without such a link, they do not contribute to the value of one's life as a whole. The isolated gustatory pleasure of the ice cream is genuinely insignificant from the perspective of one's life as whole.

When we face an opportunity to secure a pleasure, then, it can appear in two lights, depending on whether we look at the opportunity from the momentary perspective or from the perspective of one's life as a whole. From the momentary perspective, it appears to be of significant value; from the perspective of one's life as a whole, it seems of little consequence.

How does this bear on choice and action? It seems to me that this kind of discrepancy between the two different perspectives warrants a permission. Previously I said that there is a permission to do other than what is best in terms of the larger perspective because of the claims of the narrower perspective, a permission to attach *more* significance to what is important from the narrower perspective than is warranted by the larger perspective. I think, similarly, there is a permission to do other than what is best from the narrower perspective because of the claims of the wider perspective, a permission to attach *less* significance than is warranted by the narrower perspective to what is important from that perspective. So, there is a permission to attach less significance to the small pleasures and pains of day-to-day life than is warranted by the momentary perspective because of the fact that from the perspective of one's life as a whole, they have little or no significance. This kind of permission explains in satisficing terms the rationality of settling on a restaurant and forgoing the afternoon snack: not because doing so will maximize the quality of one's life as a whole, but instead because in terms of momentary well-being the result is good enough. Finding a better restaurant or enjoying the snack is of considerable value from the momentary perspective. However, from the perspective of one's life as whole they matter much less, if at all. Because of this difference, one can discount the value of enjoying the better restaurant, or enjoying the snack.

Again, let me be clear that I am saying something different from the maximizer, and that my account deems rational certain actions that the maximizer would deem irrational. This kind of permission does not require that the benefits be greater than the costs, that, for example, a life in which one forgoes chocolates for the sake of diet or work efficiency is better than one that includes eating chocolates and being a bit heavier and a bit less productive. It may be that forgoing the chocolates isn't really worth it "in the long run," yet on my view it can still be rational.[33]

Perhaps the most powerful criticism leveled against satisficing is that it is "unmotivated": No justification for one's choice can be provided. If A is better than B (e.g., a long-distance program that charges 5 cents a minute is better than one that charges 7 cents a minute) and I choose B, I can offer no justification. I cannot offer the justification that it (7 cents a minute) is good enough, because this applies equally to the better alternative, about which there is this reason to choose it and more.[34]

I don't think, however, that the objection applies to my defense of satisficing. I can provide a reason for preferring, for example, to be a fine philosopher, if not the best philosopher, or even the best philosopher

I can be. The reason is that I want to enjoy each day – to promote my "momentary well-being." Just as in the moral case one may do other than what is best from the impersonal point of view *for the sake of* one's own particular interests and concerns, one may do other than what is best from the perspective of one's life as a whole *for the sake of* one's momentary satisfaction. Crucially, in offering this justification one is not claiming that one enjoys a better life on the whole if one enjoys each day. Instead, one is claiming that there is a permission to sacrifice to some extent the quality of one's life as whole so as to make each day a little more enjoyable.

The charge that satisficing is unmotivated may have more force against the permission to do other than what is best from the momentary perspective in virtue of the broader perspective in cases like choosing a restaurant and declining chocolates. It may have more force because in preferring what is good enough from the momentary perspective one does not increase the quality of one's life as a whole: From the perspective of one's life as a whole, I've claimed, whether one finds a better restaurant or eats the chocolates makes no difference. There is no "for the sake of" to which one can appeal.

I don't think the charge sticks, however. There is still a reason for forgoing the momentary good. The reason is that it doesn't matter from the perspective of one's whole life. One might ask: If it doesn't matter from the perspective of one's life as a whole, why not go ahead and maximize momentary good? It might be a different matter if by settling on a restaurant or forgoing the chocolates one were to improve one's life as a whole. It would be different, in other words, if from the momentary perspective one preferred A to B, and from the perspective of one's life as a whole one preferred B to A. But the actual situation is that from the momentary perspective, one has a marked preference for A to B, and from the perspective of one's life as a whole one is *indifferent* between A and B. Given that performing the preferred option from the momentary point of view "does no harm" from the perspective of one's whole life, why not go ahead and do what the momentary perspective favors?

The answer, I think, is that the fact that from the perspective of one's life as a whole one is indifferent between A and B does not entail that the perspective of one's whole life has no bearing on choice between them. To think so is to think that the perspective of one's life as a whole is silent on the matter. But it isn't: Indifference is not silence. According to the perspective of one's life as a whole, A and B are equal, a matter of indifference if one chooses one or the other. If we accept, as I do, that decision making should as much as possible take the different perspectives into account – should reflect the full evaluative circumstances – then this indifference should have import. The rational permission that I suggested gives it import: In virtue of the indifference, there is a permission to discount the difference between A and B recognized by the narrower momentary perspective. The reason to forgo a momentary good such as a better meal or a few chocolates after lunch, then, is that in so doing one takes into account the different perspectives: One recognizes that there is value from the point of view of the momentary perspective in having a nice meal, and more value in a better meal. At the same time, one recognizes that from the broader perspective of one's life as a whole a better meal is of no great benefit, which gives one reason to qualify or discount the significance of getting a better meal as viewed from the momentary point of view. People often say, in such situations, that finding a better restaurant "matters" in one sense, but not in another. This saying is exactly right, and it explains why it is rational to settle on a restaurant independent of the deliberative costs of identifying a better restaurant.

Ultimately, then, my reply to the charge that satisficing is unmotivated is that the objection assumes there is a single, authoritative measure of value that provides a measure of a person's well-being or good. But this is precisely what I deny. There is no univocal conception of a person's well-being or good. Well-being is relative to a perspective, and each perspective makes genuine normative claims.[35]

This reply to the charge that satisficing is unmotivated also explains how my defense of satisficing does not lead to a dire conclusion. It avoids the dire conclusion that the full evaluative circumstances can't be taken into account because the rational permission just is a response to the plurality of evaluative perspectives. It avoids the dire conclusion Nagel reaches that we must ultimately give up on (articulable) justification because articulable reasons can be provided for our satisficing choices, reasons that appeal to the evaluations of alternative perspectives.[36]

Satisficing and Virtue (Ethics)

Some advocates of satisficing offer a "virtue-oriented" defense. Christine Swanton, for instance, maintains that "moderation" is a virtue and maximizing a vice.[37] This by itself is mere assertion: It is no defense of satisficing to simply proclaim it a virtue. Presumably what is in question is whether it is a (self-regarding) virtue, and it is question-begging to assert that it is. Something has to be said to support the claim that satisficing is a virtue and maximizing a vice.

Swanton does provide something in this regard. Maximizing, she says, is sometimes "...the expression of a vice, such as, e.g., inappropriate perfectionism, ruthlessness, cold calculativeness, exceeding personal authority, and so on."[38] Michael Stocker also offers a virtue-oriented defense as well as some explanation of what makes maximizing a vice:

> One central reason for my disagreement [with maximizing] stems from the moral psychological import of regretting the absence or lack of any and every attainable good. This regret is a central characterizing feature of narcissistic, grandiose, and other defective selves. It is also characteristic of those who are too hard on themselves, who are too driven and too perfectionistic.[39]

Both Swanton and Stocker also note that going too far in the other direction can be a vice: Just as there are character defects in seeking out every opportunity to promote one's well-being (or even one's broader interests), so too there are character defects in too much passing up of such opportunities. To do so is to manifest "laziness, culpable indifference, callousness, cowardice, weakness, excessive squeamishness, and so on."[40] Stocker says that there is vice in being "too easily satisfied, too complacent, too ambitionless, too easy on oneself, too lacking in drive, and so on."[41]

Unfortunately, these comments do little to solve the problem. To say that maximizing is "inappropriate perfectionism," or that maximizers are "too hard on themselves," "too driven," or "too perfectionistic," is to add nothing: It is simply to repeat that it is a vice. The question at issue is whether maximizing is inappropriate or *too much* of anything.

Some of the other terms of abuse simply miss the mark. Swanton says that maximizers are ruthless and cold-calculating, and that they exceed their personal authority. Stocker claims that they are narcissistic and grandiose. These charges all suggest that maximizers do not sufficiently take others into account. However, if it is self-regarding rationality that is at issue, then the problem with maximizing cannot be insufficient attention to others.

It might seem that to demand an explanation for what makes something a virtue or a vice is to beg the question against virtue-based approaches to ethics and practical reasoning generally, according to which the virtues are primary or foundational, as opposed to the good as in teleological conceptions of practical reason, or duty or the right as in Kantian or deontological conceptions. This, however, is to assume that any explanation of what makes something a virtue or a vice must be in instrumental terms: It must explain that virtues promote the good, or the performance of duty, whereas vices are contrary to the good or the fulfillment of duty. There is, however, an alternative, one frequently associated with Aristotle. According to this alternative, virtues are dispositions or traits that enable one to live a characteristically human life. Virtues are virtues, then, not (merely) because they are conducive to the good or the right, but because they reflect fundamental and characteristic features of human beings.

It seems to me that the account of satisficing I have offered provides just this kind of Aristotelian backing for a virtue-defense: Satisficing is a virtue because it involves taking into account the variety of perspectives available to human beings, where the capacity to take up the various perspectives is what is characteristic of human beings. Nagel makes just this point:

> Conflicts [between perspectives] . . . are ubiquitous. They cannot . . . be resolved by subsuming either of the points of view under the other, or both under a third. Nor can we simply abandon any of them. . . . The capacity to view the world simultaneously from [a variety of perspectives] is one of the marks of humanity.[42]

What I have said, then, builds upon, and provides needed backing for, a virtue-oriented defense of satisficing.

A virtue-oriented approach of this sort is not without problems. The first and most obvious is that the fact that viewing the world from a variety of temporal perspectives is characteristic of human beings does not make it good or desirable – does not make it a virtue. Indeed, one might think there is a fallacy in thinking so because something normative is derived from something factual.

This first objection can be handled by making clear that the claim that viewing the world from a variety of temporal perspectives is desirable is a substantive normative claim: It is not desirable because it is characteristic but because it is, on reflection, desirable. When we reflect on what it is to be a human being, and what gives human beings special value, the ability to take up different perspectives emerges as central. The ability to look at things from a variety of perspectives is what gives our lives a richness that they otherwise would not have and allows us to ask questions – questions of morality and science – that we could not were we limited to a single, narrow perspective.

This reply to the first problem raises a second and, for me more troubling, objection: If it is good or desirable to view the world from a variety of perspectives, and satisficing is a practical manifestation of doing so, then it seems that satisficing is instrumental – simply a means to the best life. In other words, what I have provided here is not a defense of satisficing at all; what I have provided instead is a new account of well-being, according to which well-being consists in viewing the world from a variety of perspectives. Satisficing with respect to those things that are normally thought to contribute to well-being – for example, nice meals, chocolates, or interesting careers – is simply instrumental: the way to give a place in one's practical life to the variety of (temporal) perspectives and so to maximally promote one's well-being.

This second objection is a powerful one. One option is to concede it but claim a certain victory nonetheless. According to the objection, sensitivity to the import of the human capacity to take up different (temporal) perspectives enriches the instrumental defense of satisficing, taking it well beyond the simple accounts that appeal to the costs of further search or the value of "leisure." Conceding the objection is to admit failure with respect to defending genuine satisficing. But it can be seen as a kind of victory nonetheless, for two reasons. First, it provides a more satisfying account of the examples canvassed at the beginning. I noted there that the various attempts to account in instrumental terms for the choices made in the examples seem forced, and to stretch plausibility. The result is that the rationality of these choices – settling on a restaurant, declining the chocolates, pricing one's house in the way described, setting lower career aspirations – might be thought suspect. This suspicion is erased, however, if one accepts the enriched account of instrumental satisficing that includes an account of well-being emphasizing the import of the human capacity to take up a variety of (temporal) perspectives. Second, if this account of well-being and its associated conception of instrumental satisficing are accepted, then satisficing seems justified with respect to just about anything commonly thought to be a good. It is a victory, then, insofar as the scope of instrumentalism would be so wide as to satisfy even the most inveterate satisficer.

Although I am sometimes drawn to the position that results from conceding the objection, I want to at least consider a second option, which is to rebut the objection. The rebuttal I want to sketch here I don't regard as conclusive. It is nonetheless powerful and suggests a promising line of thought for those of us suspicious of maximizing accounts of rationality. Central to my response is the idea that some values cannot be expressed in a ranking or preference-ordering.[43] Some values have a different structure: They function as *regulative norms*.[44] A regulative norm does not identify some good to be produced – for example, pleasure – where the more that is produced, the better. Instead, a regulative norm serves as a constraint on the pursuit of other goods. We can best get a grip on this by thinking about theoretical reason and the norms of deductive logic. In arguments, valid reasoning is desirable or good. However, it is not the case that we should produce as many valid inferences as possible. That would be ridiculous. For then it would make sense to generate (pointless) syllogisms all day long, and a proof of a given theorem with one thousand valid inferences would be better than an elegant five-line proof. Rather, reasoning validly serves as a constraint: When we reason (not for the sake of reasoning itself, but in the pursuit of something else, e.g., truth), we should reason validly. Validity provides the rules or framework within which we work: It is not an end in itself.

Examples can also be drawn from practical philosophy. Some defenders of (maximizing) consequentialist theories of morality try to square their theory with common sense by assigning intrinsic value to keeping promises and other commitments. But this leads to the absurd result that we should "make commitments willy-nilly, just so that more commitment fulfillments can exist in the world."[45] The value of keeping commitments must be understood differently: We should keep our commitments, insofar as we make them in the pursuit of other goods.

So too I claim with the value of moderation, or the value of taking into account the variety of (temporal) perspectives we can occupy. These are not ends in themselves. It would be absurd to perform as many moderate acts as possible, or to maximize either the number of situations we evaluate from a variety of perspectives or the number of perspectives we use to evaluate situations. For then it would make sense to make as many moderate purchases as one can, or eat as many moderate meals as one can. It would make sense to simply multiply the number of (temporal) perspectives we evaluate things from, when some seem entirely irrelevant or pointless, for example the perspective of eleven seconds, or three and half months.[46] The point, then, is that the good life, a life that takes into account the different perspectives available to human beings, cannot be construed as maximizing anything. For the good life is structured by a regulative norm: In our pursuit of various goods, for example pleasure or excellence in one's profession, we ought to be guided or constrained by a demand to take into account the valuations of the various (temporal) perspectives available to human beings.

This response is subject to one important objection, which is that satisficing just as much as maximizing requires that values be expressible in a ranking or preference-ordering, for just as it is only in the context of a ranking that we can speak of a choice as being best, it is only in this context that we can speak of a choice as being good enough. Satisficing, in other words, is so similar to maximizing that if we undermine the latter we at the same time undermine the former. In a recent article, Michael Byron argues in this way: Objecting to Swanton's virtue-oriented defense of satisficing, he claims that satisficing makes sense only in the context of consequentialist theories of practical reason and advises nonconsequentialists to "stop claiming to endorse satisficing." His argument is that in a nonconsequentialist framework, talk of satisficing is superfluous because "the truth of nonconsequentialism entails that choosing a suboptimific alternative is sometimes rationally permissible."[47] This, however, hardly seems like an objection. I think that Byron is getting at something different, which is that in a nonconsequentalist framework what makes a suboptimal choice rational has little to do with its being good enough. What makes it rational is that it is the expression of a virtue. But at least on my account this is not exactly the case: On my view, part of what makes a suboptimal choice rationally acceptable is that it is good enough (relative to some relevant perspectival ranking). Were the option not good enough according to that perspectival ranking, it would not be rationally acceptable. Justifications for preference, then, will include, at least implicitly, a claim that the option is good enough. This, it seems to me, warrants describing such preferences as satisficing. Moreover, on my view some things can be ranked, in particular well-being of various types, and with respect to anything that can be so ranked I have defended preferring other than what is best – what is good enough. This seems ample reason to describe my view as a satisficing view.

Byron himself observes that this is a terminological issue, and I'm inclined to agree. His worry is that describing nonconsequentialist views as satisficing views "misdirects inquiry." On his view, then, we should go "beyond optimizing" in a more radical way: We should abandon talk of maximizing and satisficing all together. Although I wouldn't be entirely unhappy with such a result, it seems to me that inquiry is equally likely to be misdirected if we drop talk of maximizing and satisficing, because according to views like mine the fact that an option is good enough is central to its being rationally acceptable. I believe that it is informative to retain this talk and describe views such as mine as satisficing views. As long as those of us who defend nonconsequentialism make clear what we are saying, and on what grounds, it seems to me that it won't confuse matters if we continue to talk in terms of maximizing and satisficing.

Conclusion: Satisficing as Humane

Scheffler maintains that a moral theory which includes an agent-centered permission realizes an "Ideal of Humanity," because it takes into account not just the impersonal point of view but also the personal point of view. It takes into account the fact that human beings have an interest in the welfare of humankind, but we also have individual lives that are of special importance to us. As a result, moral conceptions with agent-centered permissions have it that morality is "fundamentally a reasonable and humane phenomenon," one that allows morality to be "integrated in a coherent and attractive way into an individual human life." Consequentialist theories, in contrast, realize an "Ideal of Purity," because they require purifying oneself of one's particularity – eliminating one's special attachment to one's own life.[48]

I am, in effect, making the analogous claim: A theory of self-interested rationality that includes rational permissions realizes an ideal of humanity, because it takes into account both the momentary perspective and the perspective of one's whole life. Each of these perspectives is an essential part of us; Velleman notes that a person has "both a synchronic and a diachronic identity."[49] Only a theory of self-interested rationality that takes both of these perspectives – both of these identities – into account does justice to what we are as humans and construes rationality as fundamentally a reasonable and humane phenomenon. A satisficing conception of self-interested rationality, then, is a humane conception. Maximizing conceptions, which seem to take only one or the other perspective into account, are not humane: They represent a demand for an inhuman kind of purity.

Notes

I have benefited in the development of this paper from conversations with the following people: Elizabeth Anderson, David Velleman, James Joyce, Peter Railton, Jack Meiland, David Sobel, Nishiten Shah, Krista Lawlor, Manyul Im, Nadeem Hussain, and Michael Slote. I have also benefited from audiences at Central Michigan University, Yale University, Tulane University, the University of Delaware, and the University of California, Santa Cruz; also from participants in the Fourth Annual Conference on Game Theory in Ethics and Political Philosophy, Waterloo University. Finally, I wish to thank my students at Yale University, who eagerly commented on earlier drafts of this paper.

1. Self-interested rationality refers to rationality in circumstances where only the agent's good is at stake, or rationality's taking only the agent into account.

According to some, well-being simply is a matter of preference-satisfaction, in which case the more general characterization of rationality collapses into self-interested rationality. This collapse, mistaken I believe, is particularly prominent in rational choice theory, which is where maximizing conceptions of rationality are most explicitly defended.

2. Michael Slote, *Beyond Optimizing*, Cambridge: Harvard University Press, 1989. Other proponents of satisficing include Michael Stocker, *Plural and Conflicting Values*, Oxford: Clarendon Press, 1990; and Christine Swanton, "Satisficing and Virtue," *Journal of Philosophy* 90 (1993): 33–48.

3. See, for instance, Philip Pettit, "Satisficing Consequentialism," *Proceedings of the Aristotelian Society* supp. LVIII (1984): 165–76.

4. Two distinct satisficing claims must be distinguished at the start. The first is that preferring an option that is good enough to one that is better is rationally *permitted*, in which case preferring a better option is also rational, perhaps even more rational. The second is that preferring an option that is good enough is rationally *required*, in which case preferring an option that is better is irrational. Such rational permissions and rational restrictions are analogous to the agent-centered permissions and agent-centered restrictions that distinguish so-called deontological theories from consequentialist theories in moral philosophy. It is generally agreed that agent-centered permissions are less paradoxical and therefore more plausibly defended than agent-centered restrictions. I think the same is true in the rational case, and therefore I seek here to defend only rational permissions.

5. These examples are for the most part taken directly from Slote, *Beyond Optimizing*.

6. Herbert Simon most famously develops this line of thought, which emphasizes costs of deliberation or computation, under the rubric of "bounded rationality." See, for instance, "Theories of Bounded Rationality" and "Decision-Making as an Economic Resource," both reprinted in his *Models of Bounded Rationality: Behavioral Economics and Business Organization*, vol. 2, Cambridge: MIT Press, 1982. Jon Elster, *Sour Grapes*, Cambridge University Press, 1983, complains that there are costs to determining whether one is at the point where the costs of further deliberation exceed the benefits, which leads to a regress that supports a robust conception of satisficing that goes beyond what Simon is willing to endorse.

7. David Schmidtz, *Rational Choice and Moral Agency*, Princeton University Press, 1995, emphasizes this kind of instrumental satisficing, which he refers to as "local satisficing" serving the interest of global optimizing.

8. A variety of other strategies are available to maximizers to explain away apparent cases of rational satisficing. They could, for instance, do what has been done in defense of maximizing theories of morality such as utilitarianism: maintain that it is not individual actions but something else – for example, rules, motives, habits, or character traits – that are to be evaluated directly in terms of maximization, with actions evaluated indirectly, in terms of whether they comport with rules, motives, or whatever, which maximize. This strategy is problematic just as it is in the moral case because it is not clear why if utility or the good is the foundation of practical reasoning it should not be applied

equally to rules, motives, and acts. See Stephen Darwall, "Rational Agent, Rational Act," *Philosophical Topics* XIV (1986): 33–57.

9. Stocker, *Plural and Conflicting Values*, 320, makes this point: "... in making that claim they are, in effect, trying to saddle those who hold that they knowingly choose the lesser over the better with evaluative arrogance or stupidity. In this particular case, they are claiming that I somehow must see my ease as having greater importance and value than what I could achieve. Yet, except in special circumstances, I would have to be arrogant or stupid to think this. The better understanding is that I see that my ease lacks this importance, but that I nonetheless believe that I am justified in taking it."

10. Shelly Kagan, *The Limits of Morality*, Oxford: Clarendon Press, 1989, 13, and "Does Consequentialism Demand Too Much?" *Philosophy and Public Affairs* 13 (1984): 239.

11. See Norman Daniels, "Wide Reflective Equilibrium and Theory Acceptance in Ethics," *Journal of Philosophy* 76 (1979): 266–82.

12. The import of a narrative structure in life has been emphasized by Alasdair MacIntyre, *After Virtue*, University of Notre Dame Press, 1984; Charles Taylor, *Sources of the Self: The Making of Modern Identity*, Cambridge: Harvard University Press, 1989; and David Velleman, "Well-Being and Time," *Pacific Philosophical Quarterly* 72 (1991): 48–77.

13. Slote, *Goods and Virtues*, Clarendon Press, 1983, 23–4.

14. Velleman, "Well-Being and Time," 51. Slote, *Goods and Virtues*, offers a different analysis: The first politician's life is more desirable because certain times in one's life, for example what Slote calls the "prime of life," are more important to the quality of one's whole life than others, for example one's childhood. I prefer Velleman's account, for essentially the reasons he provides.

15. Daniel Kahneman, et al., "When More Pain Is Preferred to Less: Adding a Better End," *Psychological Science* 4 (1993): 401–5. Kahneman and his colleagues provide an analysis more similar to Slote's analysis of the case of the politicians: They claim that how bad the pain is at its peak and how bad it is at the end influence preference more than the duration and intensity (the total quantity) of pain. They call this the "peak and end rule."

16. We better remember more recent events *ceterus paribus*: More significant events that are in the further past may well be better remembered than insignificant events in the nearer past.

17. This assumes, falsely perhaps, that imaginative memory just as much as actual memory has a bias toward the more recent past.

18. This in part explains the particular tragedy of the Vietnam War and the injured veterans: Their suffering seems pointless because the war – for a variety of reasons – is viewed as pointless, unlike the pitcher whose later suffering is the result of a worthwhile endeavor.

19. Thomas Nagel, *The View from Nowhere*, Oxford University Press, 1986, 5.

20. Velleman, "Well-Being and Time," 60, claims that "self-interest is not a unitary dimension of value. Rather, a person has two distinct sets of interests, lying along two distinct dimensions – his synchronic interests, in being well off at particular moments, and his diachronic interests, in having good periods of time, in particular, a good life."

21. Samuel Scheffler, *The Rejection of Consequentialism,* Oxford: Clarendon Press, 1982, suggests this account, though not to defend it but to subject it to criticism.
22. Nagel, *View from Nowhere,* 7.
23. Nagel, "The Fragmentation of Value," in his *Mortal Questions,* Cambridge University Press, 1979, 133.
24. Velleman, "Well-Being and Time," 66, 68, agrees: "I hesitate to assume that the more comprehensive of these perspectives has exclusive authority.... The good that something does you now is not just the phantom of a restricted method of accounting: it's an autonomous mode of value."
25. Scheffler, *Rejection of Consequentialism,* 56.
26. Scheffler, *Rejection of Consequentialism,* 14.
27. My view here should not be confused with that of Schmidtz, *Rational Choice and Moral Agency,* despite the fact that he too offers a defense of satisficing by appeal to the conflict between narrower and broader perspectives. Schmidtz defends only instrumental satisficing: Satisficing with respect to a narrow perspective is rational because it serves to maximize with respect to the larger perspective (of one's life as a whole).
28. It also avoids appealing to another maximizing ploy, which is to maintain that in the long run the person who takes leisure is able to accomplish more because of the rejuvenating power of taking some "time off." Of course this is true. My point is just that this need not be the (only) justification for taking time off for some current enjoyment.
29. Slote, *Beyond Optimizing,* ch. 6, and Stocker, *Plural and Conflicting Values,* 320, argue similarly.
30. I would endorse such a permission, of course.
31. There is an analogy here to Keynes's famous critique of mainstream economics. He warned that "in the long run we're all dead."
32. There is an alternative, though I think less plausible, way to account for this: We can ignore such minor pains when evaluating our whole life because we can assume that they are perfectly mirrored by minor pleasures such that it is a wash.
33. This argument, I concede, depends on the controversial thesis that minor pleasures and pains do not matter at all from the perspective of one's life as a whole. Although I have said some things in favor of the thesis, I have not offered anything like a defense of it here. Such a defense is beyond the scope of this paper. There is a related, weaker thesis that might be thought more amenable: Minor pleasures and pains contribute to the quality of one's life as whole, but much less than they do to one's momentary well-being. Though I accept the stronger thesis, I believe this weaker thesis is all I need, because what motivates the kind of discounting I've suggested is an evaluative discrepancy between perspectives. Because of limitations of space, I will also not argue for this here.
34. Pettit, "Satisficing Consequentialism." Also see Schmidtz, *Rational Choice and Moral Agency,* 38; and Michael Byron, "Satisficing and Optimality," *Ethics* 109 (1998): 84–6.
35. Another powerful objection to my defense of satisficing derives from the analogy between rational permissions and the agent-centered permissions

defended by Scheffler. Kagan argues that Scheffler's argument can be taken in either of two ways, and that both are problematic. First there is the *negative* argument, according to which the personal point of view merely stands in the way of doing what is best from the impersonal point of view. It is a regrettable but inevitable aspect of our psychology that we view matters partially, from the personal point of view, one that we would eliminate if only we could. Second, there is the *positive* argument, according to which the personal point of view is not a regrettable hindrance but is rather a point of view that reveals distinctive values, ones that are unique to it and therefore unavailable to a person limited to the impersonal point of view. We should not eliminate it even if we could, then, for in so doing – in rendering ourselves totally impartial, in rendering ourselves perfect moral persons – we eliminate much that is valuable. Against the negative argument Kagan complains, rightly I think, that at most what the negative argument gets us is that some morally flawed actions are not blameworthy, for example because given the difficulty of performing the correct action (of overcoming the personal bias), blaming the offender will lead to worse consequences than not. So long as the personal point of view is regarded as no more than a hindrance, it can only excuse moral failing. Against the positive argument Kagan complains that no good case has been made that the distinctive values are compromised by limiting ourselves to the impersonal point of view. The analogous argument against rational permissions claims that either (a) the momentary point of view is a regrettable hindrance and merely excuses rational failing or (b) the momentary view must be shown to reveal genuine values not available to the perspective of one's life as a whole. I take up this challenge elsewhere and exclude it here because of limitations of space. (See Michael Weber, Ph.D. dissertation, *Satisficing: The Rationality of Preferring What Is Good Enough*, University of Michigan, 1998.) I maintain there that (a) whereas defenders of satisficing such as Slote and Stocker rely too much on the negative argument, which supports only blameless irrationality, (b) just as the positive argument can be defended in the moral case, so too can it be defended in the rational case. What makes the personal point of view more than a regrettable hindrance is that, as Susan Wolf, "Moral Saints," *Journal of Philosophy* 79 (1982): 419–39, argues, moral saints – those with only an eye to the impersonal point of view – are rather dull and miss out on much that is valuable in life; analogously, what makes the momentary point of view more than a regrettable hindrance is that those with an eye only to the quality of one's life as a whole are a rather dull bunch, missing out on genuine values, for example the value of spontaneity and simple "pleasures of the moment."

36. Though my defense can avoid the charge that satisficing is unmotivated, it might seem open to a different objection: It is not satisficing at all, because any preference deemed rational is atop some perspectival ranking. I may, for instance, be rationally permitted to prefer what is good enough relative to my life as a whole, but only because doing so is best in terms of my momentary well-being. So I may be rationally permitted to prefer to be a good philosopher rather than the best philosopher, or the best philosopher I can be, so as to make each day a bit more pleasant. But in so doing while I am satisficing

relative to the quality of my life as a whole, I am maximizing relative to my momentary well-being. Rational choice, then, always involves some kind of maximization. The charge, quite simply, is that the model I have suggested does not significantly differ from the picking model I rejected earlier. I don't think this is right, however. The rational permissions I defend, just like the agent-centered moral permissions Scheffler defends, sanction options that are good enough, and not best, by any measure. Consider first the moral case. From the impersonal point of view, let's assume that donating $100,000 to Oxfam is better than donating $50,000, which is better than donating $0. From the personal point of view, we'll assume it is just the reverse. Scheffler's agent-centered permission, so long as n is greater than 2, sanctions donating $50,000, which is not top-ranked on either the impersonal or the personal ranking. It sanctions this option, and not the option of donating $0, because $50,000 multiplied by n where $n > 2$ is greater than $100,000, where $0 multiplied by n will never exceed $100,000. Now consider a purely self-interested choice. From the perspective of the quality of one's whole life, let's assume that being the best philosopher one can be is better than simply seeking to be a quite fine philosopher, which is better than forgoing philosophy altogether in favor of the life of a beach bum. From the perspective of momentary well-being, we'll assume that the rankings are just the opposite. The rational permission, as I conceive it, sanctions seeking to be a quite fine philosopher, which is not top-ranked from either the perspective of one's life as whole or the momentary perspective. It is sanctioned really for two reasons: (a) because one can discount the value assigned by the personal point of view to being a beach bum because it is low ranked by the perspective of one's life as a whole, such that it is surpassed by seeking to be a quite fine philosopher; (b) because one can discount the value assigned to being the best philosopher one can be by the perspective of one's life as a whole in virtue of its low ranking from the personal point of view, such that it is surpassed by seeking to be a quite fine philosopher (but not presumably by being a beach bum). On my view this can't be explained in precise mathematical terms. But it seems to me, as I've indicated earlier, that the mathematical precision of Scheffler's account is a weakness rather than a strength.

37. It is misleading, I think, to equate satisficing and moderation. As Schmidtz, *Rational Choice and Moral Agency*, 31, notes, satisficing contrasts with optimizing (or maximizing), whereas moderation contrasts with being immoderate. The immoderate person has extensive wants; those of the moderate person are less extensive. A maximizer seeks to maximally satisfy his wants, whether they are extensive or not, whereas the satisficer seeks less than the maximal satisfaction of her wants, regardless of their extent. A satisficer, then, can be either moderate or immoderate, as can a maximizer.

38. Swanton, "Satisficing and Virtue," 43.

39. Stocker, *Plural and Conflicting Values*, 321.

40. Swanton, "Satisficing and Virtue," 43.

41. Stocker, *Plural and Conflicting Values*, 321.

42. Nagel, *The View from Nowhere*, 134.

43. My response is derived largely from Elizabeth Anderson, "Reasons, Attitudes, and Values: Replies to Sturgeon and Piper," *Ethics* 106 (1996): 538–54.

44. I borrow this term from Barbara Herman, *The Practice of Moral Judgment*, Cambridge: Harvard University Press, 1993.

45. Anderson, "Replies," 542.

46. And if there are other nontemporal perspectives we can take up, for example the perspective of a bat, then it would make sense to do so whenever possible, for example when buying a television. It may make sense in certain philosophic and scientific contexts to consider the perspective of a bat, but not when buying a television. This makes clear that the value of taking up different perspectives is a kind of regulative norm: It comes into play in the pursuit of other things, and how it comes into play is determined by what other things we are pursuing.

47. Byron, "Satisficing and Optimality," 90–1. Pettit, "Satisficing Consequentialism," also suggests that satisficing is so similar to maximizing that it is hard to see how one can reject the latter without rejecting the former.

48. Scheffler, *Human Morality*, Oxford University Press, 1992, 4–6.

49. Velleman, "Well-Being and Time," 67.

6

Satisficing: Not Good Enough

Henry S. Richardson

Introduction

The idea of satisficing either expresses the correct but relatively banal insight that the pervasive need to trade off incommensurable values puts optimizing deliberation out of reach, or else it articulates a specific, non-optimizing strategy of decision. In company with the proponents of satisficing, I believe that optimizing is seldom an apt concept for modeling deliberation. As a broad approach to human rationality emphasizing, as H. A. Simon famously did, that our limitations as deliberators mean that optimizing is rarely a rational strategy, satisficing constitutes a valuable insight; however, when satisficing is worked up into a competing strategy of decision – as it has been by a number of recent philosophers – the idea of satisficing gets into trouble, as I will show. The core idea of satisficing is that "one ceases to search for alternatives when one finds an alternative" that one deems to be "good enough."[1] Working this idea up into a decision-making strategy requires specifying a suitable metric of what is "good enough." As I shall argue, showing a suitable deference to the banal facts about tradeoffs among incommensurable values while at the same time having to remain distinct from optimizing pushes the proponent of satisficing as a decision-making strategy to specify what is "good enough" in terms of a highly idealized account of what someone's preferences are. This does establish satisficing as a distinctive strategy of decision but one that rather incoherently grafts a highly idealized metric of what is good enough onto an underlying effort to recognize the far-from-ideal state of our deliberative capacities.

Negatively, then, I will argue that satisficing is an unsatisfactory replacement for optimizing as a deliberative strategy. More positively, I will argue that the core insight about the inaptness of optimizing, as well as many of the sorts of concrete cases adduced by proponents of satisficing, can be better accommodated by understanding how practical commitments function in our deliberations. Thinking in terms of practical commitments – for example, final ends – supersedes the need for any overall metric of goodness, whether for purposes of locating what is best or for purposes of locating what is good enough.

The first order of business, then, is to understand the reasons why those who would work satisficing up into a strategy of decision almost invariably turn to preference satisfaction of an idealized sort as their metric of what is good enough. For it is not simply that this is the most common way to interpret satisficing; it is also the only workable way to avoid both banality and optimizing while letting the notion of what is good enough do most of the work.

Measuring What Is "Good Enough"

As a strategy of decision, satisficing is the idea that one sorts through alternatives until finding one that is "good enough" in some relevantly global sense. To locate the relevant kind of global perspective, we should note that satisficing is always defined as proceeding relative to some *endeavor*, that is, relative to the pursuit of some goal or end. Hence, there are two items that might reflect a global or a local perspective: (i) the endeavor with respect to which one is satisficing and (ii) the metric of satisfaction, or of how much is "good enough."

Can satisficing with regard to a global endeavor be a rational strategy? Yes, unless the perspective of this endeavor is defined or thought of literally as an "all things considered" one. Carefully noting that an individual's good and the satisfaction of an individual's preferences are two different things, Michael Slote has argued that an individual can rationally satisfice with respect to the project of pursuing his or her own good.[2] He has also mentioned the possibility that an altruist can satisfice with respect to the project of pursuing the good of others.[3] These two possibilities are linked, and they help explain each other. One reason that one might hold back from optimizing in the pursuit of one's own good is that one also cares about the good of others and – explicitly or implicitly – recognizes a need to find an appropriate balance or tradeoff between the two.[4] Similarly, satisficing altruists may recognize the importance of leaving room for their own "ground projects" or of avoiding the foibles of moral sainthood.[5] These cases of satisficing with respect to a relatively broad or relatively global goal seem perfectly coherent. What seems a nonstarter, as a candidate for rational action,[6] is satisficing with respect to the absolutely global project of – what shall we say? – *pursuing the good.* The satisficing egoist and the satisficing altruist are each perfectly intelligible, as we readily see that there are sets of reasons not addressed by their endeavors to which we might appeal in explaining why the satisficing strategy makes sense. Not so, however, with the endeavor of pursuing the good. To be sure, in pursuing the good, it may often be best to stop canvassing options at some point and go ahead and choose; from this absolutely global perspective, however, it seems that we can understand this only as "subtle optimizing," as David Schmidtz has called it.[7] That is, this declaration of closure must be the optimal action, taking account of the costs of further deliberation.

Although satisficing is thus intelligible with respect to some quite broad endeavors, such as seeking one's own happiness or that of others, examples of purportedly rational satisficing usually depict individuals engaged in considerably more specific projects. A homeowner is selling a house and decides that a particular offer is good enough.[8] An executive is picking an outfit for the day and decides that a given blouse will do.[9] An engineer is designing a highway and goes with the materials that recent experience suggests work well enough, rather than test anew all plausible candidates for a surfacing material.[10] I will treat these examples as paradigmatic cases in which satisficing seems appropriate and will return to them both to analyze that appearance and to make the case that the notion of practical commitments offers a better way of understanding their non-optimizing aspect.

If satisficing is not intelligible with respect to the absolutely global endeavor of pursuing the good, then why insist on any aspect of globalness in defining satisficing? The reason is that unless a global perspective is invoked in defining the metric of satisfaction, satisficing will merge indiscriminately with the simple and banal idea of tradeoffs. It would merge, that is, into such phenomena as choosing a wine for dinner that is not *too* costly or deciding that the argument of one's paper is explicit enough given the word limit. Furthermore, as I will be arguing below, the idea of metrics that are local to, or immanent in, our endeavors suggests an entirely different approach to practical rationality from the one implicitly adopted by those who uphold the importance of satisficing. Thus, to give a preliminary illustration: Suppose that I have decided to cook a good meal for my friends. It would be absurd to optimize with respect to that goal and cook them the best possible meal – even the best one possible given my credit rating. Instead of optimizing, I might instead characterize in purely *culinary* terms what would be "good enough": a relatively creative dish made with fresh ingredients readily available at my local market, say. "No need for filet mignon for *this* occasion," I might say to myself.

The dilemma for the defenders of satisficing results from the fact that what makes plausible the kinds of departure from optimizing that they instance is the incommensurability, or at least surface incommensurability, of the many values we seek: There is no common metric in terms of which one may adequately represent the various considerations bearing on our choices for the purpose of making those choices. (Note that, on this gloss, incommensurability of valued items does not imply that we cannot choose between them or compare their value.)[11] Allowing their analysis to remain mired – as one might think of it – in the level of the multiple, incommensurable values with which we daily truck, however, would both deprive the idea of satisficing of any generality or usefulness as a rational strategy and – as I will be able to show more fully only at the end of this paper, once we have been through the examples from several viewpoints – reduce it to being an overly complex way of making the simple point that we face tradeoffs among incommensurables.

To sum up our results so far: For satisficing to be a rational strategy, it must be applied to an endeavor more local than that of pursuing the good. For satisficing to be an interesting and distinctive decision strategy – as opposed to an unexceptionable exhortation to take account of how our finitude prevents us from rationally optimizing – its metric of what is "good enough" must be a relatively global one. If we now ask what that metric might be, we see that the first point limits our answer, for it requires us to take seriously the multiplicity of human endeavors. As we have seen, if rational satisficing is a real possibility for us, then as practical reasoners we cannot be rightly understood as ultimately seeking just one thing – pleasure, say. There must be more than one irreducibly different perspective on the good, such as those provided by the perspectives of self-interest and the common good. Beyond this, we may conclude that if satisficing is rational with respect to some endeavor, then we must be able to recognize that endeavor as the pursuit of a distinct good, of some end that the agent seeks for its own sake and not simply as a means to some one ultimate end.

Because, as Schmidtz puts it, the "goals we cherish as ends in themselves inherently tend to become incommensurable," the dependence of the intelligibility of rational satisficing on the multiplicity of endeavors valued in themselves puts pressure on what might possibly serve as a metric for what is "good enough."[12] Because goods are multiply incommensurable, no suitably global metric of "good enough" arises directly from the goods themselves. A car that is good enough in terms of handling ability may not be good enough in terms of gas mileage, and vice versa. I take it that our values do tend to be incommensurable.[13] Hence, it is important to recognize the difficulties posed for choice – and hence for straight optimization – by incommensurable values without getting stuck by them. To do so, the satisficer needs an interpretation of "good enough" that can win some distance from these incommensurabilities.

The natural and compelling interpretation that presents itself employs the language of rational choice theory – in particular, its concept of an individual's preference ranking of alternative actions. If an individual's preferences are sufficiently orderly, then they can be represented by a single-valued numerical function – a utility function, as it is called. Hence, preferences are quite sure to be able to provide a metric of more and less, and hence, potentially, of "enough." There are different variants, here. The ranking in question might be limited to the agent's "self-regarding" preferences.[14] Alternatively, the ranking might cover all features of real- ity – from the well-being of relatives to the existence of spotted newts – that an agent might plausibly care about.[15] If incommensurabilities among goods are particularly widespread and intractable, then they may prevent an individual's ranking of alternatives from being complete; even so, the ranking can provide a metric in terms of which, in many cases, an option may be declared "good enough."

In the remainder of this paper, therefore, I take the form of satisficing worth discussing as a strategy of rational deliberation to be one in which the deliberator ceases to search for alternative ways to pursue some local or specific endeavor when one finds an alternative that is "good enough" as assessed in terms of general preference satisfaction. This understand- ing of satisficing, which I have argued to be the most interesting and plausible version of the idea, seems to be fairly common in the literature. Thus, Schmidtz describes satisficing "not as an alternative to optimizing as a model of rationality but rather as an alternative to local optimizing as a strategy for pursuing global optima" and seems perfectly happy to de- scribe these global optima, for these purposes, in expected-utility terms.[16] Michael Byron explicitly interprets "good enough" in preference satisfac- tion terms (as a "threshold") as opposed to interpreting it in terms of the specific endeavors themselves (or as an "aspiration level").[17]

In what follows, I will argue that the concept of satisficing does not do a good enough job in accounting for the phenomena it was invented to explain. The central reason why not is that although satisficing is a strategy characteristic of an agent of bounded knowledge and rationality, the idea that a preference satisfaction metric can be seen as underlying all rational choice is a creature of considerable idealization. This idealization, however, puts it out of reach of a bounded agent, pursuing day-to-day strategies of reasoning.

The Idealizations of Preference Theory

To show that the version of the idea of preference satisfaction into which satisficing as a strategy of decision is pushed is highly idealized, I must first briefly explain why a less idealized version of preference theory is of no use in this context. I will then highlight the idealizations that the alternative interpretation of preference satisfaction involves. These, in turn, reveal a kind of incoherence in the idea of satisficing as a rational strategy, for it holds tightly to idealization in the very act of trying to step outside it.

We may divide preference theory into two types, depending on whether or not the idea of preferences is understood independently of actual choices. As Amartya Sen puts it,

Preference may be seen as "prior" to choice: we may try to choose what we prefer. This is indeed the natural sequence in reflective choice, seen from the first-person point of view. However, from the point of view of the outside observer, the opposite sequence may be the natural one: we observe the person's choices and surmise his or her preferences from these choices.[18]

The first of these approaches gives rise to idealizing versions of preference theory, which attempt to represent what people really prefer, or would prefer if they were able to think things through completely. The second, observer's approach, led within economics to the theory of revealed preference.

We may quickly rule out the latter, non-idealizing version of preference theory as of no use to the satisficer. On this interpretation, one's actions reveal one's preferences. If the executive picks one blouse out of the closet in order to wear it with the skirt she already has on, this is taken to reveal that she prefers so doing to any of the alternatives available. Obviously enough, this understanding of preference theory squeezes out all room for satisficing, for rational behavior simply cannot depart from the optimal, on this reading. Accordingly, the theorist of satisficing must turn to an understanding of preferences that makes them independent of what is actually chosen.

A different interpretation of preferences emerges from axiomatic utility theory – an approach that still parades under the label "rational choice theory." This theory at least purports to occupy the first-personal, deliberative perspective. On this approach, preferences are not simply read off from choices; instead, the sets of preferences worth taking seriously in deliberation are said to be those that would satisfy certain fundamental axioms, such as that of transitivity, under idealized deliberative conditions.

The reason that axiomatic utility theory depends upon a strong idealization is that in the absence of an antecedently detailed space of reasons – of factors that count for and against options – the theory radically underdetermines choice. Faced with any seeming violation of the axioms, there is always a question as to whether the appearance of violation can be removed simply by re-individuating the options. For example, if some actual set of choices appears to violate transitivity, and if agents stick with these choices on reflection, that probably means not that they are irrational but that there is, in effect, some equivocation in their rankings of A over B, B over C, and C over A. The characterization of the options has presumably failed to take account of the different respects in which these options are valuable. Once these are adequately taken into account, we will likely see that although A is indeed preferred to B, it is really A* that is dispreferred to C.[19] The axioms being quite robust, we must generally suspect that finite human agents have not had a chance to completely think through the options, nor to individuate them according to a final arraying of all of the relevant dimensions of value and a full sorting out of their interactions.

Thus, imagine that our highway engineer gets into the following informal cycle in deciding on a material for a road's wearing surface: She decides that porous asphalt is preferable to concrete on account of the former's better drainage; that the ease of laying hot-rolled asphalt makes it preferable to porous asphalt; and that concrete's durability makes it preferable to hot-rolled asphalt. There are many important goods at stake in a road surface, of which drainage, ease of laying, and durability are but three. Completely thought-through preferences that satisfied the axioms would represent the rankings our engineer would have if she could think through, for each relevantly different context (e.g., for situations with different traffic patterns and rainfall), how these different dimensions interact. Along the way, she may have need or opportunity to re-individuate the options. She might, for instance, distinguish two types of concrete: Perhaps grooved concrete affords some of the drainage benefits of porous asphalt while retaining nearly the durability of smooth concrete.

As is plain, then, axiomatic utility theory provides not a decision-making strategy or approach but rather a way of representing what it would be to be a perfectly rational agent. Because it is mathematically tractable, this sort of preference theory can suggest ways of reasoning under uncertainty and ways of approaching strategic and economic interactions; nonetheless, preference theory essentially starts off with agents who are decisive, in that they are able to rank alternatives. Because preference theory is not a decision-making strategy, it is largely silent about how to rank alternatives.

Axiomatic preference theory serves as a kind of rational theology for atheists. Our medieval forebears, armed with idealizations about the omnipotence and perfection of God, derived theorems pertaining to His existence and His willing and brought these to bear on what we have reason to do. Leibniz's account of the truth-conditions of statements about our reasons for action refers to God's infinite wisdom and intellect and the way in which He would use His rational capacities wisely to balance the incommensurable perfections of the created world. Such a theory makes it relatively difficult to account for one person's reasons' being different from another's. A modern theory more flexible in this respect is the "ideal adviser" theory, which reconstructs the truth-conditions of one's reasons for action in terms of an adviser – in effect, an idealized version of oneself – who knows all the alternatives and all of their consequences or ramifications. The ideal adviser generates advice by developing one's preferences in relation to the alternatives thus understood.[20] Hence, our modern idealizations leave more room for individuality.[21]

Because our knowledge is fragmentary and our intellects are limited, these idealizations do not directly provide useful strategies for decision.[22] Reconstructing truth-conditions for reasons-statements is one enterprise, while characterizing appropriate ways of reasoning is quite another. Although it is clear that preference theory reflects a highly idealized way of reconstructing our all-things-considered reasons for action, satisficing is a notion that belongs, rather, to the mundane level of actual practical reasoning.

The idea of satisficing arose in Herbert Simon's attempt to characterize the decision making of organizations in a way that took realistic account of human limitations. Abstracting somewhat from particular features of his view, the cognitive limitations on which he focused were the following three:[23]

- We do not know all the possible alternatives.
- We do not know the consequences of all of the possible alternatives.
- We do not know all of the evaluatively relevant differences among possible alternatives.

Although these do seem three distinct sorts of ignorance, it is worth noting that thinking in terms of axiomatic utility theory might lead one to boil these three limitations down to one. From the idealizing perspective of preference theory, the separation of an "alternative" from its "consequences" actually betrays the crude simplifications of everyday life, in which, in considerable ignorance of the often quirky and perverse consequences of what we choose, we describe our alternatives in local terms. As Kenneth Arrow emphasized, because of the way evaluatively relevant features can interact in ways we care about, our infinite advisers would actually want to consider alternative "total life histories."[24] Further, if we knew all of the evaluatively relevant differences among possible alternatives, we would not need to know *all* possible alternatives, just the evaluatively different ones. In short, all an ideal adviser would need to know would be the available comprehensive world futures "individuated by justifiers": If a difference to the way the future would go makes an evaluative difference, then that provides a basis for individuating futures; if not, not.[25]

At least for expository purposes, however, Simon treated the three listed forms of ignorance as distinct. In addition to taking account of these limitations of our knowledge, he kept clearly in view the limitations on our deliberative capacities. We have limited abilities to discern and process relevant information, limited capacities to entertain alternatives, and limited capacities for arriving at decisions. It is tough enough for us to make one decision at a time on some local issue, let alone to settle many at once. In part for this reason, we rely upon planning: We commit ourselves to partially worked-out plans at one time and generally refrain from wholesale reconsideration later on. Our plans help shape what is on our agenda for decision. That we rely upon formal or informal agendas is another feature of our decision making from which, as Simon rightly noted, preference theory abstracts.[26]

Although Simon's theory may be intended simply to be descriptive,[27] one who aims to recommend decision-making strategies would also do well to take these limitations of human deliberative capacities into account.

Against this background, my question about the idea of rational satisficing is whether it can coherently take these limitations into account for the purposes of describing our strategies of local non-optimization while at the same time buying into the idealizations of preference theory for the purposes of defining the metric of what is "good enough" that satisficers use.

A priori, the answer to this question seems clear: Satisficing so described – as it must be to be both intelligible and interesting – is not a coherent idea, for the completely thought-through preferences of an ideal adviser simply are not available to any actual agents as they are deciding whether to accept an offer on a house, choose a particular blouse, or specify a given road surface. But perhaps this seems both too quick and too uncharitable. Just as we can allow idealization in the construction of the overall theory of rational choice, can we not allow for some idealization in the application of its subordinate concepts, such as that of satisficing? Well, we can; but whether we should depends in part upon whether the resulting construct yields a good model of the everyday phenomena that this notion of satisficing is being invoked to fit. I will argue that it does not.

The Concept of Satisficing Poorly Fits the Facts

The idea of satisficing is understandably invoked to account for ways in which actual agents of limited capacities depart from optimizing, especially when incommensurable values are at stake. Even the sorts of case invoked by the literature on satisficing, however, are ill explained by reference to the strategy of satisficing. To make this point, I will return to the cases of the executive, the homeowner, and the highway engineer.

Does the executive grab a blouse that is "good enough" in preference satisfaction terms? This is a case in which the incommensurability of goods – an important part of the reason, as we have seen, that preference satisfaction emerges as the natural metric of what is good enough – occupies the foreground. Because of this incommensurability, it is natural that her thinking is not antecedently completely thought through. This implies, however, that the relevant stretches of her preference rankings are not available prior to the choice for the purpose of determining which option is good enough.[28] If this choice of blouse is a recurrent problem that tends to arise in certain typical contexts, such as dressing for the monthly board meeting, then it is certainly plausible that she will have worked out some views about what is appropriate to wear. Once those views are worked out, however, it would be silly for her not to optimize with respect to them. Our satisficing executive, remember, is coping with serious constraints on deliberation. So we may instead think of her as facing a new situation: Perhaps this is her first board meeting, or the first one at which so-and-so is present. If, for this kind of reason, she faces a need to satisfice, she will also lack the relevant range of preferences by reference to which to work out which option is good enough.

Perhaps this is unfair: Perhaps the suggestion is that, in satisficing, one works out on the fly which option is good enough, in preference satisfaction terms. Yet this suggestion matches nothing in our introspective experience. This may be shown first for a case like our executive's, where the point is relatively obvious. After laying it out for this case, I will turn to one that appears more favorable to the satisficing idea.

The phenomenological mismatch between satisficing and the kind of thinking our executive will naturally engage in can be put in terms of the contrast between monotonic and nonmonotonic reasoning.[29] The notion of a preference ranking that underlies the satisficing idea suggests a monotonic mode of reasoning. Once it is established that she prefers blouse A to blouse B, that conclusion can be taken as fixed, and she can go on to fill in the rest of her ranking without worrying about overturning that conclusion. Once the ranking is sufficiently filled in, the preferences can be represented in terms of a monotonically increasing function, and the satisficing level can be set at some point within its range. Working on the fly, she just needs to sense where she is in that range, and whether she has reached the point that is good enough. In fact, however, our ordinary deliberation involving incommensurable goods or subordinate ends is decidedly nonmonotonic: It is subject to frequent reversals and changes of mind. Anticipating my analysis in the next section, it would be natural to represent our executive as having three commitments:

(C1) If I'm going to a board meeting, I should wear something businesslike.

(C2) If I'm going to a board meeting, I should wear something elegant.

(C3) If I'm going to a board meeting, I should wear something sober.

In parallel with the highway engineer's informal cycle, we see easily how each of these conditional commitments could serve in turn to defeat the conclusion of the previous one. This is a decidedly nonmonotonic way of proceeding, one that remains phenomenologically enmeshed in the level of the subordinate goods or ends, and it does not seem to have available to it anything like an inchoate sense of the all-things-considered ranking. Yet being only a case of *prima facie* intransitivity – each step ranking the options only in some respect, and not all things considered – this is not a case in which an all-things-considered preference ranking is impossible. It is just that it is not even inchoately available to the agent as she deliberates.

I said a few paragraphs back that if worked-out preferences are available, then it is silly not to optimize with respect to them. We can now see more fully why this is. It is certainly possible that our executive has a number of blouses that are each sufficiently businesslike, elegant, and sober to be considered good enough for her board meeting. If so, then any one of those would seem to be good enough. Here, though, "good enough" means, not "rises to an adequate level of preference satisfaction" but "satisfies each of the constraints reasonable to impose on the choice of a blouse to wear to a board meeting." Furthermore, none of these constraints can be adequately grasped simply in terms of the categories of the more or less. Rather, each ramifies into a welter of contextually specific norms of professionalism, elegance, and sobriety that have many contextually specific elements and aspects.

That the incommensurability of values often prevents preference rankings from being even intuitively available to agents as they try to work out what an acceptable option would be does not imply, however, that there are no cases in which satisficing is a useful and sensible strategy. What about the case of the homeowner, in which the dollar price appears to offer a natural dimension of comparison?

Michael Slote introduces the case of the homeowner in the following terms:

An individual planning to move to a new location and having to sell his house may seek, not to maximize his profit on the house, not to get the best price for it he is likely to receive within some appropriate time period, but simply to obtain what he takes to be a good or satisfactory price. What he deems satisfactory may depend, upon other things, on what he has paid for the house, what houses cost in the place where he is relocating, and on what houses like his normally sell at. But given some notion of what would be a good or satisfactory price to sell at, he may fix the price of his house at that point, rather than attempting, by setting it somewhat higher, to do . . . the best he can. . . . [H]e is a "satisficer" content with good enough and does not seek to maximize (optimize) his expectations.[30]

In this description, of course, if what is "good enough" were defined by the agent directly in dollar terms, that would count as an aspiration level rather than as a utility threshold. This example differs from that of the executive, however, precisely because the dollar scale appears to be just a convenient stand-in – or *numéraire*, as the economists like to say – indexing preference satisfaction. Hence, this is a case in which, it appears, the dollar index might serve to tame the incommensurability of values that was so prominent in the case of choosing blouses.

This appearance, however, is misleading. To see why, we need only consider how it is that an individual might attempt to set a threshold in a non-arbitrary way in such a case. After all, the underlying ideal of preference-based rationality cannot itself explain how one might decide that a given level of preference satisfaction is good enough. In the idealized terms of preference theory, more preference satisfaction is indeed always better. Anticipating this point, Slote in fact alludes to three possible rationales for determining that a given selling price would be good enough: (1) that it exceeds what the seller paid for the house (or perhaps, exceeds that amount compounded by a decent annual rate of return); (2) that it covers, or may be expected to cover, the costs of purchasing a house at his new location; and (3) that it is not less than what comparable houses in his neighborhood have recently sold for. Each of these possible rationales is a good one. In fact, I want to suggest, each rises beyond being a mere heuristic for this case, as each represents, at least indirectly, a consideration that the homeowner might plausibly care about on its own. The first and the third rationales reflect the importance of not being a fiscal fool or an irresponsible investor of one's family's assets. The second reflects a prudent concern to avoid getting into a real financial bind. These values – avoiding being convicted, in one's own eyes or those of others, of being a fiscal fool, and avoiding a situation of financial anxiety – are not commensurable. Hence, despite the initial appearance, we are back in the same situation as the one we arrived at in analyzing the executive's case: The notion of "good enough" is here indeed intelligible, but only against the background of conflicting, incommensurable aims or values. In a parallel fashion to the prior case, a price that the agent considers "good enough" turns out to be one that meets all the constraints that he considers reasonable to impose on an acceptable dollar offer.

It may be objected that there is at least one kind of case in which the fixing of a price that is good enough can be thought of in preference terms. Suppose that the seller is not going to buy another house at all but rather is going to use the money to finance a retirement spent roaming the globe. Although there are obviously more and less expensive ways of roaming the globe, our homeowner has decided how much money it will cost to finance a retirement that will yield him an adequate level of satisfaction. This dollar value, in turn, can establish what selling price is good enough. In such a case, is not the level of preference satisfaction used to establish what is good enough?

I answer that it would be such a case only if determining the cost of an adequate retirement were itself a case of satisficing in preference satisfaction terms. Otherwise, what matters is an aspiration level defined in dollar terms, not in preference satisfaction terms. It is no more plausible that one could decide what sort of retirement activities would be good enough by referring to a preference satisfaction metric than that one can choose blouses that way. The case of the highway engineer raises no new hope for the proponent of satisficing; but because it does, to the contrary, involve a different way in which that description goes wrong, it is worth discussing separately. The new factor salient in this case is that the engineer's deliberations will almost surely be informed, if not constrained, by a set of specifications worked out by the previous deliberations of others. Previous generations of highway engineers have worked on the question of what surfaces to use and will have narrowed down the field of possibilities. Further, they will have produced generalizations about what sorts of surfaces to prefer under what sorts of conditions and will have codified their results. Hence, it would be silly and unprofessional for the engineer to survey all possible surfaces in order to calculate which is optimal. The engineer's case, therefore, differs from the foregoing in that there almost surely is involved an additional and different kind of constraint that it is reasonable to impose on the choice. The constraint is a procedural one: The choice must comport with the usual and customary practices of highway engineers.[31]

What we seem to lack, then, is any plausible case in which reasonable choice behavior is rightly described as satisficing – where that notion is interpreted, as I have argued that it ought to be, as implying that what is good enough is defined in terms of preference satisfaction. Still, one might claim that reference to satisficing is a useful, if approximative, characterization of these sorts of cases. That claim could stand, however, only if there were not a better way of understanding what is going on in them. I will now argue that there is.

Ends as Commitments and Limits

To make sense of the kinds of cases that draw the satisficing characterization, what we need to understand is how practical commitments can play a role in deliberation. Neither preferences nor desires have a committal aspect. Intentions, in sharp contrast, are plainly committal, often in such a focused way that they can be thought of only as the products of deliberation, rather than as input for deliberation.[32] Hence, what we are searching for is a notion that combines some of the committal aspect of intentions with some of the flexibility found in desires and preferences. I will characterize this idea of practical commitment in general and then suggest that final ends are a kind of practical commitment that can well make sense of the cases of the executive, the homeowner, and the highway engineer. Before I can lay out these ideas, however, I must further explain why the notion of desire is not helpful in this context.

In understanding these cases, we clearly need to get beyond the simple idea of conflicting desires. If desires are thought of causally, along the "quasi-hydraulic" lines that McDowell has criticized,[33] then it will also be natural to think of the strongest one prevailing. If our psychology were so simple, there would be little bulwark against a kind of automatic optimizing of the sort that occurs when water finds its own level. Even on contemporary functionalist understandings of desire that are developed in a way that is not necessarily causal, desire will lack a sufficiently committal structure to enable us to make sense of why someone would stop short of optimizing.[34] Michael Smith, for instance, interprets desires in terms of the idea of "direction of fit," which in turn he interprets (and contrasts with beliefs) in terms of a dispositional counterfactual: "A belief that p tends to go out of existence in the presence of a perception with the content that not p, whereas a desire that p tends to endure, disposing the subject in that state to bring it about that p."[35] Lacking the quasi-hydraulic definiteness of the usual causal accounts, this more abstract characterization of desire leaves up in the air how it is that conflicts of desire can be addressed. Smith's own answer is: via reasoning – specifically, via an attempt to reach reflective equilibrium around one's conception of ends.[36] With this last general statement I agree[37]; however, I think that we can better pave the way for understanding how reasoning can be extended to settling conflicts among aims – and more specifically, how we operate in the cases that tend to draw the satisficing characterization – if we enrich our psychological vocabulary by including a notion of practical commitment.

I come to this alternative idea in a moment; first, though, let me put in other terms what is unsatisfactory about the idea of desire. Another way to phrase the critical point is that desires are too irresponsible to be of much help in modeling what is going on in these cases. Because we simply expect desires to conflict all the time, there is neither any conceptual pressure to regiment them nor any conceptual structure in them that is apt for building further structure. I can persist in wanting both to have my cake and to eat it, even after I have recognized that I cannot do both; and although my decision to eat the cake may (tautologically) indicate that this desire was the stronger one, it is not readily capturable by any shift in my structure of desires.

As we make our way responsibly through the world, we must cope with the limitations of our awareness and of our reasoning capacities. If we had no such limitations, we could proceed as preference theory seems to suggest: We could confront each situation anew and think through in a complete way all of the organically interacting components of each alternative option that we face. If we thus proceeded, we could persist in operating with a belief-desire psychology. In fact, however, our practical psychology has adapted to the limitations that put such an approach out of reach. We do not apply a pure set of wants or preferences to a completely described set of outcomes each time we decide what to do. Instead, we operate on the basis of commitments, which combine the evaluative judgment that something is worth pursuing (in a certain way, perhaps) with a motivational attachment to that enterprise. Because practical commitments unite aspects of desire with aspects of belief, they are more "responsible" than desires and provide a better building block for arriving at somewhat systematic conceptions of what one ought to do.

Our final ends represent a particularly interesting and important subset of our practical commitments. As I have elsewhere suggested,[38] we may understand the notion of a final end – something sought for its own sake – by first working out a more general understanding of what it is to pursue one thing, x, for the sake of another thing, y. As with simple desires, there is certainly a counterfactual or dispositional element involved. Because there are two different goods involved, it must be put a little differently: One would pursue x even if the only good thereby attained were y. Something is sought for its own sake only if one would pursue it even if no other good were thereby attained. The sort of disposition expressed in such counterfactuals also entails certain limitations on deliberation, and specifically on one's further dispositions to reconsider, or not to reconsider, one's decisions. Thus, the disposition to pursue x even if the only good thereby attained were y entails that one will tend not to reconsider one's decision to pursue x upon learning that only y is thereby to be attained. On this account, an end has a desire-like direction of fit, as it, too, reflects a disposition to pursue something.

Yet there is more to ends than that. Because something can be sought both for its own sake and for the sake of something else, final ends lend themselves to being ranged in a hierarchy. That is so because, in addition to the dispositional aspect, the general notion of pursuing one thing for the sake of another also entails a reflective judgment that often imports an asymmetry.[39] Suppose that I enjoy exercise for its own sake but also value (or pursue) it for the sake of my health. This tends to suggest that I do not value my health for the sake of exercise. Yet if health and exercise are each things that I would pursue on their own, why this lack of full symmetry? The reason, I suggest, is that although pursuing x for the sake of y entails an evaluative judgment to the effect that it is appropriate (or acceptable or correct or *comme il faut*) to let one's pursuit of x be regulated by reference to the pursuit of the superordinate end, y, the relation might not hold the other way around. Hence, if I pursue exercise for the sake of health, then I judge that it is appropriate to look to my health to determine how far to push myself in exercise and when I ought to hold back. If I instead pursued health for the sake of exercise, I would instead be willing to neglect those aspects of health that did not contribute to my exercising and might sacrifice the health of my old age for the sake of being able to exercise well in my prime. Hence, (commitment to) an end also has a desire-like direction of fit that results from this kind of evaluative judgment. A final end is one we judge to be, within some range or in relevant respects, self-regulating.[40]

This duality in an end's direction of fit does not make ends impossible. In this respect, they are unlike "besires" as tendentiously characterized by Smith. On his account, a besire that p is a unitary psychological state that combines the features of the desire that p and the belief that p. If "besire" is thus defined, if the definitive features of the belief aspect and the desire aspect are understood in terms of direction of fit, and if direction of fit is, in turn, cashed out in terms of the dispositional counterfactuals given above, then Smith has a convincing case that there can be no besires. It is incoherent to suppose that there is a single mental state that both tends to disappear and to persist in the presence of a perception with the content that not p. Ends – and more generally, commitments to pursuing one thing for the sake of another – do not suffer this incoherence, as their dispositional aspect and their judgmental aspect have differing contents.[41] In particular, the judgment involved in (being committed to) pursuing x for the sake of y is that it is appropriate to look to y in modulating one's pursuit of x (and not vice versa).[42]

On account of this aspect of self-regulation, final ends involve a kind of self-limitation. In this respect, they stand intermediate between the old-fashioned, quasi-hydraulic desires of philosophical lore and the more idealized desires or preferences commonly hypothesized by decision theorists. Your traditional desires *for food* or *for sex* build no limits into their content; limitation comes with obstacles and with satiety, when the desire in question wanes in strength.[43] Idealized desires or preferences *that p*, in stark contrast, have as sharp and limited satisfaction conditions as does p itself. (For this very reason, we must suspect that desires of this latter form have their natural home in the idealizations of preference theory.[44]) A final end we take to be appropriately self-regulating; and this means that we at least take it to have sufficient normative structure to generate some appropriate limits. Food – or eating – is not a plausible candidate for a final end (mere eating being more likely merely instrumental to staying alive), whereas eating fine French food might be a final end for someone (while also, perhaps, being sought for the sake of camaraderie). And French cuisine – here I have picked an obvious case – clearly is the focus of a highly developed set of social practices to which many norms are internal. Similarly immanent links pertain to the end of cooking a nice meal for friends. In other cases – as with exercise – the relevant norms may have a somewhat more biological basis.[45] But "all forms of life," as Martha Nussbaum puts it, "contain boundaries and limits."[46] This self-regulating or self-limiting feature of ends is worth emphasizing, as it highlights their divergence from the sort of "value dimension" that one might "weight" so as to arrive at an all-things-considered metric.[47] This is not how we should think of ends.

With this alternative conceptualization of moral psychology in place, we can better explain what is going on in the supposed cases of satisficing.

The Cases Recast in Terms of Conflicting Ends

Let us return, then, to the executive, the homeowner, and the highway engineer. Because elements of the redescription of these cases in terms of conflicting final ends has already cropped up in my criticism of describing these as cases of satisficing, not much suspense remains; but we need to consolidate the conclusion that they are better described in these terms.

The values with which our executive is struggling – businesslike appearance, elegance, and sobriety in appearance – may not be ones that she has internalized as final ends. She may, after all, remain quite alienated from the sartorial expectations of her workplace. Whether or not she values these as final ends, however, she likely operates with them as if they were final ends. She needs to figure out what she would wear if she were committed to these ends of professionalism, elegance, and sobriety in appearance.

There are two importantly different possibilities for our executive: First, she may readily find a blouse that satisfies each of these commitments (or "as if" commitments). If she does, then, as we have already seen, that blouse is clearly "good enough" on a basis that can be understood wholly apart from preference satisfaction. My sketch of the moral psychology of ends has, I hope, reinforced the point that preferences are one thing and ends another. The second possibility is that she cannot find a blouse that satisfies all three commitments. What would give the appearance of satisficing, in that case, is better described as her being unable or unwilling, within her time constraints, to work out whether there is a way to satisfy all three of these commitments. Rather, she picks something on the basis of one or two of the commitments, letting the other(s) go by the boards. Because the conflict remains unresolved – rather than being worked out, for instance, by reference to a superordinate end-of-career success, say – there is clearly no available all-things-considered metric of what is "good enough." Rather, this is a case better described as one of "decision making under unresolved conflict."[48]

Here, the defender of satisficing may sense an opening. "Surely it is just in the case in which ends conflict," one may object, "that recourse to some overall idea of preference satisfaction is needed to model what a good enough response to the conflict would be and, more generally, to cope with the conflict." Part of my answer to this objection, though, has already been given – namely that an all-things-considered preference ranking simply is not available until all such conflicts have already been completely thought through. I can now point out more constructively, in addition, that there are modes of reasoning about ends, and especially conflicting ends, that cope with such conflicts rationally without invoking any kind of commensurating metric. For instance, one may try to work out a superordinate end (say, that of dressing appropriately for work) in which each of the conflicting, more specific ends, has its place.[49] One may also attempt to specify one or more of the conflicting ends – to modify one's contextual interpretation of it – so as to alleviate the conflict one faces.[50] Hence, even if one tries to resolve most contingent conflicts among one's practical commitments, one need not invoke the idea of preference satisfaction in so doing.

The case is similar with the homeowner, whose ends include being a prudent investor of his family's assets, a prudent planner for his family's financial future, and no fool in comparison to his neighbors. The seller who is initially characterized as a satisficer may well be satisfying all three of these commitments. Although he undoubtedly has other life aims that could be well served by some additional cash, these may simply not be salient for him in the context of this choice. In this case, conflict among his salient commitments is not a factor. The practical implications of his three ends – mediated, in each case, by fairly conventional ideas about what is prudent or foolish in the circumstances – can be ranked in terms of stringency. That is so because a rough dollar figure can be put on what a prudent return on his investment in the house would be, what a prudent provision for his future housing would require, and what it would take to come off as at least no fool in comparison to neighbors who have recently sold comparable houses. For this reason, he faces, not so much a conflict among the three commitments as an issue about whether to hold out for satisfying them all. Still, he may end up settling for less money than he might have gotten. Lacking a way to reduce all of his relevant commitments to a single ordering, he will likely neither optimize nor employ a satisficing strategy.

In the cases of the executive and the homeowner, conventions or practices lie in the background that help interpret the ends moving them. For the highway engineer, these are surely a matter of foreground. We may suppose that a highway engineer is professionally committed to laying, at reasonable cost, roads that drain well and last. We may be equally sure, however, that highway engineers are also professionally committed to following and respecting the norms of their profession. In many jurisdictions, norms of highway construction are officially spelled out, in part so as to help preclude construction fraud. These ordinances seem typically to indicate several canonical sets of specifications for road construction. Hence, we have two possibilities in redescribing the case of the highway engineer. The first is to follow the pattern of the executive and note that she is coping with a case of decision making under unresolved conflict, rather than deciding which option is "good enough" in preference satisfaction terms. The second is to suggest that the norms of her profession in fact dictate that she not think through, *de novo*, which material would be best but rather that she pick one of the canonical ones.

Although this last point referred to the highway engineer's commitment to certain procedures, which excludes her from considering certain sorts of reasons, the deeper phenomenon here is shared with all ends and takes us back to the psychological need for commitments.[51] The engineer's case differs from the others not in blocking certain issues from reconsideration – for that is a general feature of all practical commitments, of which ends are a species – but rather in that the norms of nonreconsideration involved are public, explicit, and purportedly authoritative. In all three cases, it is a psychological necessity to operate with certain commitments that one will not rethink unless one runs into trouble. One is tempted to say that it would be a mark of insanity, when getting dressed or when figuring out how much money one will insist on in selling a house, to try to generate a decision from the ground up, abstracting from all such previous commitments. There is no need to say this, however, for in principle there would be no way to do this. There would be no basis for forming a preference at all without reference to some things that one considered worth seeking for their own sake; and this very notion, as I have argued, entails a commitment aspect.

Conclusion

The satisficing strategy falls down in its attempt to straddle two perspectives: the everyday perspective of its purported examples and the idealizing perspective of its metric of what is "good enough." The notion of an all-things-considered preference ranking has no proper home in everyday psychology, where cases of satisficing are supposed to arise. What does instead illuminate the everyday context is the idea of a practical commitment, and more specifically that of a final end. The purported cases of satisficing that have been put forward in the literature are better thought of as cases in which people either content themselves with seeing to it that their salient practical commitments are satisfied or else face some conflict among their ends or commitments that they are unable or unwilling to resolve in the time available.

It may be thought that my analysis simply brings us back to the interpretation of satisficing that I rejected at the outset, that which interprets "good enough" in terms of evaluatively specific levels, each tied to some one value. After all, I have been rejecting the idea that agents deliberate by optimizing. I have no great objection to this way of taking my analysis. As I said above, my objection to satisficing, on this rejected interpretation, is not that it is false to the phenomena of deliberation but that it is banal. One way to underline its banality is to notice that the notion of what is "good enough" in the relevant respect will tend to be otiose. Our executive aims to wear something that is professional, elegant, and sober. It adds nothing to say that she aims to wear something that is "professional enough, elegant enough, and sober enough." That goes without saying. It is when we say it anyway, and then proceed in a general way to try to give any real content to the idea of what is "good enough," that the idea of a satisficing strategy ceases to be banal and becomes misleading.

To be sure, our executive will probably operate with a context-specific sense of what is elegant enough for what context, say. I know from my own case that I consider black jeans elegant enough for some contexts but not for others. What I believe is really going on in such cases, however, is that additional dimensions of nuanced commitment are being revealed. In addition to wanting to be elegant, I aim to be comfortable, to avoid being taken for a lawyer, and not to stand out in certain ways. Working out a conception of the good, in which one's final ends are arranged in appropriate hierarchies of pursuit, is a way to try to make such commitments explicit. Because such hierarchies have considerable regulative structure, making them explicit is also a way to try to work through conflicts among them, which are pervasive in our lives. Thinking about what is going on when practical commitments bear on a case or when they conflict in terms of what is "good enough" neither illuminates this structure nor helps provide a way to refine it. In this banal version, the idea of satisficing may be a conceptual tool that fits the facts, but it is not good enough. We can do better.

Notes

I am most grateful to Margaret Olivia Little, Gopal Sreenivasan, and the Stanford Ethics Discussion Group for their comments on an earlier version.

1. Michael Byron, "Satisficing and Optimality," *Ethics* 109 (1998): 70. See also, for example, David Gauthier, *Morals by Agreement*, Oxford: Clarendon Press, 1986, 184; John Broome, *Weighing Goods: Equality, Uncertainty, and Time*, New York: Blackwell, 1991, 7.
2. Michael Slote, *Beyond Optimizing: A Study of Rational Choice*, Cambridge: Harvard University Press, 1989, chap. 1.
3. Slote, *Beyond Optimizing*, 26.
4. Because Michael Byron intends the perspective of the "global goal of making my life go well" to be an all-things-considered one, we must take it that, in his view, because an altruist has a local goal of helping others, the altruist's life, by definition and pro tanto, goes better insofar as the others' lives go better. See Byron, "Satisficing and Optimality," 76–7.
5. Bernard Williams, "Persons, Character and Morality," in *Moral Luck*, Cambridge University Press, 1–19; Susan Wolf, "Moral Saints," *Journal of Philosophy* 79 (1982): 419–39.
6. Because my interest here is ultimately with the structure of practical reasoning, I pass over the possibility that intentional though imperfectly rational action might satisfice in the project of pursuing the good. If, as Michael Stocker has argued, there are cases of intentional pursuit of the bad (Michael Stocker, "Desiring the Bad: An Essay in Moral Psychology," *Journal of Philosophy* 76 [1979]: 738–53), then it would seem that there could also be cases of intentional action that satisficed with respect to all-things-considered

goodness. To say that, however, would not be to say that this satisficing is a rational strategy.

7. David Schmidtz, *Rational Choice and Moral Agency*, Princeton University Press, 1995, 29–30.

8. Slote, *Beyond Optimizing*, 10.

9. Schmidtz, *Rational Choice*, 39.

10. Herbert A. Simon, *Administrative Behavior: A Study of Decision-Making Processes in Administrative Organizations*, New York: The Free Press, 1997, 98.

11. I depart from James Griffin and Joseph Raz in refusing to use "incommensurable" to *mean* "incomparable." For a brief statement of my reasons, see Henry S. Richardson, "Commensurability," in Lawrence Becker, ed., *Encyclopedia of Ethics*, 2nd ed. New York: Routledge, 2001, 258–62.

12. Schmidtz, *Rational Choice and Moral Agency*, 47. The point is put contrapositively by Simon, *Administrative Behavior*, 5–6: "In balancing the one aim against the other, and in attempting to find a common denominator, it would be necessary to cease thinking of the two aims as ends in themselves, and instead to conceive them as means to some more general end." I argue for the existence of incommensurable goods in Henry S. Richardson, *Practical Reasoning About Final Ends*, Cambridge University Press, 1994, chap. V.

13. I have argued for the existence of value incommensurability in Richardson, *Practical Reasoning About Final Ends*, sec. 17.

14. See Slote, *Beyond Optimizing*, 20.

15. Appeal to such so-called "existence values" makes economists who employ cost-benefit analyses nervous. See, for example, Matthew D. Adler and Eric A. Posner, "Implementing Cost-Benefit Analysis When Preferences Are Distorted," in Matthew D. Adler and Eric A. Posner, eds., *Cost-Benefit Analysis: Legal, Economic, and Philosophical Perspectives*, University of Chicago Press, 2001, 281–2.

16. Schmidtz, *Rational Choice*, 53, 30.

17. Byron, "Satisficing and Optimality," 73. As Byron notes, a dissenter, in this last respect, is Philip Pettit, "Satisficing Consequentialism," *Proceedings of the Aristotelian Society* suppl. 58 (1984): 165–76.

18. Amartya Sen, *Choice, Welfare, and Measurement*, Cambridge: MIT Press, 1982, 1.

19. On the issue of reindividuating options so as to restore the transitivity of an individual's preferences, see Broome, *Weighing Goods*, 102–4. Although Broome speaks of reindividuating options so as to maintain continuity with earlier discussions, he argues that it would be more perspicuous to think in terms of rational requirements of indifference – that is, in terms of pairs of options between which it would be irrational not to be indifferent.

20. See Peter Railton, "Facts and Values," *Philosophical Topics* 14 (1986): 16; Michael Smith, *The Moral Problem*, New York: Blackwell, 1994, 151ff.

21. For a powerful critique of preference theory in the spirit of Voltaire's critique of Leibniz's "optimism," see Jean Hampton, "The Failure of Expected Utility Theory as a Theory of Reason," *Economics and Philosophy* 10 (1994): 195–242.

22. This point is emphasized by David Sobel, "Subjective Accounts of Reasons for Action," *Ethics* 111 (2001): 461–92.

23. Simon, *Administrative Behavior*, 93–4.

24. Kenneth J. Arrow, "Utilities, Attitudes, Choices: A Review Note," in *Individual Choice Under Certainty and Uncertainty*, in *Collected Papers of Kenneth J. Arrow*, Cambridge: Harvard University Press, 1984, 57.

25. Broome, *Weighing Goods*, 103.

26. Simon, *Administrative Behavior*, 122.

27. See Byron, "Satisficing and Optimality," 71n.

28. For the general point that preference-based modes of modeling optimizing reasoning tend to be useless in deliberation, see Richardson, *Practical Reasoning About Final Ends*, sec. 15.

29. I am indebted here to Heath White.

30. Slote, *Beyond Optimizing*, 9.

31. I do not mean to deny that executives' wardrobes and house selling are completely free from the normative constraints of custom and usage; the difference is one of relative prominence.

32. I am indebted to Heath White for this economical way of contrasting desires and intentions.

33. John McDowell, "Non-Cognitivism and Rule-Following," in *Mind, Value, and Reality*, Cambridge: Harvard University Press, 1998, 213.

34. In Henry S. Richardson, "Thinking About Conflicts of Desire," in *Practical Conflicts: New Philosophical Essays*, eds. Peter Baumann and Monika Betzler (Cambridge, England: Cambridge University Press, forthcoming 2004), I develop a richer, Aristotelian conception of desire that is better suited to capturing the notion of a commitment.

35. Smith, *The Moral Problem*, 115. Smith comments in a footnote appended to this passage that this contrast is rather rough but could be refined along decision-theoretic lines.

36. Smith, *The Moral Problem*, 158–60.

37. See Richardson, *Practical Reasoning About Final Ends*, esp. chap. 8.

38. Richardson, *Practical Reasoning About Final Ends*, sec. 7.

39. I am grateful to Gopal Sreenivasan and the members of our moral reasoning seminar for helping me see that I had earlier exaggerated this point.

40. The reason for the qualification is related to the reasons we may have to seek final ends also for the sake of some more final end: The former may need *some* regulation by reference to the latter.

41. Here I am indebted to Margaret Olivia Little, "Virtue as Knowledge: Objections from the Philosophy of Mind," *Nous* 31 (1997): 63–4.

42. It is also possible to combine desire and evaluative judgment in simpler ways while still steering clear of Smith's problem. See, for instance, Michael E. Bratman, "Reflection, Planning, and Temporally Extended Agency," *Philosophical Review* 109 (2000): 54–5, which analyzes the kind of commitment involved in "an agent's endorsement of a desire in terms, roughly, of a self-governing policy in favor of an agent's treatment of that desire as providing a justifying reason in motivationally efficacious practical reasoning." The reflective judgment involved in this policy is also distinct in content from the object of the desire thus endorsed.

43. Note that we cannot say that the desire for food is really the desire that one has some food, for the latter would be satisfied by a single scrap of bread, whereas the latter is likely not.

44. See the classic development of desires as propositional attitudes in Richard C. Jeffrey, *The Logic of Decision*, 2nd ed. University of Chicago Press, 1983, esp. 59–60.

45. For examples, see Philippa Foot, *Natural Goodness*, Oxford University Press, 2001.

46. Martha C. Nussbaum, "Non-Relative Virtues: An Aristotelian Approach," in Martha C. Nussbaum and Amartya Sen, eds., *The Quality of Life*, Oxford University Press, 1993, 267.

47. This picture of weighting subordinate considerations, which are thought of as satisfied either more or less, is quite pervasive. See, for example, S. L. Hurley, *Natural Reasons: Personality and Polity*, Oxford University Press, 1989, chap. 11.

48. The phrase is from Isaac Levi, *Hard Choices: Decision Making Under Unresolved Conflict*, Cambridge University Press, 1986.

49. See Richardson, *Practical Reasoning About Final Ends*, chap. 10.

50. Richardson, *Practical Reasoning About Final Ends*, chap. 4.

51. On the notion of exclusionary reasons, see Joseph Raz, *Practical Reason and Norms*, Princeton University Press, 1990.

7

Why Ethical Satisficing Makes Sense and Rational Satisficing Doesn't

James Dreier

Introduction

I will argue that rational satisficing and ethical satisficing suffer from the same problem, namely, that they are in danger of making no sense because their conceptions of the good cannot be made out independently of a conception of the proper aim of actions.[1] In the case of rational satisficing, the main argument comes from the foundations of decision theory. In the case of ethical satisficing, I borrow an argument from Philippa Foot.

In the end it turns out that ethical satisficing survives the problem, whereas rational satisficing does not. I will motivate the distinction by appealing to an intuitive feature of commonsense morality, namely, supererogation.

Rational Satisficing

The literature on rational satisficing is loaded with interesting examples, but none of them has ever struck me as an example of rational satisficing. They always appear to be examples of something else, not always of the same thing, but always of something that defenders of maximizing could accommodate within their theory. One of these is the example of Hannah. Suppose Hannah has put her house on the market, and naturally she wants the best price for it. Because she can't wait indefinitely for bids to come in, she decides to accept the first bid that comes in above a certain satisfactory price that she chooses in advance. Suppose she picks $200,000 as her threshold. If someone offers her $205,000 the first day the ad appears in the local real estate listings, she'll take it. Of course, she would *rather* have a higher bid, and she knows that by accepting the $205,000 offer she may well be missing out on a higher offer. But she has decided that anything over $200,000 is "good enough," or satisfactory.

Hannah's strategy seems quite reasonable. At least, it seems reasonable if we assume that Hannah doesn't have any reason to expect much higher offers if only she waits another few days, and also that another $10,000 wouldn't make an enormous difference to her prospects of buying another house, or the like; and certainly other features added to the story could make her strategy look unreasonable. But it certainly *could* be a reasonable strategy.

Why is it reasonable? Is it just reasonable on the face of it to accept an offer one deems "good enough" even though a higher offer would be better? Surely not. If Hannah comes home after work to find three voicemail offers for the house, it would not be reasonable to accept the lowest of the three even if the lowest is over $200,000.[2] Nor, it seems to me, would it be reasonable for her to accept an offer of $200,000 if her real estate agent were to tell her that two other prospective buyers were almost certain to make much higher offers tomorrow. Near certainty, in this context, is nearly as good as certainty.

What conditions have to be met before Hannah's strategy seems reasonable? We could probably come up with quite a number of necessary conditions. But here are two that seem especially important: First, there must be no offer *better* than the "good enough" offer that is likely to show up shortly. Second, the extra money Hannah would likely gain by waiting a little longer must not be terribly significant to her. We could put it this way: Hannah's strategy is reasonable for her because there is a kind of tradeoff between money and time. Getting the deal done soon is better, and getting more money is better, and the longer she waits the more money she is likely to get for the house. The threshold she sets and the strategy of setting a threshold are reasonable if she picks an amount that trades time against money in the most reasonable way, given what she wants and what she knows.

Decision theory, in its classic form, is often understood to give decision makers formal and explicit advice about how to make tradeoffs like Hannah's. It is often understood to combine three factors in providing Hannah with a strategy for selling: First, it tells her to assign utility numbers to waiting times, presumably lower numbers to longer periods. Second, she is to assign numbers from the same scale to dollar values for the house, with higher numbers to greater dollar amounts in proportion to how much those dollar amounts matter to her. And third, she is to assign probabilities to prospects of receiving offers of various amounts given that she wait various periods of time. These three collections of numbers she can then use to calculate the expected utility of various strategies, and she will be rational if she picks the strategy with the highest expected utility. If this version of decision theory is correct, then Hannah's satisficing strategy of setting a threshold of $200,000 and accepting the first offer over the threshold has a higher expected utility than any available alternative strategy.

By definition, the expected utility of a strategy, S, is given by the formula

$$eu(S) = u(A_1 \& S) \, pr(A_1|S) + u(A_2 \& S) \, pr(A_2|S) + \ldots + u(A_n \& S) \, pr(A_n|S)$$

where the A_i form a partition (so that the conjunctions of the A_i with S partition the space of outcomes of the strategy), and the function $pr(X \mid Y)$ assigns conditional probabilities: the probability of X given Y. Intuitively, the idea is that we can figure out how good a strategy is by taking its various possible outcomes, weighting their goodness by their probabilities, and summing the products. If some possible outcome is extremely good, it will contribute a lot to the goodness of the strategy if it is likely, but it might contribute little to the goodness of the strategy if it is unlikely.

Decision theory thus explains in a precise way the rough conditions we sketched. By setting her threshold at $200,000, Hannah reduces her chance of getting a much higher offer. If she would be very likely to receive a much higher offer were she to wait a little longer, and if waiting longer does not reduce her utility, and if getting a lot more money would increase her utility by a great deal, then the expected utility of setting a higher threshold (or some other type of strategy) would be greater than her actual one. But if she cares little for the extra money she might get over $200,000 (so that the utility of these forgone prospects is not great), and if it matters a lot to her to get the house sold quickly (so that the utility of prospects of larger dollar amounts received after a longer wait would not be relatively small), and if the chance of getting much larger offers would not be large (so that the multipliers of the better prospects would be small multipliers), then her chosen strategy is reasonable.

Now, the advice that decision theory gives to Hannah may seem onerous to follow. What if Hannah doesn't have any clear idea of the probabilities associated with the various outcomes given the various strategies she might adopt? Even coming up with plausible estimates might be a dreary prospect. And how exactly is she supposed to go about assigning all those utility numbers? By definition, your utility for X is greater than your utility for Y just in case you prefer X to Y. But having assigned, say, an arbitrary utility of 100 to the prospect of selling her house for $200,000 in one week, how does Hannah know whether to assign 110, 195, or 1,000 to the prospect of selling for $205,000 in five days? David Schmidtz writes:

> Suppose I need to decide whether to go off to fight for a cause in which I deeply believe or to stay home with a family that needs me and that I deeply love. What should I do? My friends say I should determine the possible outcomes of the two proposed courses of action, assign probabilities and numerical utilities to each possibility, multiply through, and then choose whichever alternative has the highest number.
>
> My friends are wrong. Their proposal would be plausible in games of chance where information on probabilities and monetarily denominated utilities is readily available. In the present case, however, I can only guess at the possible outcomes of either course of action. Nor do I know their probabilities. Nor do I know how to gauge their utilities. The strategy of maximizing expected utility is out of the question, for employing it requires information that I do not have.[3]

Schmidtz's friends go on to suggest instead that he make the best estimates he can of the relevant parameters and use those, but Schmidtz notes that he has no reason to trust a formula full of estimates.

Schmidtz's friends are devotees of what I will call Crude Decision Theory. Crude Decision Theory can indeed be useful in special circumstances, like deciding whether to accept the doubling cube in backgammon or how much to direct your multinational corporation to spend on research. Schmidtz is right, though, to say that as a guide to ordinary decisions it is useless (or worse). The most compelling objection is that we do not, ordinarily, know how to assign utility numbers to outcomes.[4] In the special cases of games or boards of directors, there are (or anyway may be) good reasons to let numbers of points or dollar profits stand in for utilities, but in most of our lives we have no such proxies. The problem is not only that we find it hard to be precise about our own utility functions, but that there is some quality we know well but find it hard to quantify. The problem is worse than that. It is that 'utility' is here a bit of technical jargon, so that without some theoretic explanation (beyond the usual paraphrase, "strength of preference") we don't even have any clear idea of what quality it is that we are supposed to quantify.

What Is Utility?

Or do we? There are some candidates, at one time or another and by some philosophers or other thought to be plausible candidates, for qualities whose quantities should stand in for utilities. Even the tradition of decision theory has seen some (confused, I think) candidates for qualities that "measure" utility. Michael Slote writes, "Even those opposed to consequentialism and utilitarianism as moral theories have tended to think that (extra-moral individualistic) rationality requires an individual to maximize his satisfactions or do what is best for himself...."[5]

If satisfaction is an experience, if it is, say, enjoyment of something you like or want, or if we have or are given some independent conception of what is best for a person, then at least the more severe problem would be solved. We would still need some explanation of how to quantify enjoyment or the good for a person, but at least we would have some definite account of what quantities we are supposed to be plugging into the expected utility formula. Crude Decision Theory might be filled in by a story about this quantity, and eventually by a further story about how to determine the utility for any given prospect (and person). In that case, Crude Decision Theory would be a competitor to a serious satisficing theory of rational choice: The one would tell us to maximize the expectation of the quantity; the other would say that we should (at least sometimes) be choosing so as to get *enough* of that quantity, and that we have satisfied the strictures of rationality when we have reached that threshold, even if we could have gotten more.

Slote gives an example in which it is fairly plausible that satisficing (understood as a competitor to maximizing expectation in the Crude version) is rational: the example of the Snacker.

Imagine that it is mid-afternoon; you had a good lunch, and you are not now hungry; neither, on the other hand, are you sated. You would enjoy a candy bar or Coca Cola, if you had one, and there is in fact, right next to your desk, a refrigerator packed with such snacks and provided gratis by the company for which you work. Realizing all this, do you, then, necessarily take and consume a snack? If you do not, is that necessarily because you are afraid to spoil your dinner, because you are on a diet or because you are too busy? I think not. You may simply not feel the need for any such snack. You turn down a good thing, a sure satisfaction, because you are perfectly satisfied as you are. Most of us are often in situations of this sort, and many of us would often do the same thing. We are not boundless optimizers or maximizers, but are sometimes (more) modest in our desires and needs.[6]

If you are *perfectly* satisfied as you are, then clearly you could not increase your satisfaction by slurping a soda. But it is clear enough what Slote means us to imagine. We are supposed to imagine that we are *content*, even though we know that we would *enjoy* a snack. The felt experience of enjoyment would straightforwardly add to whatever satisfaction we feel now, but upon reflection (or maybe without thinking about it) we would rather not snack.

I think many people will react to the example by admitting that the sort of thing Slote describes is quite familiar but doubting that it sheds much light on the theory of rationality. Or if it does point to some fact about rationality, it points to the inadequacy of the notion of utility that is being put to use. Bentham might think it obvious that rational agents are driven by the prospect of pleasurable experience, but not many philosophers today find such a crass hedonism attractive. Rationality doesn't require us to *maximize* enjoyment – not because rationality imposes no maximization constraints but because rationality doesn't tell us to pursue enjoyment at all. Nor, for that matter, does it require us to pursue our own good. Most of us accept that much of Hume's remarks about what 'tis not contrary to reason.

This difficulty infects many of the initially plausible examples of satisficing, I believe. Some independently conceived quantity is suggested or stipulated, and then we are invited to react to the example by agreeing that the agent is not rationally required to *maximize* that quantity but could rationally satisfice it instead. But the examples are spoiled by the fact that the quantity in question is just not a plausible candidate for the decision theorist's utility. Certainly, a person could rationally fail to maximize it; for that matter, one could quite rationally ignore it altogether, though it might be unusual or even bizarre not to care about it at all. Shortly I will present what I'll call True Decision Theory. According to True Decision Theory, *there is no independent conception of utility.* A person's utility function is a construct, developed by the decision theorist as a convenience. If that is correct, then Crude Decision Theory is hopeless. The quantity (the expectation of which) it tells us to maximize has no independent existence; it is meaningless in advance of the theoretic construction of decision theory's central theorem. And, as I will explain, if utility is an artifact of that theorem, then the advice of Crude Decision Theory is empty.

True Decision Theory

Standard decision theory starts by assuming that a person's preferences are characterized by an ordering that ranks things from more to less preferred. The "things" in question are variously events, propositions, or states of affairs, depending on the formalization; I will take them to be propositions.[7] There need be no most preferred proposition, no *summum bonum*, nor any least preferred, though there may be. Suppose your preferences do work this way. For any pair of propositions, there is a definite matter of fact about which you prefer (to be the case); one way it could be definite is that you are indifferent between a certain pair of propositions. Then decision theory says that if your preference relation satisfies a certain set of axioms, there will be an expectational utility function that represents your preferences.

There are three technicalities to fill in. First, what axioms? Second, what is meant by "expectational"? Third, what is it for a utility function to "represent" someone's preferences? I will explain these in reverse order. A utility function, which is just a function from propositions to real numbers, represents a preference ordering just in case it assigns larger numbers to the more preferred propositions. Formally, a function u represents a preference relation R iff:

$$(p)(q)[pRq\ (u(p) > u(q)]$$

When you are indifferent between a pair of alternatives, your preference is represented by a utility function that assigns the same number to those alternatives.

A utility function is expectational just in case it assigns to each prospect a utility equal to that prospect's expected utility. Previously I gave the formula for the expected utility of a strategy. Here is that formula:

$$eu(S) = u(A_1\ \&\ S)\ pr(A_1\ |\ S) + u(A_2\ \&\ S)\ pr(A_2\ |\ S) + \ldots + u(A_n\ \&\ S)\ pr(A_n|S)$$

So long as the A_i partition logical space, this formula gives the expected utility of S no matter what sort of proposition S is. It need not be a strategy. For instance, S could be the prospect that the Red Sox win the American League East division race, A_1 could be the proposition that if the Sox win the AL East they go on to lose in the first round of the playoffs, A_2 the proposition that if the Sox win the AL East they lose in the ALCS, A_3 the proposition that if the Sox win the AL East they lose in the World Series, and A_4 the proposition that if the Sox win the AL East they win the World Series.[8] Suppose that a certain Red Sox fan, Cole, takes the probability of A_1 to be .5, the probability of A_2 to be .3, and the probabilities of A_3 and A_4 to be .1.[9] So the expected utility of S will be

$$.5u\ (A_1\ \&\ S) + .3\ u(A_2\ \&\ S) + .1\ u(A_3\ \&\ S) + .1\ u(A_4\ \&\ S),$$

that is, the expected utility of the proposition that the Red Sox win the division will be .5u(Red Sox lose in the first round) + .3u(Red Sox lose in the ALCS) + .1u(Red Sox lose in the World Series) + .1u(Red Sox win the World Series). Then for an expectational utility function u to represent

Cole's preferences, the number that u assigns to the proposition that the Red Sox win the division must be the same as that expected utility, the weighted sum of the numbers u assigns to the A_i propositions.

I will not explain the axioms in any detail.[10] The interesting ones involve probabilities and preference, and they are generally thought of as constraints of coherence. For example, a constraint that Leonard Savage called the "sure-thing principle" says (roughly speaking) that if one strategy yields outcomes preferred to the outcomes yielded by a second strategy no matter how the world turns out, then one must prefer the first strategy to the second. The crucial fact is that if a person's preferences do conform to the axioms, then there is an expectational utility function that represents those preferences. The Representation Theorem shows how to construct such a function, given a collection of preferences that satisfy the axioms, and it also shows that all expectational functions that represent the given collection will be simple transformations of one another.[11] What if a person's preferences do not satisfy the axioms? Then no expectational utility function represents that person's preferences.

Now I can explain True Decision Theory. Take our Red Sox fan, Cole. Cole can tell us which outcomes of the baseball season he prefers to which others. If we had the time, patience, and inclination, and if Cole would stand for it, we could find out his complete preference ordering for outcomes and also get him to give us probability estimates for each.[12] If these preferences conform to the axioms, then we can make up an expectational utility function for Cole. In principle, we could then go on to extend the utility function so that it covers not just baseball but all propositions, again assuming that his preferences in general conform to the decision theoretic axioms. Pretend that we have done this. Now it will turn out that in each and every decision Cole faces, he always prefers the option with the higher expected utility. True Decision Theory does not advise Cole to choose the option with the higher expected utility. Rather, it constructs a utility function for him that will always assign a higher utility to the option he prefers. And because the function is expectational, the utility it assigns to each option will also be the expected utility of that option.

According to True Decision Theory, there is simply no question of a person's making some kind of mistake in calculation and choosing the option with the lower expected utility, much less any possibility of a person's deliberately adopting some other strategy than expected utility maximization. True Decision Theory allows for no such possibility. Either your preferences satisfy the decision theoretic axioms, or they do not. If they do, then expected utility maximization takes care of itself. Whenever it might *look* to some Crude theorist as if a person chose some option with a lower expected utility than an alternative, that would just show that the Crude theorist had not properly identified the utility function that emerges from the construction given in the Representation Theorem. If, on the other hand, someone's preferences do *not* conform to the axioms, then the construction doesn't work and we have no utility function for that person to maximize.

David Schmidtz's friends were not True Decision Theorists. They were Crude Decision Theorists. As an alternative to Crude Decision Theory, satisficing looks considerably more plausible, at least in many circumstances. But if that's all that satisficing has going for it, then it doesn't have much, because Crude Decision Theory is organized around a mistake. Satisficing, I suspect, inherits that mistake. The mistake, as I have said, is to think that there is some independently identifiable quantity called "utility" that a person could identify and seek to maximize. I will now argue that this is indeed a mistake.

True Decision Theory Corrects a Mistake

Suppose we ask Cole which he likes more: the prospect of the Red Sox going into game seven of the World Series with Pedro Martinez on the mound, or the prospect of the Red Sox being ahead three games to two but with Martinez unavailable for the remainder of the Series. With some reflection, Cole could presumably say which he likes more. We are just asking him which prospect he prefers. (He might say, "It depends"; but we mean, given what you know and expect now, which do you prefer all considered?) Maybe he says he prefers the first prospect: game seven with Pedro pitching. Now we ask: How *much* more do you like that prospect than the other? Cole will be at a loss. He has no idea how to answer that question. Part of his problem is that he has no unit of measurement. Maybe we could provide one. "Let the difference between your preference for watching a ball game, on the one hand, and your watching a ball game while eating a hot dog, on the other, be *one utile*. Now what is the difference in utiles between the two World Series prospects?" The scale we have offered might be *some* help, but to think that it determines the answer to all further questions about utility is an illusion. What sort of difference would amount to thirty utiles? The difference between watching a game without a hot dog and watching one while munching thirty hot dogs? Of course not. Eating one hot dog that tastes thirty times as good? What if we just say, "Take that one utile, which you understand, and multiply it by thirty"? But that's no help. Cole knows how to multiply numbers, but not how to multiply utiles.

Decision theorists can help. Let A be the complex proposition that the Red Sox will begin game six of the Series ahead three games to two, but with Martinez unavailable for future starts. Let B be the proposition that the Red Sox will begin game seven of the Series with Martinez on the mound. Call the following "The Lottery": There is a one in thirty chance that B, and otherwise (with a chance of 29/30) A. And call the following "The Tasty Game": A is true, and furthermore Cole has a hot dog to eat while he watches the game.

Now we can ask Cole to compare The Tasty Game with The Lottery. Which does he prefer? The comparison is hard to make because the alternatives are rather complicated, but Cole could just think of it this way: If A were the case and I had a hot dog to watch the game with, would I give up the hot dog for a mere 1/30th of a chance to change the situation from A to B?

If Cole is indifferent between The Lottery and The Tasty Game, then, according to classic decision theory, the difference in his utility between A and B is exactly thirty times his utility for a hot dog. If he prefers The Lottery, then that utility difference is *more* than thirty times his utility for a hot dog, and if he prefers The Tasty Game, then the difference is *less* than thirty times his utility for a hot dog. This is how a utility scale is *defined* for Cole in True Decision Theory. Utility numbers are assigned to propositions according to the agent's preferences over lotteries, and commensurating options by balancing them with lotteries is the way that the utility function is guaranteed to be expectational. If utilities are assigned in this way, then Crude Decision Theory is false. There is no independent quantity that rational agents seek to maximize. Rather, utility simply is, by virtue of the theoretic construction, that quantity whose expectation is maximized in all of the agent's choices.

The argument is not, I know, watertight. I haven't ruled out the possibility that there is some way to specify an independent and quantifiable quality, to be called "utility," and then to make it plausible that we are each rationally required to maximize its realization in our choices. More to the point, it is conceivable that a proponent of satisficing could spell out some such conception of utility and then try to make it plausible that we are at least sometimes rationally required to choose an alternative with *enough* utility, but rationally permitted to choose one with less utility than some other available one. Although there might be such a conception of utility, it is not the conception used in decision theory. Proponents of satisficing will have to explain what it is.

Consider Slote's Snacker again. The Snacker could have a snack – he knows that one is available, but he chooses to abstain. According to True Decision Theory, the Snacker's utility for the proposition that he snack is higher than his utility for the proposition that he abstains just in case he *prefers* to snack. If he prefers to abstain, then his utility for abstaining is higher. Unless Slote means us to understand his Snacker to *prefer* to snack, even though he *chooses* to abstain when the snack is readily available, his Snacker is indeed choosing the option with the higher utility. He is not merely satisficing, but maximizing. Could the Snacker be choosing the option that he does not prefer, all things considered? It is hard to see how that is possible. If it is possible, then it is hard to see how it could be rational. True Decision Theory provides a theoretic reason to think that *all* purported examples of satisficing are really examples of maximizing expected utility. The theoretic construction of one's utility function will guarantee that the alternative preferred is the one with the higher expected utility, so long as one's preferences conform to decision theory's axioms. And if they don't, then the construction breaks down, and there is no saying what one's utility is for any option.

First Conclusion: Against Rational Satisficing

I conclude that there is a general theoretic reason to doubt that there is any such thing as rational satisficing. There is no independent conception of the goodness at which all rational action aims. An independent conception would be one specifiable in advance of a construction, like the standard construction of a utility function in decision theory, whose point is to build a quantitative property at which all (of a particular agent's) rational action can be seen to aim, out of choices or preferences. If there is no independent conception, then all rational action is action that maximizes utility and does not merely satisfice.

Here is how I could be wrong: First, I could be wrong about independent conceptions of goodness. Maybe my canvassing of the alternatives missed a plausible account of something at which all rational action aims, something that also turns out to be sensible to satisfice rather than maximize. I can't rule that out, but I think we should be skeptical unless and until proponents of satisficing provide some such account. Second, the final sentence of the previous paragraph could be false. It may be that even though the only conception of goodness we have is a conception of that at which all rational action aims, and that we have to construct a substantial conception by drawing on whatever ideas we have about which choices are better than which others, it might still turn out that satisficing is sometimes rational. The goodness-defining construction might be unlike the construction used in decision theory. It might cook up a measure in some ways like utility but without utility's defining characteristic, that it represents (in the technical jargon explained above) the agent's preferences. I can't see how an alternative like this would work, but I can't rule it out.

Ethical Satisficing

Ethical satisficing is structurally similar to rational satisficing. Ethical satisficing theory says that it can be morally right to choose an alternative that is good enough (in general, because its consequences are good enough) even though there is a better alternative available. In this section I will argue, first, that there is some reason to think that the objection I leveled against rational satisficing can be carried over to work against ethical satisficing. The way has been paved by Philippa Foot. Second, though, I will suggest that in fact ethical satisficing is importantly different from rational satisficing, because the ethical conception of the good is different from the rational conception of the good in such a way as to make it more plausible that ethical goodness can be understood independently of the aims of ethical action.

Foot's Argument

"A consequentialist theory of ethics," writes Philippa Foot, "is one which identifies certain states of affairs as *good* states of affairs and says that the rightness or goodness of actions (or of other subjects of moral judgment) consists in their positive productive relationship to these states of affairs."[13] By this account, a satisficing utilitarianism would count as consequentialist,[14] but Foot is actually concerned with the usual maximizing types of utilitarianism and other versions of (agent-neutral) consequentialisms. Her paper "Utilitarianism and the Virtues" aims to undermine a powerful rhetorical advantage that consequentialist theories enjoy. It is this advantage that explains the sticking power of utilitarianism (and its kin) in the face of stunningly counterintuitive and to most of us absolutely unacceptable implications. "What is it," Foot asks, "that is so compelling about consequentialism? It is, I think, the rather simple thought that it can never be right to prefer a worse state of affairs to a better."[15] This may seem obvious. In any case, I am sure it is quite right.

In resisting consequentialism, we feel that we must shoulder the burden of explaining why it might sometimes be rational to do what will have a worse outcome. And the sense of paradox in what we feel we must insist upon is nearly impossible to dispel. Consequentialists deploy what is by now a well-known strategy in theoretic ethical disputes: Whenever the opponent manages to make it plausible that something of value is lost when an agent maximizes good consequences, the consequentialist just slurps up that value and tosses it into his basket of goods-to-be-maximized. Common-sense moralists then want to say that the consequentialist has entirely missed the point. But consequentialists rightly insist that the opponent say clearly just what the point is, and it is, to say the least, extremely hard to see how to say it in a way that resists the slurping-up strategy.

Foot's strategy is ingenious, and I think correct. She argues that "we go wrong in accepting the idea that there *are* better and worse states of affairs in the sense that consequentialism requires."[16] Of course, we do talk in ordinary conversation about things – not one particular kind of thing or another, but just "things" – being better or worse, say, than they used to be. "The doubt is not about whether there is some way of using the words, but rather about the way they appear in the exposition of utilitarian and other consequentialist moral theories."[17] A state of affairs can be good for me, good for you, or good for General Motors, but not just good *simpliciter*. But isn't it just a good thing, for instance, that the starving people of the world be fed? Certainly, that makes sense. Foot goes on:

[W]hat can truly be said about the important place that the idea of maximum welfare has in morality... is not that in the guise of 'the best outcome' it stands *outside* morality as its foundation and arbiter, but rather that it appears *within* morality as the end of one of the virtues.[18]

That the importance of maximum welfare is appreciated correctly from within virtue theory is, obviously, controversial. The broader point is much more generally compelling. The idea of a good state of affairs (or "best outcome") gets its content by being embedded in a moral theory. It has no independent content, so consequentialists cannot build support for their view by leaving it unspecified and claiming that whatever the goodness of states of affairs turns out to be, proper moral conduct must be a matter of maximizing it.[19]

The point is not that consequentialism is incoherent because it assumes that there is such a thing as a good state of affairs. Foot's aim is not to argue against consequentialism but only to undercut a certain argument *for* it, what I called a rhetorical advantage it enjoys. If some version of consequentialism is true, then there *is* such a thing as the goodness of states of affairs. States of affairs will turn out to have moral goodness by degrees. That goodness will be precisely what we all morally ought to seek to maximize, our common end when we adopt the moral point of view. Utilitarianism is, after all, a coherent moral theory (or anyway it is for all Foot says). But to suppose, in an argument between consequentialists and their opponents, that there is such a thing as the moral goodness of a state of affairs is to beg the question in favor of the consequentialists. In other kinds of theories, there will be no such thing. The clearest way to see this is not by looking at an alternative moral theory but to consider other normative schemes within which there is nothing that counts as *that at which everyone adopting the normative perspective aims.* Law is a good example: To be a law-abiding citizen is not to aim in common with all other law-abiding citizens at some state of affairs. Etiquette is another. From the perspective of manners, an important aim is to avoid embarrassing others in social situations. Could this be *the good,* from the point of view of etiquette, which a good-mannered person will seek to maximize? No,

because good manners, not being solely a matter of purposes, also require that certain things be done or not done: e.g. that hospitality not be abused by frank discussion of the deficiencies of one's host as soon as he leaves the room. [Foot notes: It is customary to wait until later.] So if invited to take part in such discussions a well-mannered person will, if necessary, maintain a silence embarrassing to an interlocutor, because the rule here takes precedence over the aim prescribed.[20]

Just to complete the point: It might turn out that the embarrassment to the interlocutor exceeds what would be caused by frank discussion of the host; even so, the well-mannered person will be silent. What the example shows is plainly not that etiquette is irrational or paradoxical. Rather, it shows that there is no such thing as a "good state of affairs from the point of view of etiquette."

Now to my own point. Clearly, Foot's objection that there is no *independent* notion of a good state of affairs, but only the possibility of moral goodness for states of affairs getting content from a moral theory, is closely related to my claim in the first part of this paper, that the goodness that all rational action by definition seeks is not independently identifiable but rather constructed in a theoretical way from the agent's preferences. I might complete the analogy by arguing that the only ethical theories from within which the idea of a good state of affairs makes sense are maximizing theories. Then my conclusion would be that ethical satisficing does not make sense. However, I will not complete the analogy with such an argument, and I will not draw such a conclusion. It seems to me that rational satisficing and ethical satisficing are not quite analogous.

How Ethical Satisficing Might Be Different

An element of commonsense moral thinking is at once closely parallel to (maybe even identical with) satisficing and also so powerfully intuitive that it is hard to believe it could turn out to be senseless. That element is supererogation. In commonsense moral reasoning, we take it for granted that there are supererogatory acts, and it would be incredible if the very idea of supererogation turned out to be incoherent. In the next section, I will explain why I think supererogation is akin to ethical satisficing. I will also present a puzzle: How is supererogation possible? Then, in the section after, I will try to answer the puzzle. Finally, I will return to satisficing. Does the solution to the supererogation puzzle carry over to rational satisficing? If so, then my argument in the first part of the paper was wrong. But in the last section I will argue that the solution does not carry over.

It is at least arguable that we do have a commonsense notion of a morally good state of affairs that is independent of our idea of whatever it is that ethical action can be seen to aim at. John Rawls famously says:

It is essential to keep in mind that in a teleological theory the good is defined independently from the right. This means two things. First, the theory accounts for our considered judgments as to which things are good (our judgments of value) as a separate class of judgments intuitively distinguishable by common sense, and then proposes as a hypothesis that the right is maximizing the good as already specified. Second, the theory enables one to judge the goodness of things without referring to what is right.[21]

Of course, Rawls assumes here that there *is* such a thing as our intuitive sense of what is good independent of what we think is right. He gives this interesting example:

[I]f the distribution of goods is also counted as a good, perhaps a higher order one, and the theory directs us to produce the most good (including the good of distribution among others), we no longer have a teleological view in the classic sense. The problem of distribution falls under the concept of right as one intuitively understands it, and so the theory lacks an independent definition of the good.[22]

Our intuitive understanding, as Rawls reports it, counts the 'good' of distribution as a part of the *right*, and not as an element of the *good*, even insofar as we judge that people ought to aim at, for instance, equality in distribution. If Rawls is right, then the intuitive notion of the good is not merely induced by our judgments of what right action should be striving for. The commonsense conception of the good must then have more flesh than Foot allows.

It is not clear to me that Rawls is right about the example.[23] Following Foot's line, we might say that as long as a theory prescribes that one always seek to promote equality in distribution, that theory counts equality as a good (equality contributes goodness to states of affairs). It is at least not obvious that this is a counterintuitive thing to say. (Equality, after all, is a good thing.)

I think it's more promising to look to virtue theory itself for some help. First notice that there are perfectly good examples from virtue theory of kinds of systematic normative judgments that do not lend themselves to capture in a theory of good states of affairs – the examples from law and etiquette are fine ones, but we can also find examples at home in ethics. Think of courage: To be courageous is not to seek to bring about some special kind of state of affairs.[24] I don't display any courage by causing you to act bravely, even though I bring about the same state of affairs that you bring about by acting bravely.

The example of courage isn't helpful to advocates of satisficing. What would a virtue have to be like to support the satisficers' case?[25] To start with, it seems to me that we need to find some quantifiable (measurable) property, P; a degree of realization of P, say r; and a plausible virtue, V, such that choice in accordance with V amounts to realizing P to degree r. The idea is that realizing less than r in your choices will mean falling short of V, whereas striving for more than r will not mean having V to a greater degree. Now if we can also think of P as being good (or being a good-making property), then, I say, we will have a plausible example of ethical satisficing.

Let's fill in the schema with a couple of examples from the crafts. First suppose that you are making soup. P will be the property of saltiness, which you realize in the soup by adding salt. If you leave out the salt entirely, you are a bad cook, and you lack a certain nameless virtue V. If you add a little salt, but less than r, then you are doing better but you still fall short of full V. Adding exactly r means that you have V fully. Good soup! But adding more than r doesn't make you more V (it's a virtue, after all). In fact, if you toss in five or six cups of salt then you are an awful cook. Is V therefore a satisficing virtue? No. Adding salt to make the soup salty to degree r makes it better, but adding more makes it worse. So it is implausible to think of saltiness as a good in soup. (We would probably say that good soup is just salty enough, rather than saying that good soup is salty, or that the saltier soup is, the better.) The problem is that there is too much symmetry. Less than r is worse, but so is more than r. That's why P (saltiness) isn't easily thought of as a good (even a culinary good). So we'd better have another example.

Suppose you are a mason, and your job is to build a wall around a sheep enclosure to keep out the coyotes. Here P will be the height of the wall, r will be whatever height does keep coyotes out, and V is again a virtue with no natural name. In this example, the symmetry of the soup is broken. If you build a wall of height r, then you have carried out your job in accordance with V; less and you are not such a good mason. Building a wall much higher than r – say, a thirty-foot wall – displays no extra virtue at all, but it doesn't make the wall worse (at least not in respect of keeping out coyotes). Here it does (to me, anyway) seem right to say that height is good in a wall. So this V is a better candidate for a satisficing virtue.

But not quite good enough, I think. The problem is that a taller wall is not better, not once r has been reached. Indeed, it is sensible to say that a wall of height r is as good as can be (in respect of height, anyway), so that *maximizing* goodness also requires that a mason build a wall of that height and does *not* tell him to build it higher. Satisficers win a hollow victory if their view is plausible only in those cases in which it agrees with a maximizing conception! What more is needed? We'd better return to ethics proper.

The Paradox of Supererogation
On the face of it, supererogation is easy to understand. We have moral duties, which provide us with decisive moral reasons to do or refrain from doing various things. Sometimes there are special extra things we could do, "above and beyond the call of duty," that would be especially good, often because they would produce especially good results, but we are not obligated to do them. For example, suppose you are riding a bus and as the doors are about to close, the hat of the lady sitting next to you blows out the window. You leap up and bound out to the street just as the doors close, sprint down the block to grab the hat, turn and race after the bus, catching it after four blocks as it stops at a traffic light, and hand the hat through the open window to its owner. Good for you! The man sitting next to you could just as easily have done the same, but

he didn't, and he did nothing wrong. You are commendable, you did something commendable, better than what he did, but even so he did nothing wrong. What you did was supererogatory. The idea seems easy enough to understand.

But seen another way, it is puzzling. Morality, we are inclined to think, is a matter of what reasons one has *from the moral point of view*. When there is a supererogatory act available, it would be better for you to perform it. So surely you have a reason, from the moral point of view, to perform the act. You may have some reason not to perform it, but at least typically you will have no reason *from the moral point of view* to refrain from it (if you do have some such reason, then it will ordinarily be outweighed by the reason you have to perform, because by hypothesis it is better to perform). But now it is hard to see how it could be permissible, from the moral point of view, to refrain from doing something that you have an undefeated reason (from that very point of view) to do. Everything from the moral point of view speaks in favor of your going to fetch the hat, and nothing at all speaks against it. It what sense is it "all right," "permissible," "not wrong" to fail to act?[26] There seems to be no sense at all. Supererogation, according to this way of seeing things, turns out to be impossible.

The impossibility of supererogation looks to me to be the same as the impossibility of rational satisficing. If I am right that something's being better from a certain point of view is the same thing as one's having a reason to do it (or bring it about, etc.) from that same point of view, then the coherence of supererogation is the same as the coherence of satisficing. Satisficing appears to ignore reasons that one admits one has. And so does merely doing one's duty when a supererogatory act was available. Yet satisficing theory says that it can be reasonable to satisfice, and commonsense morality says that it can be morally acceptable to fail to perform what is supererogatory.

Alastair Norcross and Frances Howard-Snyder argue that consequentialists cannot believe in supererogation, and they conclude that consequentialists ought to reject the whole idea of moral wrongness, instead evaluating everything on a scale from better to worse.[27] If that's true, my inclination is to take this to be a reason to doubt consequentialism. Supererogation seems obviously to make sense, as does the idea of something's being morally wrong. When theoretic considerations imply that such things don't even make sense, my inclination is to doubt the implicating theory. By contrast, rational satisficing does not seem to me to make much sense, but the argument against it looks to be no better than the argument against supererogation. If, like me, you think that the conclusion that there is no such thing as supererogation is a sort of *reductio* of whatever theoretic premises were used to derive it, then maybe you ought to doubt my theoretic argument against the possibility of rational satisficing. To conclude, let me try to distinguish the cases.

Why Ethical Satisficing Makes Sense and Rational Satisficing Doesn't

Maybe the solution to the Paradox of Supererogation is something like this: It is tempting to think that when I consider a supererogatory act I find that other, nonmoral reasons compete with my moral reason. From the moral point of view, I simply ought to perform the supererogatory act, but prudential or maybe other kinds of reasons weigh in against it. Then from some all-things-considered point of view, my *duties* seem to count heavily by comparison with my other reasons, but my reasons of supererogation are not so heavy. The explanation for why it seems permissible for me to skip what is above and beyond the call of duty is that, although I do have some reason to rise to a saintly level, I have better (albeit nonmoral) reasons to do something else.

This explanation isn't right as it stands. If it were, then our verdict for people who fail to go beyond the call of duty would be that they act wrongly, though it is understandable and rational that they do. Failing to perform would not be morally permissible, because one would have moral reasons for performance and no moral reasons for nonperformance. Choosing not to do the supererogatory act would be like shoplifting a sweater that you really, really want and can't afford. But they are not alike: Stealing the sweater is morally wrong, and failing to fetch the hat isn't.

Still, I want to suggest something like that explanation. Maybe there isn't just one "moral point of view." Maybe there are (at least) two. To borrow from virtue theory, one point of view we can adopt is the point of view of the perfectly virtuous agent (one of Susan Wolf's moral saints, perhaps); or, less ambitiously, just the beneficent agent. From this perspective, there is everything to be said in favor of fetching the stranger's hat and nothing to be said against it. Failing to fetch the hat is falling short of perfection (in this dimension) and not permissible at all. But we can also adopt a less ambitious perspective – that of the just person (maybe 'dutiful' would be a better word). From the point of view of justice, there isn't anything to be said in favor of going to all that trouble to get a stranger's hat. If I do go to all the trouble, that doesn't make me more just. The suggestion is that judgments of wrongness are made from the point of view of this less demanding virtue, whereas judgments of what would be better or worse are made from the more ambitious point of view.

It may be asked what I have reason to do from the moral point of view, *all-things-considered.* How am I to adjudicate between these points of view? Shall I do what beneficence requires, or only what justice requires? But I don't see why there should be any answer to this question. What makes us think that there is any *all-things-considered moral* point of view? There must be some point of view from which I can consider all my reasons together, granted. Otherwise I could not decide what to do; because I can do only one thing, I have to choose. But this perspective needn't be moral at all. As far as I can see, it is quite coherent (and plausible) to think that there are two moral points of view I can adopt, one from which I have reason to fetch the hat and the other from which I don't, and these two points of view ground the judgments that it would be better to fetch it but not wrong to keep my seat. Naturally, I have to decide what to do, so I have to balance all the considerations at some point, but at that point I am no longer adopting a distinctively moral perspective.

We might add that (normally at least) the reasons I find from the point of view of justice or duty are especially stringent and strong. So reluctantly I put the sweater back on the shelf, even though I really, really want it. Reasons of supererogation are not so strong. They don't seem so compelling – though they do count – when other, perhaps prudential, reasons compete. This much *seems* right, but it is speculative. A more solid account awaits some explanation for why justice should be weightier than beneficence.

In any case, my suggestion for how supererogation is possible is that there are two perspectives from which the two different sorts of ethical standards are derived. What looked like a contradiction is merely a conflict: From the one perspective certain facts are reasons, and from the other they are not. Although it is true that at some point the two perspectives must be commensurated, the conflict is *not* reintroduced as a contradiction because the point of view from which we make our all-things-considered judgment needn't be an ethical perspective.

Could something similar be true of rational satisficing? The story would have to go like this: We can adopt an especially exacting perspective on what we are to do, and from that perspective we recognize which choices and outcomes are better and worse. A different, less ambitious perspective allows a kind of laziness: Differences among acts all of which are over a certain threshold have no significance from this perspective. From the permissive perspective, there is nothing wrong with my choice as long as it is good *enough* (i.e., above the threshold).

This story doesn't sound too bad when described in the sketchy way I have just described it. However, I don't see how it could be a plausible story about rationality. Rationality is not a matter of appreciating reasons from some particular perspective. It is a matter of appreciating whatever reasons one actually has. So if I do not, in fact, have any reason at all to choose the very very very good option instead of the merely very very good option, then it is hard to see how the options deserve those labels. Furthermore, if option A really is *better* than option B, then it just *does* provide me with some reason to choose it, a reason that outweighs whatever reasons I have to choose B. If I do choose B, then I have ignored that reason. How could that be rational?

To prevent my explanation from being needlessly woolly, let me return to a couple of examples. Suppose that when I see the stranger's hat blow out the bus window, I hesitate and deliberate. Adopting the most exacting ethical perspective, I see that it would be a better thing to jump out of the door and retrieve the hat. Adopting the less stringent ethical perspective, I see that I have no duty to retrieve it. From the first perspective my reasons favor a hasty exit, but from the second perspective they do not. What to do? All things considered, now, I notice that I will be late for the hockey game if I go fetch the hat. I really want to see the faceoff. Yes, it would be better, in the sense of more beneficent, if I get the hat. But it is not wrong to continue to the game. All things considered, my own personal interests outweigh the ethical ones in this case. This story makes perfect sense.[28]

Now suppose I am considering an offer of $200,000 for my house. I know that if I turn it down, it is likely that tomorrow I will get substantially higher offers. It is therefore better – a better choice – to wait, because the outcome of the choice is likely to be substantially better. Adopting a less ambitious perspective on the situation, I decide that the $200,000 offer is good enough. From this perspective, although it would not be sensible to sell my house for $1,000, I have no reason to wait an extra day to get substantially more than $200,000. What to do? When I consider all things, let's suppose, I notice that it would be nice to get the whole ordeal over with right away. Yes, it would be better to get more money, but it is not *irrational* to settle for less and move on with my life. Does this thought make sense? I can't see how. If the value (to me) of finishing the sale is really greater than the (expected) value of waiting, then it is not irrational to sell now, for the lower price, because the balance of my reasons favors selling now. But in that case, it is not better to wait!

The outcome of waiting will be worse, from my own perspective. On the other hand, if waiting another day really is better, then the balance of my reasons favors waiting, in which case it could not be rational to sell now. In neither case does it make sense to think that waiting will be better but that selling now is rational.

Let me sum up. Ethical satisficing is (in one form) deciding not to perform a supererogatory act. It can make sense, I have argued, because the reasons that make the supererogatory act better might be outweighed, all things considered, by some nonmoral reasons I have, reasons that do not make failing to act ethically better. Rational satisficing cannot make sense. There is no such thing as a reason that weighs in my deliberations all things considered but that doesn't make its choice rationally better. The perspective of rationality just is the perspective of all things considered.

Notes

1. Rational satisficing is usefully distinguished from ethical satisficing in Hurka, "Two Kinds of Satisficing," *Philosophical Studies* 59 (1990): 107–11.
2. Michael Slote sometimes seems to think that it would be reasonable to accept the lowest of the three offers. For now, my point is that it does not seem immediately and intuitively reasonable.
3. David Schmidtz, *Rational Choice and Moral Agency*, Princeton University Press, 1995, 28.
4. It is not so compelling, I think, to object that we ordinarily do not know probabilities. The tradition of decision theory is, by and large, a tradition of subjectivist probability; the probabilities that get plugged into the formula are really your degrees of belief that the various outcomes will occur. Although these may be *fuzzy*, they cannot be unknown. Nor is it as compelling to object that in ordinary decisions we have no idea what the outcomes might be. If we really have *no* idea, I say, then I suppose any (undominated) decision is as good as any other!
5. Michael Slote, *Beyond Optimizing*, Cambridge: Harvard University Press, 1989, 141.
6. Slote, *Beyond Optimizing*, 143–4.
7. I suspect that a more adequate theory would have to take *properties* as the fundamental objects of preference, in order to capture the essentially *de se* nature of many ordinary preferences, but that improvement will not concern me in this paper. See James Dreier, "Accepting Agent Centred Norms: A Problem for Non-Cognitivists and a Suggestion for Solving It," *Australasian Journal of Philosophy* 74 (1996): 409–22, esp. 415–19.
8. Remember, the propositions need only be logically possible!
9. These probabilities sum to one, as the probabilities of the elements of a logical partition must. Note that each of the A_i is a *material conditional*, the

probability of which must not be confused with the similar-sounding conditional probability.

10. A clear exposition of the axioms, as well as a proof of the theorem, can be found in Chapter 4 of Michael D. Resnik, *Choices*, Minneapolis: University of Minnesota Press, 1987.

11. They will be affine transformations of each other – that is, if two utility functions u and v are both expectational and both represent, say, Cole's preferences, then we can find constants a and b such that for every proposition p, $u(p) = a(v(p)) + b$. The Kelvin, Fahrenheit, and Celsius temperature scales are affine transformations of one another. Any pair of expectational utility functions that represent the same set of preferences will be related to one another as temperature scales are related to one another: The size of the degree can differ, and the zero point may be set arbitrarily, but aside from those differences the structure of the scales will be constant.

12. Maybe we *couldn't* find out, for some principled reason. What matters here is that there *is* such an ordering. Maybe Cole cannot give us probability estimates, because he doesn't have the relevant concepts of probability; in that case we can supply estimates for him by asking him, for example, whether he'd rather have a coupon redeemable for Red Sox tickets just in case the Mets win more than 75 games, or one redeemable for the same Sox tickets just in case the Mets win 75 games or fewer. If he'd rather have the first coupon, then he takes the probability that the Mets win more than 75 games to be greater than one-half.

13. Foot, "Utilitarianism and the Virtues," in Samuel Scheffler, ed., *Consequentialism and Its Critics*, Oxford University Press, 1988, 225.

14. John Broome remarks to this effect in *Weighing Goods*, New York: Blackwell, 1991, 7.

15. Foot, "Utilitarianism and the Virtues," 227.

16. Foot, "Utilitarianism and the Virtues," 227.

17. Foot, "Utilitarianism and the Virtues," 228.

18. Foot, "Utilitarianism and the Virtues," 239.

19. The idea of maximizing welfare may have content independent of any moral theory. The point is, as Foot says, that in consequentialism "something is supposed to be being said about maximum welfare and we cannot figure out what it is." Foot, " Utilitarianism and the Virtues," 232.

20. Foot, "Utilitarianism and the Virtues," 239.

21. John Rawls, *A Theory of Justice*, Cambridge: Harvard University Press, 1970, 25.

22. Rawls, *A Theory of Justice*, 25.

23. John Broome is skeptical; see *Weighing Goods*, 14–15.

24. If the sort of state of affairs that a virtuous person is supposed to bring about can be specified by reference to the person, then there is some hope of characterizing courage in the consequentialist way. But in the text, by 'state of affairs' I always mean what ethicists usually call an *agent-neutral* state of affairs.

25. Swanton, "Satisficing and Virtue," *The Journal of Philosophy* 90 (1993): 33–48, answers this question in some detail. My answer is somewhat more schematic.

26. The reasoning in this paragraph follows some reasoning of Shelly Kagan, *The Limits of Morality*, Oxford University Press, 1989, 371–4, where Kagan is investigating how a defender of agent-centered options can avoid moral decisiveness. His point is that it is hard to see how an option can avoid turning out to be a requirement.

27. Alastair Norcross and Frances Howard-Snyder, "A Consequentialist Case for Rejecting the Right," *Journal of Philosophical Research* 18 (1993): 109–25.

28. Here I have to add that I am not claiming to have solved the problem that Kagan raised in the pages of *The Limits of Morality* cited above. I am claiming to have solved a related problem, inspired by Kagan's discussion. Kagan's actual problem is harder to solve, because it amounts to providing a thorough justification for options rather than removing the air of incoherence that surrounds them when viewed in a certain light. I think his demand would be satisfied by an explanation, mentioned but not offered in my text, for why and in what sense considerations of duty should be stronger or weightier all things considered than considerations of beneficence. But as I say in the text, I can only speculate about the existence of an explanation like that. I don't have one.

8

The Plausibility of Satisficing
and the Role of Good in Ordinary Thought

Mark van Roojen

When we think about whether it ever makes sense to choose something that is simply good enough even when other better things might instead be chosen, it seems that it can. We can readily be offered examples in which it seems that is just the choice we sensibly make. To use one oft-cited example,[1] it makes sense to accept a reasonably good offer on a house one is selling rather than hold out for a higher price. It may be just as reasonable to hold out for more, but provided the offer is good enough, there is nothing irrational or unreasonable in accepting the first sufficiently good offer.

Thus the examples seem to show that satisficing – that is, to choose the merely good enough over an option which is better yet – is sometimes rational. However, many philosophers have wanted to argue that things are not as they seem. They wish to defend the idea that satisficing is rational only if it serves as part of an overall strategy to maximize. In service of this position, they have available a general strategy for dealing with examples that purport to show otherwise. This strategy is to ask the advocate of satisficing what it is about the lesser option that justifies one's choosing it over the greater. Once a reason is offered, the clever proponent of maximizing can incorporate that consideration into a more sophisticated characterization of goodness, so that options which satisfy the consideration will, other things equal, be better than alternatives. Then, using this more sophisticated way of constructing a notion of goodness, the defender of maximizing can argue that the supposedly merely satisfactory option is in fact better than the alternative.

Thus, in the foregoing example of selling the house, an advocate of maximizing can argue that by taking the first sufficiently generous offer,

the seller really is maximizing the good, although perhaps not maximizing the selling price. The reasons why it makes sense to take the first good
offer include the fact that one cannot be certain of getting a better offer,
that one will have to spend more time waiting for a better offer if it is
to come, that the uncertainty during that time will create some anxiety,
and that such anxiety is not worth the extra money that the seller might
get. Thus, the advocate of maximizing the good might argue, the seller
is maximizing expected good if not money.

In this paper, I want to resist this sort of argument while granting it
its due. I believe that the defenders of maximizing are right to ask for
reasons to choose an option that is admittedly less than the best. And, the
formal trick of constructing an ordering incorporating the very features
that ground the reason offered in defense of maximizing can also be accomplished. So the defense will have to proceed by arguing that not every
reason can be given its *best* characterization when presented in the form of
placing an option in an ordering from better to worse. My underlying idea
is that we really need two distinct value notions, one roughly captured by
the word 'right' as it is ordinarily used, and the other involving a notion
of goodness. Because the strategy that assimilates satisficing choices to
maximizing a more sophisticated conception of goodness tends to push
these two notions together, it has costs that are not worth paying for the
sake of theoretical simplicity.

Thus I will argue for the following nest of theses: Satisficing in conditions when one is not maximizing can be defended as rational, provided
that nonconsequentialism is rational and provided that the preferred
characterization of the resulting nonconsequentialist position is not one
in which the right action is justified in virtue of maximizing agent-relative
value. Rather, the nonconsequentialism that can serve to defend satisficing should be one in which the best characterization of certain reasons
to act does not involve maximization of value of any sort, whether agent-
relative or agent-neutral. I will also argue that there are reasons to prefer
this sort of nonconsequentialism to theories that defend the sorts of actions distinctive of nonconsequentialism by claiming that value should
be thought of as agent-relative value. An upshot of the argument will be
that satisficing cannot be well defended within an overall framework that
is consequentialist.

Some Clarification of the Subject Matter

My topic is not about the *self-regarding* rationality of satisficing or maximizing. I take it that by delimiting the issue by using the term 'self-regarding'

one has restricted the reasons to maximize or satisfice to reasons that have to do with promoting the interests of the agent in question. But once we've done that, I don't see how we can resist the conclusion that satisficing is rational only as a strategy to maximize expected personal good. And if we limit ourselves to self-regarding reasons, then any strategy that conflicts with maximization will be criticizable for not securing as much personal good as possible; and the proponent of mere satisficing will not be able to point to a competing *self-regarding* consideration which outweighs that demerit, for all of the self-regarding considerations will have already been weighed up in ranking the various options from the perspective of self-regarding rationality.

My topic is rationality without such qualifications. I will assume that the overall rationality of a choice is a function of all the considerations that can be brought to bear against and in favor of each of the options. These will often include considerations such as how well the option serves the agent's own interests, but they may also include altruistic considerations, moral considerations that are neither purely altruistic nor self-interested, and, for that matter, aesthetic considerations when they are relevant. This will allow the issue that I consider to be most basic to emerge in its most natural way: Are there considerations for or against choosing certain options that are not best captured by representing those options as maximizing some good or other?

Thus I want to defend the idea that it can indeed be rational to knowingly choose an option that is less good than the alternatives. To label the position, I will be arguing that mere satisficing can be rational, provided that nonconsequentialism can be vindicated. I do not claim that it is always rational nor even that it is rational most of the time. To clarify, what I mean by "mere satisficing" is choosing an option that is merely good enough but not the best, where that choice should not be reconstrued as part of a sophisticated strategy for maximizing overall goodness by satisficing local goodness,[2] nor for maximizing expected goodness by taking an outcome one knows to be good enough when the costs of continuing to search for a better option are high.

But I don't want to defend the claim that it can be rational to do a worse action when one knows that by doing something else one would be doing a better action.[3] When "better" is applied to actions, it no longer seems to me to be about the goodness of the option chosen, but rather about the rightness or rationality of the action. That we should rationally do what is most rational is a tautology that proponents of mere satisficing should not be portrayed as denying. The rationality of mere satisficing is thus not best construed as requiring that one "may be rationally permitted to do less than the rationally ideal or best."[4] If it is most rational to choose some particular option, then it is less rational to chose any other option.[5] Once we have ordered a series of choices by their rationality, there is no substantive issue remaining. We may decide to call any of the set of choices toward the more rational end 'rational' or we may reserve that name for only the most rational choice. But nothing of any substance can turn on this. There may be a substantive issue about whether we should criticize choices that are close enough to the most rational choice. And we could align our use of the term 'rational' with our verdicts about this issue. But in this case the substantive issue is about *us*, and not about the rationality of the agent's choices. The substantive question concerning rational satisficing is whether a choice can be as rational as it gets without optimizing some good or other defined independently of the rationality of the action itself.[6]

I should also probably stress that the issue I am pursuing is about satisficing *goodness* and not about satisficing whatever is represented according to a theory of revealed preference. It would be incoherent for a theory to define utility as whatever was maximized by a person's actual choices or dispositions to choose and then go on to say that one should act so as to do something other than maximize whatever this was. How could one follow such advice? If one did so, one would be making different choices and manifesting different dispositions to choose, and this would change one's preference ordering as conceived by the theory of revealed preference. The theory would then have to use these preferences as the basis for its advice and on that basis advise us to do something still different, and if we follow the revised advice, the theory would run into the same problem all over again.[7] For the position to make sense, the thing that we are satisficing has to be something that is not solely a function of our preferences as revealed by our choices. Because I think that there is something like objective goodness independent of our preferences that allows us to compare options, this is the notion I want to use in asking and answering the question at issue.

Enough about what I'm not defending.

A Strategy for Defending the Rational Mandatoriness of Maximizing

The kinds of situations that interest me here are those in which a person chooses an option that is good enough but that is less good than available alternatives while still believing that those better alternatives are available. Defenders of mere satisficing have proposed various examples, and, as I have already remarked, those who think that mere satisficing is irrational have a general strategy for combating arguments employing those examples. They can ask the defenders of mere satisficing to offer reasons in favor of choosing the lesser but adequate option and then use those reasons to argue that the option chosen is not after all the lesser of those available. If the advocate of mere satisficing refuses to explain why it makes sense to choose the lesser option, then the critics can offer considerations of their own and employ them to show that the option chosen is really best, or they can refuse to agree that the choice makes sense. If their reaction is the latter, who could blame them? If theorists want to argue that a choice makes sense, then they should have something to say to doubters. At least if one is a doubter and the advocates of the view you doubt don't say anything to defend it, one hasn't been given any reason to change one's mind.[8]

In the example we began with, that of selling a house, it seems relatively easy to come up with reasons for taking the first satisfactory offer. If we don't take the first satisfactory offer, one thing we will lose is the time it takes to get a better one. In general, money now is worth somewhat more money later; that's why people can make money in the loan business. By taking the money offered right now, we can immediately put it to good use, perhaps in making more money, or buying something we need or want. We also forgo the trouble and stress of dealing with additional potential buyers, realtors, and so forth in the attempt to gain still more. These reasons, which certainly count in favor of a satisficing monetary strategy, in turn give us reasons to think that we might actually be maximizing the overall good, composed of money and enjoyment and other non-monetary goods. Furthermore, there is always some chance that we will not later get a higher offer or even another offer as good, in which case this offer is the best we are going to get even in monetary terms alone. Even where that is not actually true, antecedent to knowing how things will turn out, accepting the offer may maximize expected monetary benefit.[9]

A somewhat more challenging example is suggested by Michael Slote. It may, he argues, make sense for someone to aim "to be a really fine lawyer like her mother," rather than to choose to be the best lawyer she could be.[10] So far, this does seem to capture the judgment of ordinary common sense. But this may be so only because excellent lawyering can interfere with other worthwhile pursuits, and because taken to an extreme it can interfere with enough of them to make one's life less good as a whole. If so, the example presents no obstacle to the view that suboptimal choices are less than fully rational. The woman in question can be depicted as choosing the best life for her, which is not the life in which she is the best lawyer she could be.

But Slote goes on to deny that this is what is at work in the example. He claims that common sense will endorse the woman's choice even when it is not made "from a belief that too much devotion to the law would damage other, more important parts of one's life."[11] And he mentions moderation as a trait that might explain such choices and help us to regard them as both nonmaximizing and rational. Once again, there may be reasons why moderation itself can contribute to the greater good, so that the choices can be reconstrued as optimizing after all. Moderate goals may just be more realistic and give agents the greatest chance of success. Or, small steps may be the best way to do as well as one can. Thus, aiming to be a really fine lawyer may be the best way to become the best lawyer that one can be.[12]

But the fans of satisficing can and do respond by citing the intrinsic value of moderation itself or of other virtues that satisficing or modera-tion serves. Perhaps certain suboptimal choices are the manifestation of dispositions that are involved in certain virtues. If it can be rational to value those virtues, then satisficing will be rational. This is the strategy employed by Christine Swanton. She argues:

[T]he rationality of satisficing stems from the value of acting from desirable or at least not undesirable traits. It is characteristically rational to act out of friendship, love, courage, and so on, even where such action does not directly or indirectly optimize. This rationality stems from the rational desire to be the sort of person who is a friend and acts as one, who expresses his love for someone, and so forth. Such a person will not always set aside those traits and emotions in order to optimize . . . where the cost is betraying, or not being true to, his character, his love, or even his feelings. Let us assume that the agent realizes that the optimific action is to betray his friend. But the agent does not want to be the sort of person who betrays his friend to produce a better state of affairs. . . .[13]

This is the hardest challenge for the foes of mere satisficing to meet, and in the end I will come around to defend something akin to Swanton's position. But the foes of mere satisficing will not be easily persuaded by the value of virtue, precisely because they think that this value should be added in as one of the factors determining what is better than what. With the added value of virtue in the mix, choices that seemed not to maximize value can now be reconstrued as doing so after all.

Having admitted virtue in as one of the intrinsically valuable things that makes an outcome better, there are two ways that the friend in the example may be optimizing even when he seems to be refusing to do so. First of all, as Aristotle tells us, virtues are created and destroyed by acting as though one has the virtue. Thus, if friendship is valuable, and betraying one's friend is not an action typical of friendship, then there is some likelihood that throwing the friend over would undermine the agent's character so that he would be less likely to form true friendships in the future. Thus, one future effect of betraying a friend is that one will have fewer friends over the long haul. This result would be worse than sticking with a friend when it is disadvantageous.[14]

More importantly, the value of friendship itself – and its contribution to one's own state of character – might be so great as to wipe out the disadvantage of sticking by one's friend. Swanton begins her exposition by saying that it is the value of acting from desirable traits that rationalizes the suboptimal choice. But if by this she means that acting from virtue is so valuable that it often justifies giving up other valuable things to do it, foes of mere satisficing will agree. However, they will insist that this is so because that value has to be weighed against the disvalue of continuing to manifest the trait. Apart from the intrinsic value of acting on the trait, the virtuous action does not bring about the best available outcome, whereas when we factor in this intrinsic value the balance tips back the other way. Virtuous action does, in the relevant cases, rationalize acting in a way that is otherwise less than optimal. But once the value of virtue is figured in, such choices are nonetheless optimizing.[15]

I hope that by this point the strategy of argument against mere satisficing is reasonably clear: For any consideration that can be cited as rationalizing a choice that is not optimal, use that consideration to argue that the end chosen is in fact better than the other alternatives after all. If the advocates of rational satisficing are to prevail, they will need a way of blocking the strategy. They will need an argument to show that not all considerations are best captured by factoring them into a story about what makes outcomes better. In effect, what is needed is a way of making the considerations that allow us to order choices in terms of their rationality part company from the factors that make outcomes better. To put it yet another way, we need a theoretical reason to resist reducing the right to the good or vice versa. Thus, it may be helpful to look at a longstanding debate that is often put in just those terms – that is, the normative ethical controversy about the truth of consequentialism. I'll begin by rehearsing an argument from that debate that in some ways parallels the arguments concerning satisficing. I will then offer a strategy by which nonconsequentialists can resist the arguments that parallel the foregoing anti-satisficing arguments. Finally, I will go on to show how those same arguments can be used to defend mere satisficing.

A Parallel Argument for Defending Consequentialism Against Nonconsequentialism

There is a long history of debate between theories that are intuitively consequentialist – that is, theories which evaluate the rightness of actions by looking at their consequences broadly conceived – and theories that are nonconsequentialist and therefore deny that actions can always be judged right or wrong solely in virtue of their consequences. Since Elizabeth Anscombe first introduced the term,[16] that debate has carried on in part by allowing the consequentialists to characterize consequences of actions very broadly, so that features of actions that were not relevant according to more traditional forms of consequentialism such as utilitarianism are counted as consequences of the action – for example, that a right is violated or that a lie is told will count as a consequence of violating someone's rights or of telling a lie. Consequentialists then argue that given enough latitude in characterizing the consequences of actions, they can show that right actions always bring about better consequences than their alternatives,[17] or on satisficing models of consequentialism that their consequences are good enough. Nonconsequentialists argue that even with the additional resources, consequentialism is not adequate to capture the correct view about which actions are right in key instances because there exist other considerations besides the goodness of outcomes that determine what sorts of actions are right. Generally, nonconsequentialists defend three sorts of considerations that justify actions which are not reducible to the value of their consequences. One sort involves special obligations toward others that trump considerations of overall good. Another involves constraints on permissible ways of bringing about good outcomes. And a third involves the moral permissibility of pursuing one's own commitments even when they would have to be abandoned to pursue the overall good.[18] Nonconsequentialists often argue by presenting examples of actions that they hope their consequentialist opponents will agree are right and that they think cannot be accommodated within the consequentialist framework.[19]

Consequentialists respond by bringing to bear various consequences that their opponents may have left out of account, so that the action which intuitively seems right turns out to have better consequences than the alternatives after all. For example, in explaining the rightness of refusing to violate the rights of one person to save a greater number of others, they argue that harms caused by rights violations themselves have a greater negative weight than the same sorts of harms when they are not the result of rights violations. These claims have some plausibility, and they work to defend the intuitive response to the cases at hand, so long as the harms prevented by violating the right in question do not themselves involve the violation of similar rights.

Eventually however, the debate reaches examples in which capturing the intuition that nonconsequentialists expect us to share requires bringing in agent-relative conceptions of better or worse in order to remain consistent with the idea that right actions have better outcomes than their alternatives that are not right. One sort of relevant example involves special obligations that we may have toward those close to us. Intuitively we think it reasonable for parents to choose to save their own children from among a group of children who are in danger of drowning, even if it might be the case that they are better placed to save some other child or several other children. At least at first, it is not obvious how consequentialism can accommodate this point. Isn't it obvious that saving two children brings about a better outcome than saving just one?[20] At this point, advocates of consequentialism such as David Sosa present arguments like the following:

To the extent that we believe the father should save his own son, we reflect a preference for the set of consequences available to the father that includes his saving his own son. Although very similar to each other, the sets of consequences are not equally son-savings. The total state of affairs consequent on an act, and the value of that total state of affairs, will depend on who performs the act. In this way consequentialism can be an agent-relative ethical theory.[21]

Sosa is actually wrong that what he has said so far involves agent-relative values. Agent-relative values allow different agents to view the very same state of affairs as having different values. Although Sosa's suggestion values a relational property of actions (son-saving), it does not give this property agent-relative value, for all alike are required to view the action as valuable for instantiating this property.

However, to fully capture the intuitive thought about a parent's obligations, Sosa is right that we will need genuine agent-relative values. The father in Sosa's example saves his own child not because he cares about who does the saving but because he wants *his child* to be saved. He would just as much want someone else to save his child as he wants himself to save the child, as is shown by the fact that he wouldn't elbow the lifeguard out of the way should a lifeguard be about to save the child.[22] Thus we need to allow that the best consequence for parents in the situation to be one where *their own* child is saved, if we want both to endorse the intuitive thought about the example and at the same time to save the consequentialist thesis that the rightness of actions is always a function of the goodness of the actions' outcomes. Thus, some advocates of consequentialism urge a liberal interpretation of what constitutes good consequences, one that allows the relative goodness of consequences to vary with the evaluator's perspective.

Another sort of idea favored by nonconsequentialists will also require agent-relative values, and perhaps also time-relativity. This is the notion that there are side constraints on right action – that there are certain action types which should not be done, even to achieve what all agree are benefits. Candidates include prohibitions on the killing of innocents, torture, certain sorts of dishonesty, and so on. These constraints also require agent-relative betterness orderings to remain consistent with the idea that right actions always bring about the best outcomes, for advocates of side constraints insist that it would be wrong to violate such constraints even to prevent someone else from violating the very same constraint. And, on one reading of what side constraints require, mere *agent-relativity* won't fully capture their stringency. If such constraints require a person not to act dishonestly, even when that person knows that honesty now will lead to his or her own greater dishonesty later, then one will need time-relative orderings to do the trick, ones that allow current actions to weigh more heavily than future actions.[23]

Thus some consequentialists believe that they can defend their theory in the face of counterexamples by admitting such relativized values. And many who are sympathetic to consequentialism are willing to stipulate that the addition of such values no longer makes the view consequentialist strictly speaking but go on to defend the resulting theories that invoke agent-relative or time-relative values as more adequate than more standard nonconsequentialist alternatives.

Reasons to Resist the Argument Where Consequentialism Is Concerned

A problem with this strategy of argument as a defense of consequentialism is that it is too powerful. Once we allow ourselves to individuate consequences or states of affairs in such a way that they are distinct whenever a reason can be offered to prefer one to the other, then the theory that we rationally must maximize good or expected good has no content anymore. Any choice can be described as bringing about the best consequences or expected consequences. This is the objective analogue of a similar problem for theories that require us to maximize expected subjective utility. On the one hand, if we do not allow ourselves such fineness of grain, seemingly reasonable choices will be ruled out by the theory. On the other hand, if we are allowed to individuate options in a sufficiently fine-grained way (apples when oranges are the alternative rather than just apples), then *any* set of choices can be made consistent with the theory. The theory no longer gives us any normative advice.

The problem is not quite as bad when we are in the realm of ranking options by their objective goodness as opposed to dealing with preferences. We have required that the options be individuated in such a way that they count as different options if some reason can be given for choosing between them. Thus some options that are intuitively the same will be treated as the same option by the theory because there will be nothing to choose between them. So the theory is not quite consistent with just any set of choices. But because more theories will now be characterized as consequentialist or consequence-based, less is ruled out by this sort of consequentialism. And partly because of this we still have to pay some costs.

One cost of this way of defending consequentialism is that it causes us to lose track of the ongoing debate between consequentialism and nonconsequentialism. If everyone can be characterized as engaging in consequence-based evaluation, what were the arguments about? We can recover the difference between the positions if we remember that old-fashioned consequentialists did not countenance agent-relative values, whereas a number of distinctively nonconsequentialist notions such as side constraints can be captured in a consequence-based framework only by using agent-relative or time-relative features of outcomes to individuate and rank them. Thus we can say that the debate we were engaged in was really a debate between the advocates of agent-neutral and time-neutral rankings of states of affairs and those who wanted to introduce agent- and time-relativity into the rankings. We can at least describe the positions in a way that shows that they are distinct and carry on our discussion of which sort is more likely to be correct.

But I suspect that our discussion will have lost something, at least from the point of view of a nonconsequentialist. Many reasons for distinctively nonconsequentialist choices do not present themselves as grounded in agent-relative or time-relative values. What makes the nonconsequentialist choice to honor a side constraint make sense to the agent is not that it maximizes agent-relative value to do so, though once we see that it makes sense we can construct an agent-relative ranking of the options in terms of their choiceworthiness. The reason it makes sense to honor a constraint may be, for instance, that this right which would be violated is important, and the agent-neutral benefits of violating the right are not such as to swamp that consideration.

The point for my purposes is this: Although agent-neutral evaluations of goodness and badness play a role in even most nonconsequentialist deliberation about what to do, agent-relative rankings of options don't play the same role in nonconsequentialist deliberation. Rather, the considerations that allow us to construct the agent-relative orderings present themselves in a more direct fashion, as considerations that compete with the agent-neutral goodness of an option for our attention. To use the familiar taxonomy of reasons, prerogatives that allow us to pursue special projects not conducive to agent-neutral goodness, deontological constraints on certain ways of promoting goodness, and special obligations due to special relationships all interact with the goodness of outcomes to determine what we should do. When we capture our normative theory in one agent-relative ordering that is itself a function of both agent-neutral value and these sorts of reasons, we obscure the ways in which these various kinds of reasons interact. We have lost information. I'll illustrate before going on to argue that we want a theory of rightness to generate the sort of illumination that is lost when we agglomerate all the relevant considerations into one agent-relative ordering of states of affairs from better to worse.

Recall the example of a parent whose child is among a number of children at risk. I will suppose that common sense dictates that parents are right to aim to save their own children, even when they can do more to save other children. But this does not require a judgment on our part that the state of affairs which is a son-saving is better than the one in which a parent saves another child. We might have no reason to prefer the one over the other, or even a reason for preferring that the unrelated drowning person be saved. Perhaps the talents of the unrelated swimmer are more likely to benefit humanity. Thus, if the father in Sosa's example wrongly decided to save an unrelated child, we would do nothing to redirect his energies.[24]

Nor does the rightness of the action require the agent – the father in Sosa's example – to make such a judgment. Even while viewing the saving of his son as the right thing to attempt, a father can recognize the legitimacy of our outsider's view. Just as we can allow that he did the right thing in saving his son though we wish that he had done otherwise, he can allow that from our point of view things might have been better had they gone otherwise. He might even agree that it would have been better overall if he had saved the other swimmer, because of that swimmer's great ability to benefit humanity. And recognition of such agent-neutral goodness and badness is not always idle in determining the right course of action even within a nonconsequentialist point of view. This is the important point to see in grasping the inadequacy of theories that reduce rightness to choosing the action that is best in an agent-relative betterness ordering. A great objective need on the part of some other child might delay the father's mission to help his own child. Enough agent-neutral goodness obtained even at some risk to his particular obligations to those close to him might legitimate his modifying his plans. Thus, the agent-neutral goodness of an outcome can sometimes override distinctively nonconsequentialist reasons to determine the rightness of an overall course of action, at least on the nonconsequentialist theories that get the most support from common sense.

The agent-neutral goodness or badness of a resulting state of affairs can also defeat the force of other reasons that might normally justify not bringing about a neutrally better outcome. Side constraints against doing certain act types can be overridden if the only way to prevent serious harms is to do those actions, or perhaps even if doing those actions were to bring about enough benefits. The same is likely true of agent-centered prerogatives to pursue one's own projects and goals. Whatever one is up to, certain sorts of emergency can suggest that we should put our private goals aside to prevent disaster.

Agent-neutral goodness interacts with at least some of these reasons in another way. In deciding between various courses of action required by traditional nonconsequentialist reasons, the agent-neutral goodness or badness of the various options may play a role. For example, although we might let our special obligations allow us to ignore goods and bads outside of our realm of responsibility so long as they are not overwhelming, within our realm of responsibility the goodness and badness of various outcomes may determine our choices. When various family members have competing needs, we can use the importance of those needs – a perfectly agent-neutral importance – to decide how to act. Thus from this sort of nonconsequentialist perspective, agent-neutral goodness along with a variety of other reasons to act is playing more than one role in determining what we should do.

I claim that it is much more illuminating for a moral theory to highlight these roles played by agent-neutral goodness than to fold it in along with other considerations to generate one agent-relative ranking of states of affairs from worse to better. A theory that highlights the distinct grounds of our reasons for acting in different circumstances does more to rationalize what we are up to. If asked why we are doing what we are doing, we might have to talk both about reasons grounded in the goodness of the states of affairs that would result if we did this or if we did that *and* the reasons that make it the case that only an agent-relative ranking of states of affairs will allow a consequence-based theory to capture rightness (if nonconsequentialism is correct). What exactly we would need to talk about would depend on the choice at hand and on the various alternative actions. But if someone were truly interested in why we did what we did, or why we thought doing some action or other was right, then this sort of explanation would be more illuminating than one which pointed out that the chosen alternative ranked highest in our agent-relative ordering of states of affairs from better to worse. More to the point, such an explanation would also be more illuminating than an actual enumeration of that ordering which, given the infinite variety of possible states of affairs, we would never be able to give. If we could grasp that ordering, we might by testing various hypotheses be able to work out what features of the states of affairs in question determined the ordering. In that case we could generate the reasons that determine that ordering. Then we would have some enlightenment about our reasons for acting as we do or as we should. But in fact it is the story about the features that generate the ordering that tells us what our reasons are, not the ordering in which those features are not factored out.

Not every true description of options involved in a given choice will serve as part of a rationalizing explanation of that choice. Not just any way of picking out the rationally preferred option shows that it makes sense to choose it. For example, it might help rationalize my choice of a given candy that it tastes sweet. It may also be that what it is for a thing to taste sweet is for it to stimulate certain receptors on a normal person's tongue in a certain way. But an explanation that used this feature of the candy to explain why I chose it would be less than illuminating, at least unless I knew that these were the receptors that constituted the basis for our ability to perceive sweetness. Insofar as showing that an action is right is part of showing that it is rational or that it makes sense to choose it, the story we tell about what makes actions right needs to be sensitive to this. A good account of what is right should be illuminating. It should show what it is about the action that makes it choiceworthy for an agent. This means, I believe, that a good account should display the option in such a way that it could make sense for a rational agent to choose it when it is thought of in the way employed by the theory.

Frank Jackson, no friend of nonconsequentialism, puts the point nicely in arguing that consequentialism should adopt the *expectation* of goodness rather than the actual goodness as the standard of right action:

[W]e are dealing with an *ethical* theory when we deal with consequentialism, a theory about *action*, about what to *do*. In consequence we have to see consequentialism as containing as a constitutive part prescriptions for action. Now, the fact that an action has in fact the best consequences may be a matter which is obscure to an agent.... Hence, the fact that a course of action would have the best results is not in itself a guide to action, for a guide to action must be in some appropriate sense present to the agent's mind. We need, if you like, a story from the inside of an agent to be part of any theory which is properly a theory in ethics....[25]

Jackson's last point is the crucial one. Insofar as an agent-relative ordering of all states of affairs from better to worse can be constructed only once we have figured out which actions are right, it cannot serve as a guide to rightness. If ethical theory is to depict what is going on in such a way that it represents decision making "from the inside," it will have to give us something more. If nonconsequentialism of the traditional sort presents us with the right story about what makes actions right, then a theory that keeps agent-neutral goodness apart from the sorts of considerations that justify failing always to aim at such goodness will be superior. Thus, if the various strategies to argue for nonconsequentialism succeed, a theory that puts some distance between rightness and goodness is to be preferred to one that assimilates the latter to the former.[26]

Deploying the Nonconsequentialist Resistance Argument to Defend Mere Satisficing

It should be evident that if the foregoing is correct and if nonconsequentialism is the right account of morality, optimizing goodness is not always morally required. But of course, this by itself does not show that satisficing goodness makes sense. First off, we would need a defense of nonconsequentialism, something I have not offered. Bracketing that caveat, even if nonconsequentialism were correct, not every form of choice that eschews optimizing is a form of satisficing. To satisfice, one must pay attention to the level of goodness without aiming to maximize goodness above some satisfactory level. Thus a moral theory that postulates absolute side constraints will not in virtue of those constraints rationalize satisficing, even if it requires pursuing the good when those side constraints are not violated, for on such a theory the thought that an outcome is good enough has no real role to play in rationalizing actions. Rationalization will come either from the applicability of the side constraints in question or from the fact that the option is as good as possible without violating those constraints.[27]

A nonconsequentialist theory with defeasible side constraints will, however, make sense of satisficing. The sort of theory I have in mind allows that if things get bad enough, then the normal side constraints on right action can be overridden by duties to help others. Different theories of this sort have been proposed by Thomas Nagel and by Michael Walzer in discussions of justice in wartime.[28] The idea is that normally there are constraints on what we may do to other people that prevent us from aiming to kill innocent people, torture, and so on. But if the alternative to doing so is bad enough – which is to say not satisfactory – then we may violate these constraints to avoid serious calamities. This sort of theory allows the acceptability of refusing to violate the relevant constraint to play a role in rationalizing the choice, for if the state were not at least acceptable, we would not have made that choice. This sort of theory makes sense of satisficing goodness conceived of in the agent-neutral way that I have argued even nonconsequentialists have a reason to recognize. A similar sort of defeasibility might obtain for permission to pursue one's own projects and the special obligations we might have to others. Thus, on the versions of nonconsequentialism that allow anti-consequentialist considerations themselves to be defeated in the face of importantly good or bad consequences, it will make sense for an agent to satisfice. For on such theories, as long as the action chosen has an outcome that is good enough, a person is justified by these other considerations in acting in a way that brings about an outcome that is not the best.[29]

Conclusion

If this is the best way to resist the optimizing strategy of folding all considerations into our characterization of the good of an outcome in hopes of showing that even when we seem to be satisficing we are actually maximizing, then the defense of mere satisficing requires a defense of nonconsequentialism, in fact of nonconsequentialism of a specific sort. Although any reader will likely see that this is the sort of view I favor, I have done nothing to argue for that nonconsequentialism here. So I have not shown that mere satisficing makes sense. I have shown that we can hope to make sense of it only if this sort of nonconsequentialism is correct.

Still, this in itself might indirectly provide some support for nonconsequentialism, at least for those who feel that mere satisficing can make sense. It has been suggested that satisficing consequentialism will be better able to capture the considered judgments of common sense, thereby lessening the challenge that such judgments pose to consequentialism.[30] If my defense of mere satisficing is the best available, mere satisficing will be rational only if nonconsequentialism gives a correct account of our moral reasons to act. If so, satisficing consequentialism is not a viable theory. It will suffer from the same sort of instability that rule consequentialism is often said to suffer from. Although it may tend to do better at agreeing with the judgments of common sense about what we should do, it does so at the cost of undermining its own rationale, for to be a consequentialist is to accept that the rightness of an action is a function only of the goodness of the outcomes produced. Once one has said that much, one has accepted that all reasons are such only by reference to the goodness of a state of affairs in which they are obeyed. Thus, a consequentialist will be unable to provide any reasons not to choose the best unless those reasons have already been given their due weight in determining which outcome in fact is the best. Allowing these reasons to count again as a reason not to choose the best would be a form of double counting and hence not rational. The argument I have suggested allows a satisficer to avoid being pushed into this corner by resisting the idea that all reasons to act can be captured in determining the goodness of outcomes. But the strategy works only if nonconsequentialism is correct.

Notes

In addition to the obvious debts to authors I cite in this paper, I owe thanks to a variety of people. I thank Robert Audi, Harry Ide, Nelson Potter, and Joe Mendola for helpful conversation as I was writing the paper, and Jennifer Haley for a careful reading of an earlier draft. I also owe thanks to Michael Byron and Jamie Dreier for helpful e-mail correspondence on this and related topics, and also to Jamie for sending me a draft of the paper he is writing for this volume as I was still working on this one. The argument of the sections related to nonconsequentialism owes a lot to my graduate education more than ten years ago. Especially important were a semester TA-ing for John Broome, a seminar on consequentialism with Frank Jackson, and a conversation with Richard Holton after one of the seminar meetings during which we both came up with something like the main idea of those sections.

1. The example is employed by just about everyone in this literature, starting with Michael Slote in "Satisficing Consequentialism," *Proceedings of the Aristotelian Society* 58 supp. (1984): 139–63, at 142. Slote claims to find it in the literature about rational economic behavior from which the term 'satisficing' is appropriated.

2. These terms are from David Schmidtz, "Rationality within Reason," *Journal of Philosophy*, 89 (1992): 445–66 and roughly are meant to contrast concern with one parameter of one's life and concern for one's life as a whole.

3. Thus, although I agree with one of the two theses defended by Christine Swanton in "Satisficing and Virtue," *Journal of Philosophy* 90 (1993): 33–48, I disagree with her about the other. She thinks that both of the following are true: (A) An action that has good enough results may rationally be preferred to one judged to have better results. And (B) An action that is good enough may rationally be preferred to one judged to be better. If preference here is a way of representing what one should choose, I agree with her about A, but not B for the reasons I list in the text.

4. Michael Slote, *Beyond Optimizing*, Cambridge: Harvard University Press, 1989, 130.

5. Slote at one point rather bafflingly seems to deny this. "Even granting that it is *more rational* to treat the times of one's future equally, ... it does not follow and one may deny that it is always less rational to give some preference to the near...." Michael Slote, *Beyond Optimizing*, 126. Unless the "always" in the last clause is doing all of the work, I can't actually figure out what this could mean. I take it that if *a* is more rational than *b*, it follows that *b* is less rational than *a*. Perhaps the statement is not so much his considered position as part of a broad survey of positions that seem to be made available by a careful consideration of the options.

6. Consider a parallel with the debate over consequentialism, construed as the thesis that right actions always bring about the best consequences. Someone who denies this should not be saddled with denying that the right action is always most right, or even that the right action is always best from the point of view of rightness (if that makes any sense), and certainly not with claiming that the right action can be less right than some alternative equally available under the circumstances. My saying this may depend partly on the argument below, so it would be somewhat unfair to rule out this way of construing that debate before I make the argument. Still, it is fair to underline that this way of looking at the issue is not mandatory for nonconsequentialists to accept.

7. This is what I take to be the moral of Joe Mendola's criticisms of Gauthier's notion of constrained maximization in Joseph Mendola, "Gauthier's Morals by Agreement and Two Kinds of Rationality," *Ethics* 97 (1987): 765–74.

8. David Schmidtz makes just this sort of complaint against Michael Slote: "If all we have is an intuition that an act makes sense, but cannot say what the act makes sense *in terms of*, then we would be jumping to conclusions if we said that we were approving of the act as rational." Schmidtz, "Rationality within Reason," 456. And earlier Phillip Pettit complains, "The irrationality of the policy first appears in the fact that whereas he could give a reason for choosing A – it is in his view the better option – he can give no reason for

choosing B." Philip Pettit, "Satisficing Consequentialism," *Proceedings of the Aristotelian Society* 58 supp. (1984): 165–76 at 172.

9. None of these points are new with me. They are made, for example, by Schmidtz, "Rationality within Reason," 454.

10. Slote, *Beyond Optimizing*, 2.

11. Slote, *Beyond Optimizing*, 2.

12. Schmidtz makes all of these points. Schmidtz, "Rationality within Reason," 456.

13. Swanton, "Satisficing and Virtue," 37.

14. Swanton is careful to respond to this objection (raised to her by Pettit) that it would be rational to make the sacrifice for the friend even if there were no such weakening effects. Swanton, "Satisficing and Virtue," 38.

15. It appears to me that Swanton does not really address this sort of objection head on, although some of her remarks about the relevance of agent-centered prerogatives and restrictions on promoting value (on page 39, for example) are friendly to the sort of view I will suggest is needed to rationalize mere satisficing. I suppose where we differ is in this: She thinks that all that needs to be shown is that such restrictions make sense, and that virtue theory can be used to show that they do make sense. I think you need to do more than this: You must also show that the best way of making sense of nonconsequentialist prerogatives and restrictions on maximizing the good does not require folding all considerations including these restrictions into one agent-relative ordering of outcomes from better to worse. It is to this argument that the next several sections of this paper are devoted.

16. At least I believe that it is G. E. M. Anscombe who coined the term in the late 1950s, although her use of the term is not exactly the one that has gained currency. She seems to use it for any view that allows the goodness or badness or consequences to override duties that she wants to view as absolute side-constraints on actions. Thus a theorist like Ross, whom most of us would characterize as a nonconsequentialist, would be labeled a consequentialist if current usage abided by Anscombe's original implicit definition. But though she coined the term, subsequent usage has restricted it to theories that make the rightness of actions solely a function of the value of the action's consequences, and most of us limit the relevant sort of value to agent- and time-neutral value. G. E. M. Anscombe, "Modern Moral Philosophy," *Philosophy* 33 (1958): 1–19.

17. See, for example, David Sosa, "Consequences of Consequentialism," *Mind* 102 (1993): 101–22. Although Sosa is by no means the first to argue in this way, he is among the most liberal in the resources he claims on behalf of consequentialism insofar as he wants to count theories that include agent-relative features of outcomes in the specifications of the consequences of actions. Other theorists who preceded Sosa in advocating the use of agent-relative values in determining the rightness of actions have generally eschewed the label "consequentialist" for their theories, while recognizing that their theories are motivated by extensions of consequentialist rationales. For example, Amartya Sen calls his theory 'consequence based' because it allows the use of agent-relative values. Amartya Sen, "Rights and Agency," *Philosophy and Public*

Affairs 11 (1985): 3–39. John Broome revives the term 'teleological' for theories like his that allow agent- and time-relative orderings of outcomes to determine rightness. John Broome, *Weighing Goods*, Cambridge: Blackwell, 1991: 6. It should become plain from the text that I prefer to speak as Sen and Broome do rather than to continue to call theories that allow such relativized values 'consequentialist'.

18. Samuel Scheffler groups the first two sorts of reasons together as agent-centered restrictions on action and refers to the latter as agent-centered permissions. Samuel Scheffler, *The Rejection of Consequentialism*, Oxford University Press, 1982: 22–3. Nagel labels these three sorts of reasons respectively as "reasons of obligation," "deontological reasons," and "reasons of autonomy." Thomas Nagel, *The View from Nowhere*, Oxford University Press, 1986, 165.

19. Certainly the most influential argument of this sort is Bernard Williams's contribution to Smart and Williams, *Utilitarianism: For and Against*, Cambridge University Press, 1973.

20. The response that it isn't what consequentialism requires because two children saved as opposed to one will lead to population problems down the road won't help, because that strategy would also suggest that the parent should really not have saved anybody at all.

21. Sosa, "Consequences of Consequentialism," 115.

22. To see that this involves genuine agent-relativity, we need only notice that another parent may permissibly save another child who is his own rather than this woman's child but would not be required to prevent this woman from saving his child if he found her doing it.

23. Robert Nozick, who introduces the term 'side-constraint', notices in the same place that one could model side-constraints within a quasi-consequentialist framework if one allowed agent-relative betterness relations. See Robert Nozick, *Anarchy, State and Utopia*, New York: Basic Books, 1974, 29. John Broome has a nice discussion of how agent- and time-relative orderings are needed if one is to capture the workings of side-constraints in a teleological theory on pages 3–16 of *Weighing Goods*.

24. Our unwillingness to redirect the parent might merely reflect a judgment that we should not play favorites in such a situation. The point remains that the fact that one saving is the saving of a son does not commit us to viewing the state of affairs that includes it as any more valuable than any other alternative in which a life is saved, even when we think the father should save the son.

25. Frank Jackson, "Decision-Theoretic Consequentialism and the Nearest and Dearest Objection," *Ethics* 101 (1991): 461–82, at 466–7.

26. James Dreier argues for the opposing view in part by suggesting that once we see that what I am calling "nonconsequentialist" theories can be captured with agent-relative orderings, we can defend them against the charge that they ignore the good, and also because we will be less apt to conflate objectivity with agent-neutrality, thereby making it easier for nonconsequentialists to be drawn into ways of thinking that give agent-neutral theories an upper hand. James Dreier, "The Structure of Normative Theories," *The Monist* 76 (1993): 22–40.

27. Michael Byron makes something like this point against people like Swanton who use nonconsequentialist moral theory to defend satisficing: "If, on the contrary, nonconsequentialism is true, then Swanton's conception of 'satisficing' is superfluous, since the truth of nonconsequentialism entails that choosing a suboptimific alternative is sometimes rationally permissible." Michael Byron, "Satisficing and Optimality," *Ethics* 109 (1998): 67–93 at 90–1. The paragraph that follows provides my answer to this objection.

28. Nagel, *View from Nowhere*, 176, and Michael Walzer, Chapter 16 of *Just and Unjust Wars: A Moral Argument with Historical Illustrations*, New York: Basic Books, 1977, 251–68.

29. Thus, to contrast my paper with one of the others in this volume, my disagreement with James Dreier is not over whether one can construct the preference ordering that allows us to construe all choices as maximizing utility. I agree that we can. But I doubt that this is the notion of utility that someone who defends rational satisficing should use. I claim that an advocate of satisficing might use the notion of agent-neutral goodness from plausible consequentialist theories, and that if nonconsequentialism is right, it will make sense to satisfice with respect to such goodness. I think this is where Dreier would disagree with me.

30. Michael Slote, *Common-Sense Morality and Consequentialism*, London: Routledge, 1985, 3 and 136.

9

Satisficing and Perfectionism in Virtue Ethics

Christine Swanton

1. Introduction

I understand the problem of satisficing to be that of whether it is morally permitted (at least sometimes) for agents to choose an action that is less than the best when better actions are in their power and known by them to be so. The primary motivation for accepting the moral permissibility of satisficing is to reduce the demandingness of ethics. The "demandingness objection" has traditionally been directed at consequentialism, but I shall relate the discussion to the demandingness of virtue ethics.

The demandingness objection to certain moral theories is the objection that these theories contain requirements that are too demanding on agents. There are a number of possible strategies for overcoming the objection. A vulnerable theory may allow that it is morally permitted to satisfice, or given that it is not morally permitted to satisfice, it may propose a criterion of best action that is not itself too demanding. A weaker reading of the demandingness objection suggests a third strategy: It is possible that a theory may possess a demanding criterion of rightness or requirement in that sense, but a less demanding conception of conditions under which agents can be blamed for failing to perform right acts, even when those acts are in their power and known by them to be so. Let me briefly elaborate on those three strategies.

The first strategy replaces maximizing or optimizing criteria of rightness with satisficing criteria. This option severs the putatively necessary connection between right act and best act, thereby making room for the moral permissibility of an agent's choosing (at least sometimes) an action that is less than the best, when better actions are in her power and known by her to be so. However, in consequentialist discussions, this strategy has sometimes been thought to "stray too far from the roots" of consequentialism, where rightness has been understood solely in terms of features of outcomes rather than agent-centered features such as effort.[1] A similar problem may beset satisficing virtue-ethical criteria of rightness. Just as a consequentialist criterion of right seems tied to best outcomes (why settle for anything less?), so a virtue-ethical criterion of right would seem tied to actions of supremely or ideally virtuous agents, or to actions that *best* attain the targets of relevant virtues.

The second strategy retains an optimizing conception of rightness but rationalizes a less demanding notion of right or best action. I shall explore this strategy in relation to the following virtue-ethical conception of right action:

An act is right if and only if it best meets overall the targets of relevant virtues.[2]

I explicate a virtue-ethical reply to the demandingness objection along the lines of the second strategy as follows. The idea is not to wimp out on the criterion of the right but to understand what is involved in a virtue – namely a virtue whose field is striving for excellence. This virtue, which is not as demanding as might be expected, I call virtuous perfectionism. The target of this virtue is to some extent relative to the individual – it will be less demanding for some. What is right (and best) for some agents to do may not be what is right for a supremely virtuous agent. Hence virtue ethics could resolve the demandingness objection without adopting a satisficing criterion of rightness. For example, consider an agent who is able to work for Servants (an organization whose members live in conditions like those of the people they aid) but lacks the strength to do so without imposing much cost on himself. What is right or best *for him* to do, it may be claimed, is to stay at home, given the target of perfectionism as a virtue. What is right or best for another agent (who, for example, has strength born of religious faith) is to work for Servants. Satisficing is not permitted, but an optimizing criterion of the right need not be excessively demanding.

The foregoing solution for virtue ethics may be thought not to overcome the demandingness objection for the following reason. It may be objected that even if the target of perfectionism is relative to, for example, the strength of an individual, the target of benevolence, say, may be relative to norms appropriate to supremely benevolent individuals. In such a case the targets of virtues may conflict, and, the reply continues, the right act (overall) may be an act of supreme benevolence.

This problem opens the way to a third solution. According to this solution, it is granted that factoring in the agent-relative virtue of virtuous perfectionism will make the criterion of the right less demanding than it would otherwise be. But to do what is right *simpliciter* or overall may still be thought too demanding because the targets of other relevant virtues are highly demanding. The third solution is this: An agent may on occasion not be blameworthy for failing to perform right acts, even when those acts are in her power and known by her to be so. A difficulty for the third solution is acceptance of a criterion of right action that involves a balancing between targets of virtues, some of which have agent-relative targets and some of which do not. However, this solution relies on a plausible intuition supported by consequentialist notions of right: namely that the targets of many virtues such as benevolence are not relative to, for example, the strength of individuals, but relative to some maximalist ideal: in virtue ethics or ideal or supreme virtue. By contrast, a virtue whose field is agents' striving for excellence may not require, and may even *prima facie* prohibit (for reasons explored below), performing acts of supreme virtue.

In this article, I do not aim to adjudicate between the second and third solutions. My aim is to allow for the possibility of a (relatively) undemanding virtue ethics without commitment to a satisficing criterion of the right, and without commitment to the moral permissibility of satisficing. This aim is prosecuted largely by exploring the nature of perfectionism as a virtue. The relevance of perfectionism to the problem of satisficing in a virtue ethics is this: It will be thought that because agents are morally required to perform right acts, then if right acts are best acts they are morally required to be perfectionistic. That is, they are morally required always to strive for perfection. But as Slote and Stocker have pointed out,[3] perfectionism is not unequivocally a virtue, and indeed may be an anti-virtue. This fact may motivate a satisficing conception of right action. I shall argue that a correct understanding of perfectionism as virtue need not motivate a satisficing criterion of the right, for such an understanding need not lead to a problematically demanding notion of best acts.

Section 2 provides the framework of the discussion by exploring virtue-ethical conceptions of right and best action. Sections 3 and 4 explore perfectionistic virtue and vice. The disposition of perfectionism as such is contrasted with perfectionism as a virtue. Deployment of that virtue in virtue ethics makes that theory less demanding than might otherwise be the case.

2. Right Act and Best Act in Virtue Ethics

In order to discuss satisficing within virtue ethics, we must first provide the framework of the discussion – conceptions of right and best act in virtue ethics. Only then can we understand the problem of satisficing in virtue-ethical terms.

Virtue-ethical accounts of rightness conform to the following schema:

O: The (a) right action is the (an) action that is overall virtuous.

This virtue-ethical schema or core concept of rightness can be amplified according to various virtue-ethical conceptions of rightness. These conceptions can be distinguished according to whether they are agent-centered or act-centered. A helpful and interesting taxonomic framework along these lines is proposed by Thomas Hurka in his *Virtue, Vice, and Value*.[4] According to agent-centered conceptions, "right actions are those standing in some specified relation to virtuous motives, character traits, or persons."[5] According to act-centered conceptions, right acts are those in which virtue terms are applied directly to acts, and it is not the case that such acts necessarily stand in some specified relation to virtuous motives, character traits, or persons.

I shall limit my attention to the broad category of what Hurka calls agent-centered views. These come in two broad types: those that make essential reference to persons, and those that make essential reference to virtue (or aspects of virtue) without making essential reference to persons. It may be thought misleading to call the latter conceptions "agent-centered," but I shall stick with Hurka's taxonomy. The first broad type of agent-centered criterion itself comes in two types – those which require that a right act *express* the agent's virtue (or virtuous motivation) and those that do not require this. The second type may allow for an act to be right insofar as it mimics an act of a virtuous agent, and as such it can be called, for example, a just or generous act (even though not an act expressing just or generous dispositions). The first type of agent-centered view is Slote's[6]; the second type is Hursthouse's.[7]

The second broad type of agent-centered view can properly be described as virtue-centered rather than person-centered. Such a view may describe a right act as one that hits the target(s) of a relevant virtue (or relevant virtues).[8] It should be noted that this virtue-ethical notion of rightness does not entail that the rightness of acts *never* depends on any quality of the agent, such as her motives. On the contrary, it may be the case that for an act to be called right, caring motives, for example, must be expressed by the agent. It is just that it is not part of the definition of rightness *in general* that right acts must stand in some specified relation to properties of the agent – her character or motives. For in the case of some virtue terms, as applied to acts, (good) quality of motive may not be required for rightness.[9]

In summary, the foregoing agent-centered conceptions of rightness conform to O in the following ways.

An act may be overall virtuous because

O_1: It expresses overall virtue.
O_2: It expresses good motivation overall.
O_3: It is an act that a virtuous agent would or might perform acting characteristically.[10]
O_4: It hits the target(s) of relevant virtues (e.g., justice, kindness, and so forth).

Let us turn now to the idea of best act. Given O, it seems natural to conceive of a virtue-ethical notion of *best* act as follows:

M_1: It expresses supreme virtue.
M_2: It expresses supremely virtuous motivation.
M_3: It is an act that a supremely virtuous agent would or might perform.[11]
M_4: It hits the target(s) of relevant virtues not just approximately or satisfactorily, but in the best possible way.

A problem arises for the foregoing accounts of O and M and the relations between them. If rightness were understood in terms of acts that expressed supreme virtue, it might be impossible for any agent, or virtually any agent, to perform right acts. Admittedly M_2, M_3, and M_4 are weaker than this. It may be possible for agents characteristically to perform acts that mimic the acts of those possessed of supreme virtue. However, even if possible, such acts may often be thought too demanding. Furthermore, it may be possible for agents to muster up occasionally supremely virtuous motives, but such occasions may be thought to be too rare for most, or too demanding. Finally, it may be possible for agents characteristically to perform acts that best meet the targets of virtue, because one can meet the target of a virtue without possessing all the excellences that make up the virtuous disposition, but again, such demands may be thought too stringent for the normal individual.

In the remainder of this paper I shall focus on O_4 and M_4, the target-centered conception of rightness and best action. I shall assume that it is morally required of agents that they best meet the targets of relevant virtues: In other words O_4 is identified with M_4. However, I shall claim that if we understand what is required of perfectionism *as a virtue*, M_4 is not as demanding as it might first appear.

3. Perfectionistic Virtue

This section elaborates upon the nature of perfectionist virtue. It is at first sight natural to think of 'perfectionism' as automatically the name of a virtue because it connotes a striving for excellence. Indeed, because virtue is itself an excellence of character, surely a virtue ethics would recognize perfectionism, so understood, as a virtue. Furthermore, if perfectionism is a striving for excellence, and if it is a virtue, then, surely the target of the virtue is such that, in a requirement to meet it, we are subject to a very demanding ethics. I shall argue that a correct understanding of the virtue shows that this conclusion is mistaken.

First we must question the assumption that perfectionism as a virtue is simply a disposition to strive for excellence. An Aristotelian conception of virtue should make us wary of such an assumption, for virtue is a state "in a mean," and strivings for excellence may be done in the wrong manner, at the wrong times, from the wrong motives, in the wrong circumstances, and with respect to the wrong people or objects. Perfectionism can, in short, lapse into vice, or at least into states and expressions that fall short of virtue.

In order to elaborate upon perfectionism as a virtue, we need first to employ a useful distinction of Martha Nussbaum's.[12] She distinguishes between the thin conception and a thick conception of a virtue. The thin conception simply states a virtue's field (its sphere of concern) and understands the virtue as being well disposed in regard to that field, whereas a thick conception gives an account of what it is to be well disposed in regard to that field. And, of course, there can be rival thick accounts.

On the thin account, the virtue of perfectionism can be uncontroversially understood as being well disposed with respect to striving for excellence. This assumes that striving for excellence in the right manner, at the right times, and so forth demarcates an arena of virtue. However, a substantive thick conception has to tell us what are, for example, the right motives and circumstances. Rival conceptions of perfectionism as a virtue differ on what is the correct thick account.

I shall argue that a correct thick account of perfectionism as a virtue would suggest that an adequate virtue ethics is not excessively demanding. This is so for one basic reason: Contrary to what may naturally be assumed, a correct thick account of perfectionism as a virtue does not necessarily involve emulating the acts of supremely virtuous agents.

I have granted that perfectionism is a disposition to strive for perfection or excellence but have argued that such a disposition is not necessarily a virtue. In this, 'perfectionism' resembles many other terms that appear to name virtues, such as 'being positive', 'trusting', and 'loyal'. 'Perfectionism' as a virtue term names not a disposition to strive for excellence *simpliciter* but an excellent disposition in regard to this field.

Given a virtue theoretic framework, a natural understanding of perfectionism on the thick account of the virtue is that it is a disposition to strive to emulate the acts of supremely virtuous agents. But as a thick account it is questionable. If perfectionism in this sense were a virtue, it would be natural to understand right acts as ones performed by supremely virtuous agents, and it would not be permitted knowingly to fail to perform such acts when these were in one's power and known to be so. In this case, virtue ethics would be a very demanding moral theory.

I shall argue in this section that this natural virtue theoretic understanding of perfectionism is not a correct thick account of perfectionism as a virtue. It should not be assumed that excellence in striving for excellence involves direct imitation of the supremely virtuous, for in a dynamic process of improvement one may overreach one's strength, resulting in various kinds of motivational distortions and bad consequences. Excellence in striving for excellence involves excellence in improving oneself, but that does not entail striving to emulate the acts of supremely virtuous agents. It is beyond the scope of this article to give a full account of perfectionism as a virtue, but it is noteworthy that psychologists have interesting things to say about nonvirtuous forms.[13]

According to Karen Horney, for example, perfectionism, as a trait, *can* be a vice, being a mark of the "expansionist" type.

Such a person identifies himself with his standards. This type feels superior because of his high standards, moral and intellectual, and on this basis looks down on others. His arrogant contempt for others, though, is hidden – from himself as well – behind polished friendliness, because his standards prohibit such irregular feelings.[14]

Indeed, Horney distinguishes between two types of neurotic perfectionism. In the expansionist type, perfectionism involves an attempt to assert superiority, but in the self-effacing type it is expressive of overly self-berating tendencies. In both types, perfectionism is expressive of problematic depth motivations: self-condemnation. She describes typical behavior of the self-effacing type in this example:

Even after a good performance (perhaps in giving a party or delivering a lecture) they still will emphasise the fact that they forgot this or that, that they did not emphasise clearly what they meant to say, that they were too subdued or too offensive, etc.[15]

Whether such pieces of behavior are manifestations of perfectionistic (self-effacing) vice depends on such facts as whether these behaviors are part of a pattern of self-berating behavior where the objects of displeasure are nonexistent or trivial, whether the failures in presentation are perceived to be important (because the material conveyed is perceived to be important), whether those perceptions are themselves well founded, and so on.

Distinguishing the facts of perfectionistic virtue from states inferior to virtue is not necessarily easy. Even if it is clear that some perfectionistic strivings express a weak compensatory need to assert superiority, however, it may also be the case that hostility at, for example, decline in standards and mediocratization is well warranted. It may be a matter of fine judgment whether such expression should be seen *overall* as a mark of integrity, courage, and respect for the value of excellence, or whether it bears too much the hallmark of weakness. It should also be noted that motivation is not the only dimension of difference. The wrong manner of asserting a demand for excellence is also less than virtuous. Whether perfectionistic strivings are seen as a mark of virtue in, for example, generosity, industriousness, integrity, courage, and justice depends in part on the manner of such striving. If the manner appears hostile or threatening, or condescending or supercilious, for example, efforts at being a role model of excellence may backfire; on the other hand, a more judiciously displayed respect for excellence may shake complacency or compliant acceptance of prevailing norms. Personal circumstances and talents are also important determinants of vice or virtue. Assiduous striving for artistic excellence is not virtuous in the totally talentless, especially if they are neglecting their loved ones or shirking their responsibilities in the process.

Whether perfectionist strivings should be seen as marks of virtuous perfectionism depends on a host of factors, including depth motivations, intentions, degree of wisdom (including self-knowledge such as knowledge of one's strength and talents, seriousness of effects on others, and the extent to which one has responsibilities to those others), the worthwhileness of the ends to which one is devoted, and the likelihood of one's success in achieving them, even with effort.

I have shown that a disposition to strive to emulate the actions of those with supreme virtue is not in itself a virtue, for such a disposition may express distorted depth motivations or be manifested at a cost that is too great. That is, such strivings are not sufficient for perfectionistic virtue. To show that perfectionistic virtue is not excessively demanding, however, we have to show that such strivings are not necessary for virtue. The demandingness objection is not met if it turns out that (virtuous) perfectionism requires not only emulating those of supreme virtue but also doing so with, say, strength, self-love, and lack of resentment. In the next section, I shall show that perfectionism should be seen as a dynamic virtue that is to some extent relative to imperfections of the agent. Perfectionism as a virtue does not require that we strive to emulate the supremely virtuous in an excellent way, for the demand to strive to emulate the supremely virtuous may be an inappropriate demand.

To show this I shall discuss a distinction between ordinary and supreme virtue.

4. Ordinary and Supreme Virtue

The distinction between ordinary and supreme virtue allows whether virtuous perfectionism is excessively demanding to be an open question. The notion of 'ordinary' in 'ordinary virtue' is deliberately left vague, because what counts as 'ordinary' can have several dimensions. We may call ordinary virtues the virtues of ordinary lives, the virtues of those with ordinary strength, or ordinary talents. The idea is that action in line with supreme virtue, even where such action is within the agent's power, may not be required by virtuous perfectionism.

The distinction between ordinary and supreme virtue in some form or other is found in a number of virtue theoretic sources. In Aristotle, the virtues of magnificence and *megalopsychia* are not available to all. In Nietzsche, not only are the "virtues" of the herd to be contrasted with those of the *Übermenschen*, but we are even exhorted not to be virtuous beyond our strength.[16] Hume explicitly distinguished heroic virtue from the virtues of goodness and benevolence, which are contrasted with things we call "great in human affections."[17] Finally, in Christian ethics, though it is clear that love is either to be seen as the supreme virtue, or is embedded in virtues such as patience, humility, kindness, and compassion, it is unclear (at least to me) how heroic (saintly) such virtues are meant to be. Tolstoy apparently tortured himself and made his life and the lives of those near him miserable by trying to live according to the edicts of the Sermon on the Mount. From a Christian standpoint, are we all to live according to these edicts?

In light of the distinction between ordinary and heroic or saintly virtue, how are we meant to understand 'best action' and 'right action'? In Nietzsche there is often a relativity: What is best (and right) for the herd is not best for the strong, the heroic, or the excellent creative type, but one can understand a notion of best action *simpliciter* – namely actions expressive of supreme virtue. In Aristotle, some virtues such as magnificence and *megalopsychia* are not universal, and it is not clear that all of us should even aspire to attain those circumstances which make those virtues possible. In that case, generous but not magnificent acts can be right.[18] In Christian ethics, maybe, this relativity is not present; a right or best action is one that Jesus would or might perform, assuming that such acts are in our power. In the remainder of this article I want to show that perfectionistic strivings toward actions demanded by supreme virtue may not be required and may even be ill advised.

How might a distinction between "heroic" or "supreme" virtue and "ordinary" virtue allow room for a (relatively) undemanding form of virtue ethics? On the face of it, one might say, it leaves no room, for as long as acts of supreme virtue are in one's power, the agent should perform them. However, the distinction does complicate this simple picture, for it calls into question how we are to understand perfectionism as a virtue.

Is virtuous perfectionism to be measured by the standards of supreme virtue or by the standards of ordinary virtue? To what extent is virtuous perfectionism relative to the strength or other features of the agent? Consider a person who could create truly outstanding artwork or inventions were she to devote less time to her family, but she turns her back on such a life of creativity. Or consider an agent who could perform acts of supreme benevolence, for example by living and working with the poor in Cambodia for the organization Servants. Though "ordinarily" virtuous, she does not have the strength to perform such acts without considerable personal suffering. She is constitutionally rather weak, she has no religious faith to sustain her, and she is made miserable by others' suffering. How should we understand virtuous perfectionism with respect to such agents?

One possible way of understanding virtuous perfectionism in line with the distinction between ordinary and heroic virtue is to follow some suggestions of Nietzsche, who appears to hold that virtue is relative to types of individuals, but that the best acts are those that express the virtues of the best type. Although such acts are best, we are not necessarily of a "type" that should perform them. Without necessarily agreeing with the way Nietzsche draws the relevant distinctions, we may note that he speaks of at least two kinds of ordinary virtue: the "virtues" of the herd, and those of the weak. Of the former, he claims in one place:

> On the other hand, the herd-man in Europe today makes himself out to be the only permissible kind of man and glorifies the qualities through which he is tame, peaceable and useful to the herd as the real human virtues: namely public spirit, benevolence, consideration, industriousness, moderation, modesty, forbearance, pity.[19]

Of the latter, Nietzsche claims in *On the Genealogy of Morals*: "To demand of strength that it should *not* express itself as strength . . . it makes as little sense as to demand of weakness that it should express itself as strength."[20] Nietzschean claims may suggest the following solution to the problem of the demandingness of virtue ethics: It is natural to understand O in terms of M. But maybe this is a mistake. Maybe there should be a two-tiered conception of rightness: rightness for those with ordinary virtue and rightness for those with supreme virtue. Though in ordinary parlance virtue seems to be a threshold concept (otherwise nobody, or virtually nobody, would be virtuous) and thereby a concept that is contrasted with "perfect" or "ideal" virtue, I find the two-tiered solution unattractive, for it ignores the aspiration to transcend ordinary virtue – an aspiration that may be permitted and even at times required – and it neglects the dynamic aspects of virtuous perfectionism.

Without subscribing to a Nietzschean position of "virtues for the herd," or to a strong relativization of virtue, one may however acknowledge some sense to his point: namely, that virtues are contoured to some extent by differences in individuals, including their strength, and choices to lead ordinary lives. Acts of supreme virtue are not necessarily the target of *virtuous* perfectionism. In short, even if virtuous perfectionism is morally required, at least *pro tanto*, it is not on this view required that we all do the best we can, as measured by the standards of "supreme" virtue. Though agents *may* be admired for being "virtuous beyond their strength" in performing an act of this type, the virtue of perfectionism may not require them to perform such an act. It is important, though, to note the following point: They are morally required, over time, to improve their strength, even while leading ordinary lives, moving more or less gradually from states of self-control to ordinary virtue to more admirable forms of virtue. No formula spelling out requirements can be given for this moral development: Its rate, degree, and nature will depend intimately on circumstances. There is no formula for determining when, for example, a highly talented pianist should pursue a concert career beyond the limits of his psychological strength, or a woman with dependent children to move her family in order to help those in the Third World.

I have claimed then that there may be actions possessing the following characteristics:

- They are the best acts as measured by standards of supreme (heroic or saintly virtue).
- They are within the agent's power (and known by the agent to be so).
- Given the circumstances of the agent, they are not *mandated* by requirements of *virtuous* perfectionism *in the agent* (given those circumstances).[21]

However, it has not been shown that *overall* virtue may not demand such acts. In short, it has not yet been established that a virtue ethics accepting O_4 and its identification with M_4 is not overly demanding in its moral requirements. Though acts of supreme virtue may not always be the target of *perfectionism* as a virtue, perfectionism is only one virtue, issuing only in *pro tanto* requirements.

The performance of right acts (overall) may be highly demanding if the targets of other virtues relevant to assessing rightness, such as benevolence, do not take into account facts such as the strength and circumstances of the agent. It is true that I have not adjudicated between the second and third strategies available to a virtue ethics wishing to overcome the demandingness objection (see Section 1). However, if employment of the second strategy results in a virtue ethics that is too demanding in its requirements, we may yet claim that failure to do what is required need not result in blameworthiness, for we might claim that unless there is some sort of emergency, one cannot blame agents who, in developing themselves morally, meet the target of a virtue whose field is striving for excellence.

I have suggested then that virtue ethics can meet the demandingness objection without subscribing to a satisficing criterion of rightness. It is important to realize, however, that this conclusion is relative to one species of virtue ethics, namely one that accepts O_4 and M_4 as criteria of right and best act, respectively. The solution turns on the idea that *best* meeting the targets of some virtues (notably perfectionism) does not necessarily require emulating the acts of supremely virtuous agents. This solution is not available to those virtue ethicists who subscribe to M_1, M_2, or M_3, for those criteria are expressed in terms of acts or motivations of supremely virtuous agents.

Though a satisficing criterion of the right has not here been defended, it is permitted to "satisfice" in a weaker sense. Though agents are required to perform best acts (understood in terms of M_4), the norms for what is best may not, in relation to certain agents, be those appropriate to supremely virtuous agents. Furthermore, if best acts on this understanding are still too demanding, for reasons stated previously, the agent may be "permitted" to "satisfice" in the following sense: Though morally required to perform best acts, agents who fail to do so may not be subject to blame, even where such acts are in their power and known by them to be in their power.

Notes

1. See Tim Mulgan, "Slote's Satisficing Consequentialism," *Ratio* 6 (1993): 121–34.
2. This conception is explicated in Christine Swanton, "A Virtue Ethical Account of Right Action," *Ethics* 112 (2001): 32–52.
3. See Michael Slote, "Moderation, Rationality, and Virtue," in Sterling M. McMurrin, ed., *The Tanner Lectures on Human Values VII*, Salt Lake City: University of Utah Press, 1986, 56–99; Michael Stocker, *Plural and Conflicting Values*, Oxford University Press, 1990.
4. Thomas Hurka, *Virtue, Vice, and Value*, Oxford University Press, 2001.
5. Hurka, *Virtue, Vice, and Value*, 220.
6. See Michael Slote, *Morals from Motives*, Oxford University Press, 2001.
7. See Rosalind Hursthouse, *On Virtue Ethics*, Oxford University Press, 1999.
8. Swanton, "A Virtue Ethical Account of Right Action."
9. See further Swanton, "A Virtue Ethical Account of Right Action."
10. The formulation in terms of 'might' is preferred by Linda Trinkaus Zagzebski in *Virtues of the Mind: An Inquiry into the Nature of Virtue and the Ethical Foundations of Knowledge*, Cambridge University Press, 1996.
11. Because a supremely virtuous agent does not act out of character, we do not need the qualification "acting characteristically."
12. See Martha Nussbaum, "Non-Relative Virtues: An Aristotelian Approach," in Peter A. French, Theodore E. Uehling Jr., and Howard K. Wettstein, eds., *Midwest Studies in Philosophy XIII*, University of Minnesota Press, 1988, 32–53.
13. See further for depth motivational aspects of virtue, Christine Swanton, *Virtue Ethics: A Pluralistic View*, Oxford University Press, 2003, esp. Ch. 8.
14. Karen Horney, *Neurosis and Human Growth: The Struggle Toward Self-Realization*, New York: Norton paperback, 1970; first published 1950, 196.
15. Horney, *Neurosis and Human Growth*, 317.
16. *Zarathustra*, trans. Walter Kaufmann. 4th Part, "On The Higher Man" 13, *The Portable Nietzsche*, New York: Penguin Books, 1976, 403.

17. David Hume, *Treatise of Human Nature*, L. A. Selby-Bigge, ed., Oxford University Press, 1968, 599, 603.

18. There is debate within Aristotle scholarship about how this claim squares with the following doctrine of the unity of the virtues: A person can have one virtue if and only if he or she has them all. I agree with Stephen M. Gardiner, "Aristotle's Basic and Non-Basic Virtues," in D. N. Sedley, ed., *Oxford Studies in Ancient Philosophy* XX, Oxford University Press, 2001, 261–95, who claims that "for most people, these virtues [such as magnificence] cannot be put into practice, because they lack the external goods necessary to exercise them" (270), but that they are nonetheless genuine, distinct virtues. Hence I agree with his claim that the doctrine of the unity of the virtues does not apply to such virtues.

19. Friedrich Nietzsche, *Beyond Good and Evil*, trans. R. J. Hollingdale, New York: Penguin, 1973, §199. Two questions should be distinguished. Are the "herd-virtues" virtues for the herd, but not virtues for the best type? Are "herd-virtues" not virtues for anyone but are extolled (mistakenly) as virtues? In my experience, a set of "virtues" with analogous issues is uncompetitiveness (where even in team sports in many schools, competitiveness is removed by not keeping score, and sport is played solely "for fun"), inoffensiveness, being "positive" (where critical challenge is described as negative), being a "team player," and being compliant. The issues concern where lines should be drawn between virtues, and vices of excess.

20. *On the Genealogy of Morals*, trans. Douglas Smith, Oxford: World's Classics, 1996, First Essay 12, 29.

21. It may appear that I have subscribed to a satisficing criterion of rightness in one of Thomas Hurka's two senses, namely the comparative interpretation. According to this interpretation, a satisficing criterion of the right demands that an agent's required contribution meet a threshold, but the threshold is relative to options that are available to her. On my view, there is agent-relativity (of a different kind) in the target of perfectionism as a virtue, but attaining this target is partially constitutive of what it is *best* for the agent to do. See Thomas Hurka, "Two Kinds of Satisficing," *Philosophical Studies*, 59 (1990): 107–11.

10

Could Aristotle Satisfice?

Michael Byron

Introduction

It is widely known that Herbert Simon introduced the notion of satisficing in order to provide an alternative to maximizing conceptions of rationality. What may be less well understood is that he sought to avoid what were (to his mind) equally unpalatable treatments of practical reasoning. Simon observed that social scientists were divided in their treatment of rationality. Economists granted *homo œconomicus* an absurdly omniscient rationality. On the other hand, social psychologists often explained behavior solely in terms of affect, edging rationality out of the account.[1]

Simon's account of rationality, in contrast, aims to stake out a middle ground by taking account of the ways in which human rationality is bounded, while eschewing the elimination of rationality in favor of affect. In particular, the bounds of our rationality include limitations on our knowledge of the consequences of our actions, ignorance regarding what value we will ultimately attach to those consequences we do foresee, and finite capacity to grasp the alternatives available in any choice situation.[2] The decision rule Simon developed within this account of bounded rationality he called satisficing, and he contrasted it with maximizing, which, he claimed, only the unbounded rationality of *homo œconomicus* can even hope to attain.

The intuitive motivation for a satisficing decision rule is straightforward. If the rationality of *homo œconomicus* is not feasible for us, and if we wish to have some explicit standard of rational choice that *is* feasible for us, then we need a rule that presupposes a limited, bounded rationality. Simon's proposed standard requires rational agents to select an action all of whose possible outcomes the agent regards as satisfactory. In that way, no matter what happens, the agent is assured of a satisfactory outcome. Recent accounts of satisficing, such as those that I will discuss here, set aside Simon's satisficing rule and its requirement that we rate each possible outcome as satisfactory or unsatisfactory. Instead, these alternative satisficing theories ask us to search for the first alternative or action whose outcome we expect to be satisfactory. Simon's original rule employs a simplified valuation function according to which it is *not* necessary to place every outcome in an ordinal ranking, and it banishes probabilities from rational choice. Both of these simplifying features make Simon's rule computationally minimalist (as he intended). Still, something about the newer satisficing rule seems quite natural: The new rule captures the idea that the satisficer stops searching upon finding the first satisfactory alternative, where the agent serially evaluates alternatives as to their likelihood of satisfying his or her preferences (or some similar measure of satisfaction). Whereas Simon's decision rule is computationally minimalist, the newer satisficing rule simplifies by providing a principled way to limit the number of alternatives evaluated. It is thus a "stopping rule."

Aristotle, in a different historical and philosophical context, sought a middle path of his own for the account of practical reason. On the one hand, Plato's rationalist ethics made the *pathe* (passions) and *epithumia* (appetites) the causes of all wrongdoing, and he had insisted that only an intellectual grasp of the form of the good provides a basis for rational (and moral) choice.[3] Like our economists in this respect at least, Plato's account of practical reason puts a heavy burden on our rational capacities. On the other hand, the sophists of Aristotle's time had developed an elaborate relativism, according to which discourse about the good merely reflects the competing *pathe* of speakers and their communities. Unlike that of our social psychologists, the sophists' account does not seek to eliminate reason from the explanation of behavior, but it does minimize the notion of rational choice by suggesting that no set of *pathe* – and so no judgment about goods – is ultimately more rational than any other. Aristotle developed a path between these two sorts of views, according to which reason had a role in governing the *pathe* and *epithumia*, and yet those elements were important components in the explanation of rational and moral behavior.

Some recent discussions of satisficing have been couched in terms that Aristotle would have understood. Christine Swanton claims that satisficing is or expresses virtue[4]; Michael Slote contends that satisficing might contribute to a good life, and so be an intrinsic good[5]; and David Schmidtz seeks to establish a place for satisficing in the account of practical reason.[6] All of these authors distance themselves from Aristotle in the course of embracing satisficing. It is not obvious that an Aristotelian view of practical reason can help itself to a concept that is at home in contemporary accounts. For instance, an Aristotelian might be hard-pressed to incorporate the Kantian conception of rational will developed by Christine Korsgaard.[7] I would like to explore the suggestions of these authors and evaluate the extent to which an Aristotelian could embrace the concept of satisficing.

In the course of doing so it will not be necessary to rely on a complete exegesis and interpretation of Aristotle's ethics. Instead, I will need just a few theses, claims that I hope will be uncontroversially and recognizably Aristotelian.

- Human beings have a common nature and function (*ergon*).
- Human flourishing is the successful performance of that function.
- The virtues are excellences that enable one to flourish.
- Reason and the virtues play a crucial role in the attainment of flourishing.

I realize that these theses are notoriously obscure, and their obscurity is part of the rationale that the authors I discuss might give for rejecting an Aristotelian ethics or account of practical reasoning. Where necessary I will elaborate these claims, but I wish to leave them as open as possible. My aim is not to convict anyone of being anti-Aristotelian (though some might welcome that charge); rather, given that contemporary authors have abandoned some of these claims and the theoretic backdrop that supports them, I wish to examine what someone who accepts many of these ideas would have to do in order to accommodate the intuitively attractive notion of satisficing.

What Is Satisficing?

Satisficing, as I will use the term, refers to the strategy of choosing an alternative or action whose outcome is or is expected to be satisfactory rather than optimal. Everyone writing about satisficing seems to agree on at least that much. Slote and other defenders of a radical form of satisficing insist that it is often rationally permissible to choose a satisfactory, suboptimal alternative even when a better alternative is known to be available.[8] Slote conceives of optimality in terms of well-being, or an individual's personal good. An optimal alternative is one that best promotes the agent's good in given circumstances. A satisfactory but suboptimal alternative is one that promotes the agent's good to some satisfactory degree but is not the best possible alternative in that respect. In a well-known example, Slote claims that it might be rational to decline a candy bar after lunch, even if one knows that one would enjoy it and that eating the candy bar would thereby increase one's well-being.[9] Slote intends this case to illustrate how radical his claim is: Declining the candy bar is rational, he says, because it is permissible not to seek what is best. So it is important to his case that eating the candy bar *would* be a better alternative – by the agent's own lights – in terms of promoting the agent's well-being.

Slote claims that his conception of satisficing exemplifies the idea of "rational supererogation." This notion is supposed to parallel moral supererogation. A morally supererogatory action is praiseworthy in part because it exceeds the demands of duty. Some people take heroic actions, for example, to be admirable but not morally required. The category is supposed to capture a class of actions that are morally good actions but somehow too demanding to be morally required of all who might find themselves in the same circumstances. If we recognize the intuitive appeal of such a class of actions, then we may find a maximizing account of the good implausible. The reason is that, if some actions are good but not required, then morality cannot be simply a matter of maximizing the good. For if the maximizing account were right, then morality would require that we do the best available action, and supererogation would be impossible.

Similarly, Slote argues, it is sometimes rationally permissible to choose an action that is less than the best, though we may still admire or respect someone who strives to do the best. Some actions are "rationally supererogatory": They are rationally permissible, but performing them is somehow more than rationality requires. One might, for instance, look for the best deal on a new television. That's certainly rational, but most people would agree that settling for something less could also be rational: It is not *irrational* to spend a little more. If "rationally supererogatory" actions exist, then no maximizing conception of rationality is quite correct. For if the maximizing account were correct, then rationality would require us always to do the optimal action, and rational supererogation would be impossible.

David Schmidtz denies that accepting a satisfactory alternative is rational when a better one is readily available.[10] Schmidtz contends that, if I must choose between A and B, if both are available, and if I prefer A, then all else equal the fact that A and B are both satisfactory cannot make

it rational for me to choose B. Because it is not a difference between A
and B, he says, it cannot make a difference to my choice: If I prefer A and
that's the only relevant consideration, then I should choose it. Schmidtz's
move here links the notion of rationality to that of action for a reason, in
particular action for the sake of some end. That is, Schmidtz approaches
the assessment of the rationality of action in terms of whether or to what
extent an agent had a reason to act. This link might seem obvious, but
it is one that is sometimes lost. I think part of what leads Slote to the
idea that we may rationally choose B even when we prefer A is that he
loses touch with the intentionality or directedness of rational action. He
focuses instead on "rational permissibility," or what you can do without
being convicted of irrationality or unreasonableness. Schmidtz, in contrast, links rationality with the idea of what we have reason to do, and as
a result he rejects Slote's brand of satisficing.

Schmidtz follows Slote in characterizing satisficing as the employment
of a stopping rule. When I am evaluating my options and I do not want
to spend all day looking for the best one, I might like to have some principled way to know when to stop. The satisficing rule says: Stop when you
discover a course of action whose expected utility exceeds some threshold
of satisfaction. That is, pick the first satisfactory alternative. Satisficing is
thus justified, when it is justified, by its cost savings: By saving time and
other resources on my search for alternatives, I can have a satisfactory
alternative and my (remaining) resources too. And for many choices, a
satisfactory alternative is good enough. The interesting question at this
point will always be, as I suggest below, "Good enough for what?" In the
meantime, it is worth noting that Schmidtz's conception of satisficing is
at home in a maximizing conception of rationality. This is so, as I have
argued elsewhere,[11] because Schmidtz's satisficer must aim at optimality overall, and satisficing is justifiable in terms of this goal just when it
provides a net cost savings, as it often does. In other words, satisficing is
rational when it saves time, and that time will be useful for other, perhaps
more valuable, pursuits for the person seeking the best life possible.

Does Satisficing Express Moderation?

A most intriguing discussion of the connection between satisficing and
virtue is Christine Swanton's. She attempts to defend the rationality of satisficing (using basically Slote's radical conception) on the ground that satisficing behavior is rationally permissible when it expresses a virtue such
as moderation. She writes, "On my view, the rationality of the satisficer's

choice is to be understood in terms of the rationality of *expressing* the habit of moderation."[12] We will examine what she means by this in a moment. First, though, we need to explore the concept of 'moderation' at work here.

Moderation seems to be the habit of being a contented satisficer, and this conception makes Swanton's justification of satisficing problematic.

> It is questionable whether one has the virtue of moderation when one is prepared to maximize.... For, as Slote points out, the virtue is one in which it is not the case that, in all contexts, one *cares* about opportunities to maximize. It is precisely the virtue of being content with adequate rather than maximal personal good. It is not merely the virtue of not always being disposed to calculate about the maximal quantity.[13]

Notice that Swanton defines moderation as the state of being content with adequate, not maximal, personal good. Hence my suggestion that moderate folks are contented satisficers. I don't wish to quibble over a word: That's what Swanton (or perhaps Slote) means by moderation, and they are free to use the word that way. I would note that this "virtue" does not resemble Aristotle's virtue of temperateness (to use a different word). Recall what Aristotle says about the temperate person in the *Nicomachean Ethics*: "If something is pleasant and conducive to health or fitness, he will desire this moderately and in the right way; and he will desire in the same way anything else that is pleasant, if it is no obstacle to health and fitness, does not deviate from the fine, and does not exceed his means" (1119a16–20).[14] This virtue concerns what is pleasant, especially what is pleasant to touch or taste. Temperate people have a reasonable level of desire for healthy pleasures, Aristotle says, and he explains further that the absence of such pleasures generally causes them no pain. They have a reasonable level of desire for other pleasures as long as those pleasures are not unhealthy, shameful, or ruinously expensive.

Notice that in a sense the temperate person *does* optimize. In an obscure passage where Aristotle discusses the idea that a moral virtue is a mean, he also claims that, in another sense, it is an extreme. "That is why virtue, as far as its essence and the account stating what it is are concerned, is a mean, but, as far as the best [condition] and the good [result] are concerned, it is an extremity" (1107a6–8). Considered as a habit of feeling and desiring pleasure, temperateness is a mean because the temperate person has neither too little nor too much. But considered as a virtue and an element of a good human life, it is the best. And so the temperate person, by striving to be temperate, aims at the best and thus optimizes. This way of speaking can mislead, because it might suggest that the temperate person aims to *maximize* some quantity or property, and that is not the case; the best amount of pleasure, for example, is rarely the maximal amount (if the idea of "maximal amount of pleasure" is even intelligible). On Aristotle's view, flourishing cannot be characterized in terms of a single quantity amenable to maximization. Nor is any individual virtue to be conceived in terms of maximizing some quantity. It is not even the case that flourishing is a simple group of goods that might be brought together in some optimal fashion. And so in the ordinary sense of maximizing, Aristotle's account of human flourishing is not a maximizing account. All the same, temperateness does not involve choosing what is merely satisfactory either, and so temperate action is not in itself the result of satisficing choice.

Like Swanton, Aristotle seems to think that the temperate person will not maximize pleasures, for that would reflect a too-strong desire. But as indicated by the passage quoted above, Aristotle thinks that an overriding consideration is whether a desire deviates from "the fine." Moderately strong desires for healthy pleasures do not so deviate; other desires may, however, deviate from the fine, because of either their strength or their objects. This concern with the goodness of the desire is a crucial feature of temperateness that has disappeared from Swanton's conception of moderation. Its absence may be detected in her characterization of moderation as "the virtue of being content with adequate rather than maximal personal good." For here the question arises: adequate for what? Aristotle *could* have characterized temperateness as the virtue of being content with less-than-maximal pleasure, where the notion of adequacy would be cashed out with respect to his conception of flourishing. Temperate people pursue and enjoy only as much pleasure and only the varieties of pleasure as are consistent with promoting their flourishing. But I must postpone further discussion of this question and first consider the idea that satisficing is rational because it expresses the virtue of moderation.

Swanton follows Michael Stocker in thinking that motivated action, or action for reasons, need not be done for the sake of its consequences. She contends that "some motivations are not goal-directed at all, but are 'expressive,' as in 'I did it *out of* friendship'."[15] She adds: "The assumption [that motivation always concerns consequences] is false, however: even if the point of cultivating a virtue lies in its probabilizing agent flourishing, one fails to possess the virtue of, e.g., justice if one's motivations for just action concern one's own flourishing. In general, the virtuous agent does not standardly or always act *for the sake of* some consequence at all; but rather simply acts *out of* or *from* the virtue in question."[16] In other words, if you now do what is just only for the sake of your own individual benefit, then you have not in so acting exhibited or expressed the virtue of justice. Swanton thus proposes to extend the concept of motivation beyond a concern for the consequences of actions, to include "expressive motivations" as well. And so, on her view, I might rationally choose to do what is just from justice, even when the just action does not maximize personal well-being, agent-neutral value, or perhaps anything else.

In one way, Swanton seems to agree with Aristotle in what she says here about justice: If my *sole* concern in doing what is just is my own well-being, then I am not (thereby) just. Aristotle can agree: The just person does what is just for its own sake, knowing that it is just, and from a fixed habit or disposition to do such actions (applying the general remarks about the virtuous person's actions at 1105a26f to the virtue of justice in particular). Hence by doing the action *solely* for my own sake and not for the sake of justice, I would exhibit the fact that I am not (yet) just.[17]

But Swanton may mislead when she claims that "the virtuous agent does not standardly or always act for the sake of some consequence at all." The claim is susceptible of two distinct interpretations: (1) There is no goal such that all of a virtuous agent's actions are done for the sake of that goal; or (2) some of a virtuous agent's actions are such that they are not done for the sake of any goal whatever. Reading (1) is consistent with Aristotle's view: Although flourishing is the ultimate end, it is an Aristotelian commonplace that virtuous action need not aim at directly promoting one's own flourishing, or indeed any other single end.[18] We do best when we pursue a variety of final ends – ends pursued for their own sake, and perhaps incommensurable ends at that. Swanton, however, seems to need in addition the more radical reading (2), because she intends to say that some virtuous actions have "expressive" motivations and not "goal-directed" motivations. But (2) itself is ambiguous.

The ambiguity concerns the term 'consequence': Swanton claims that virtuous action need not be done for the sake of its consequences. On one construal, 'consequence' refers to the causal consequences of a course of action. I might flip the switch to turn on the light. I might drink some water to slake my thirst. These actions have consequences that can be desired as ends: I want light or drink. I perform the action as *a means* to the desired consequence. Actions that we perform for the sake of consequences in this sense we do because they are instrumentally valuable in bringing about the desired end, and we might not otherwise do them. Were the light on, I would not flip the switch; were I not thirsty, I might not drink water now.

Given a broader reading, however, the term 'consequence' might refer to any goal, whether the causal consequence of an action or not. Some goals must be specified by reference to how they are to be attained. To become a ballplayer, I must play ball. To become a teacher, I must teach. The distinction I am drawing is sometimes made between two kinds of *means*: Sometimes called "mere" means or instrumental means, one kind is externally related to its end. Flipping a switch is one way to produce light, but there are others; drinking water is one means among others of slaking thirst. The other kind of means, sometimes called "constitutive means," is internally related to its end, in the sense that no specification of the end aimed at by such means is possible without at the same time at least suggesting what the means are. You cannot reasonably aim to be a teacher without intending to teach.[19] Our actions can be related to our goals in at least these two distinct ways. And these two ways raise different possible interpretations of Swanton's claim.

If by 'consequence' Swanton refers only to the narrower sense just described – the causal consequences of an action, such that action is a mere means to the consequences – then Aristotle would agree that not all action is done for the sake of consequences. Indeed, he draws this distinction himself in the opening passages of the *Nicomachean Ethics*.[20] Yet Swanton's contrast between "goal-directed" and "expressive" motivations could suggest that the latter have no goal whatever.

If so, then Swanton might intend 'consequence' to include any type of goal. On that reading she is committed to the view that an action might be done for the sake of nothing at all. It seems possible that we might sometimes act for no reason: If you find me tearing a sheet of paper into tiny pieces, you might ask why I was doing that. And to this question I might reply: "Oh, no reason, it's just absent-minded distraction." But it would be another matter altogether to claim that *virtuous* action might be done for the sake of nothing at all.[21]

To see why there can be no goal-less virtuous actions, we need to examine the role that virtues play in motivation. Swanton wants to say that an action can be rational if it expresses a virtue: Someone acted *out of* temperateness or *from* courage. That way of speaking has a satisfactory Aristotelian interpretation. It suggests that the person possesses the relevant virtue, and that the virtue caused the action.[22] But notice that saying this much does not yet show that the action could lack a goal. Consider an act done from courage: Suppose you overcome an aversion to swimming in order to demonstrate to your daughter that she has nothing to fear from climbing into the pool. It might be correct to say, with Swanton, that you did the act from or out of courage. But is that your reason for doing it? If I saw what you were doing and knew that you disliked swimming, I might ask why you were in the pool. You might say that you wanted to show your daughter that she has nothing to fear. And when you state your intention in doing the action, you explain *that for the sake of which* you do the action. Every intentional action has an intended end, and every virtuous action is intentional. Thus, every virtuous action has an end or goal.

Swanton might reply as follows: Consider the courageous person's response when asked, "Why are you doing that?" The person might say instead, "I'm doing this out of courage." Perhaps this reply captures the sense in which the action expresses the motive. But notice that the "why" question admits of different interpretations. I might persist: "Oh, I understand what *made* you do it; I was asking what you hoped to *accomplish* by doing that." That is, the "why" question might inquire about the cause of the action (courage), or it might inquire about the goal of the action. Now from an Aristotelian perspective, reasons are also causes: They state the final cause of the action, that for the sake of which it is done. The virtue itself, in contrast, is part of the efficient cause of the action. The fact that a virtue causes an action does not and cannot by itself show that an action might altogether lack an end or goal.[23]

None of this is to deny that an end might be (solely) expressive: I might aim merely to express my affection for you in doing a particular action.[24] In such a case, the action itself constitutes the end and is no mere means to it. I aim at nothing beyond the expression. I might in such a case say, "I did it out of friendship," meaning that my affection caused the action; but once again, to say that does not show that the action had no goal. The goal was perhaps, in this case, to express my affection and no more. Other actions might involve expressions of affection that had further intended ends: Perhaps I meant my expression of affection to move you to help me, or to deceive you, or to amuse you. And in such cases, the expression of affection might be the means to an independently specifiable end. In both cases, the action has an end, something for the sake of which it is done. It seems to me that the only actions done for the sake of nothing are actions done for no reason. And virtuous action cannot be done for no reason. This point about action is quite general, not uniquely Aristotelian.

So a charitable reading of Swanton would attribute to her another target, namely the strictly instrumentalist thought that rational action always aims at some end that is independent of the action, and to which the action is an antecedently specifiable means. Her use of the term 'consequence', as I have indicated, might well denote as much: Virtuous action is not done merely for the sake of such consequences. Aristotle remarks that virtuous action is done for its own sake (1105a33). The performance of a particular kind of action might itself be the end aimed at, rather than some independent end. If this is all Swanton means by "expressive motivations," then her view so far seems harmonious with Aristotle, who would deny that virtuous action is always and only a means to flourishing. Aristotle might also embrace the idea, implicit in Swanton's argument, that virtuous action cannot be conceived as maximizing the value of consequences (in the narrow, external sense).

So how should we assess Swanton's claim that satisficing is rational because it expresses moderation? If moderation is merely the disposition to satisfice, then satisficing is trivially moderate. What remains to be seen, however, is whether such moderation is virtuous, and Swanton (following Slote) offers no argument contending that it is. The fact, if it is a fact, that some actions have "expressive motivations" and are not mere means to an end does not by itself show that satisficing *qua* expression of moderation is or can be rational. Aristotle might agree that satisficing is rational if or when it expressed temperateness. And some instances of satisficing could express temperateness: I might not seek the biggest and best slice of cake, but merely one that's good enough, and I might do so out of temperateness. Swanton distances herself from the Aristotelian concept of temperateness, and in so doing she surrenders the appeal to the rationality of virtue as described by Aristotle's theory. The surrogate in her view seems to be the argument that, because virtue ethics entails that acting virtuously is good, and because it is rational to be good, it follows that if satisficing is virtuous then it is rational.

How Is Satisficing Related to Practical Wisdom?

In general, the answer to the question of whether satisficing is rational depends on whether it is rational to settle for what is "good enough." The answer to this question will in turn depend on two further issues: First, how good is "good enough," and second, good enough for what? These questions are related. Consider them in order.

First, how good is "good enough"? This question depends for its content on the context in which it is posed. In theories that develop a preference satisfaction or expected utility account of satisficing, what is "good enough" is judged by reference to a threshold expected utility or related quantity. In other theories, the threshold may be some aspiration level of value, such as money, pleasure, cake, and so on. Many people have observed that not just any threshold will make satisficing rational. An absurdly high threshold would collapse satisficing into optimizing, or at any rate into pursuit of the best available option. In such a case, the satisficer would never be satisfied and would end up choosing the best available option anyway. A very low threshold would be equally irrational in many contexts, because it would amount to taking the first option that came along.

Some contexts, of course, might call for optimizing or for taking the first option. Sometimes we seek the best, regardless of expense, and nothing less will do. It can be quite rational to do so in significant matters, though it would usually be silly when seeking a pencil. We also sometimes take the first option, which works fairly well for taxis but would likely be a poor strategy when looking for a spouse. Few defenders of satisficing, however, would claim that it is *always* rational to satisfice. Rather, they typically claim that in many cases it is; and in general we should say that the threshold or aspiration level should be neither too high nor too low. We might have reason to satisfice, then, when we lack or do not care to employ the resources to seek the best option but prefer not to accept the first option to come along. Satisficing represents a decision rule intermediate between these extremes.

An action that implements the satisficing rule – a satisficing action – is never as such a virtuous action, at least not on an Aristotelian view. No action is, merely as such, intrinsically virtuous.[25] For an action to be virtuous, it must be done deliberately, for its own sake, and from a fixed disposition or habit. These are also, of course, criteria for *vicious* action. What distinguishes virtuous from vicious action is that the former alone is done from a correct conception of flourishing. For satisficing itself to be a virtue, it would have to be a habit. So even if I had a habit of satisficing under certain situations, and even if my threshold or aspiration level seemed reasonable, you would still need to know something about my conception of flourishing in order to know whether my habit of satisficing reflects correct choice or something more akin to laziness. No amount of tinkering with the decision rule can render its application virtuous, independent of the agent's possessing a correct conception of flourishing.

The strategy of satisficing is nothing more than a cost-saving strategy with strictly instrumental value, and this claim is borne out by the fact that it is always in point to ask the satisficer, "Good enough for what?" The satisficer chooses the first alternative deemed to be good enough, but the concept of satisfactory – what is "good enough" – makes essential reference to some further end. The satisficer chooses in light of that further end: In general, satisficing is rational when it provides a cost savings to the rational deliberator. The cost savings comes in the form of time and other resources not devoted to further deliberation. This savings is valuable not for its own sake but for the sake of some further end(s) to which one may then devote those resources.[26] One consequence of this claim is that it is impossible to satisfice with respect to one's ultimate end, as doing so would leave one without resources for answering the question "Good enough for what?"[27]

Consider two stock examples. I might satisfice when I try to sell my car. I know roughly how much the thing is worth, but I dislike taking the time required to meet with prospective buyers, show them the car, give them a test drive, and so forth. If a buyer offers me a sum near what I think it is worth, I may choose to accept the offer on the grounds that it is satisfactory. Why might doing so be rational? It could be rational if the value of the time I save in taking an early offer compensates me for the disparity in price between the offer and the perceived value of the car. But why should I care about time? Not for its own sake, surely, but for the sake of other projects to which I would prefer to devote that time. When you ask me why I accepted the offer, I will say that it was good enough, and if you ask, "Good enough for what?" a complete answer will specify those further ends of mine in the light of which I decided to accept the offer. More likely, though, you would receive an incomplete answer, such as "I dislike the hassle of selling stuff."

Schmidtz discusses the decision to choose a satisfactory toothpaste. Perhaps one could find the best toothpaste, but it is just not worth it. "There are cases where we do not care enough about the gap between the satisfactory and the optimal to make it rational to search for the optimal."[28] Once again, satisficing emerges as rational in virtue of cost savings: I could put in the time and energy to discover the best toothpaste, but then what would I have? The best toothpaste – big deal. I would rather use the time on other pursuits. A satisfactory toothpaste is good enough, given the costs *and* benefits of finding a better one. Once again, satisficing emerges as a choice strategy with strictly instrumental value.

Here is an objection to this way of thinking: Why must the question "Good enough for what?" always receive an answer in terms of some further end? Why couldn't one say, "Good enough for *me*!" perhaps thereby expressing one's moderation? Such an answer certainly seems to be common enough. On reflection, however, we should understand that it is not responsive to the question. If I choose a particular course of action and say, "That's good enough," I will ordinarily mean that the alternative is good enough for me. So to reply to the question "Good enough for what?" as suggested is merely redundant. The question asks what features of the alternative in question I find satisfactory and, more important, why I have opted not to seek a better alternative under the circumstances. And if I answer this question, I will refer to my further ends, in light of which I judge my satisficing to be rational.[29]

The applicability of this question to every instance of satisficing suggests that the strategy would play much the same role in an Aristotelian conception of deliberation as it does on instrumentalist accounts. An Aristotelian account of deliberation gives the practical syllogism a prominent role, and the practical syllogism begins with a premise concerning what flourishing requires.[30] The other premise details the circumstances of choice, and the syllogism's conclusion is either an action or a decision (depending on which Aristotelian you talk to). The phronetic agent (the one with *phronesis*, or practical wisdom) decides and acts correctly in each case. So, where satisficing is rational, phronetic agents know that flourishing does not require seeking and choosing the best thing or maximal amount of the kind under consideration. Satisficing emerges as the strategy of choosing what is "good enough" here and now for the sake of the cost savings that the strategy affords one in one's pursuit of flourishing.

Does this account show that an Aristotelian account is a maximizing account of rationality after all? Many Aristotelians adopt what Schmidtz, following Scott MacDonald,[31] calls an "inclusive ultimate end," which is simply the goal of living the best life possible. That end includes a range of other goods, coherently organized and systematically integrated into a life. This is one way to read Aristotle's discussion of flourishing in the first book of the *Nicomachean Ethics*: The best life for us includes the achievement of a range of goods, including quite a number of external goods in addition to the moral and intellectual virtues. Yet Schmidtz is also right to point out that exactly which actions any given person must do under particular circumstances cannot be inferred from any substantive maximizing principle, as is possible for utilitarians for instance. "The material corollaries of this final end will be different for different people, since what is the best life for an individual will depend on that person's circumstances, tastes, and talents."[32] Schmidtz contends, and Aristotelians can agree, that aiming to live the best life possible will entail somewhat different lives for different people, and so no substantive maximizing decision rule can yield the best life for everyone. And even for a particular individual, the demands of *phronesis*, of systematically integrating into a life the various goals and ends one values, are not such that they can be captured by an algorithm or maximizing rule.[33]

What about Antiperfectionism?

One might wonder whether satisficing is itself a constituent of a good human life, or perhaps whether satisficing expresses a virtue that is a constituent of a good life. (We have already explored this question to some degree in examining the relation between "moderation" and satisficing.) Stocker, for example, argues that "antiperfectionism" is a virtue,[34] and Swanton develops the point by contending that satisficing can be rational insofar as satisficing choices manifest the virtue of antiperfectionism. For example, consider a variant of Slote's candy bar case. Swanton describes what she calls an "immoderate satisficer":

> Like Slote's moderate satisficer, he too is unfortunate enough to have a fridge in his office provided by the company, which, alas, contains candy bars. He considers it best to abstain from a candy bar, given his values. He decides, however, that though eating on this occasion is a minor peccadillo, it is a "not bad enough" option to avoid, given the strength of his desires and other contextual features. In short, he intentionally chooses the inferior option because it is "good enough" in the sense of not bad enough. . . .[35]

Swanton argues that this man's choice to eat the candy bar can be rational not because it expresses the virtue of moderation – which she insists it does *not* express, because it is by design an instance of immoderate behavior – but instead because it expresses antiperfectionism. She claims that, "although (a) all-things-considered his life would be better if he were not self-indulgent, it is nonetheless the case that (b) making this effort would be hard on him, and (c) now he wants to lead the kind of life where he is not so hard on himself."[36] After reiterating that the agent's all-things-considered judgment is that declining the candy is best, Swanton claims that "the motive of not being too hard on yourself, which provides the motive for [this instance of] satisficing, is the expression of a virtue – antiperfectionism. Thus, inasmuch as taking the bar is weak, even weak-'willed,' it is not inappropriately weak. According to the virtue of antiperfectionism, it is sometimes appropriate to fail to be rationally supererogatory."[37]

How might Aristotelians respond to this argument? First, recall that weakness of will, or akratic action, is a paradigm of irrationality from an Aristotelian perspective. The akratic satisficer has acted in a way that reason bids him not to act. His action is explicable, if it is, in terms of his passions and not his reasons, and that is one kind of failure in rationality. So at this level, an Aristotelian would deny that akratic action is (even possibly) rational. If Swanton believes that the action is akratic (and her claim seems to be that, though weak, it is not "inappropriately" so), then for an Aristotelian that should count against the action's rationality.

But set this point aside. Swanton defends the rationality of the akratic satisficer not because he is acting on his best reasons but because his action (purportedly) manifests a virtue, and because action that manifests a virtue can be rational. So presumably if Aristotelians wish to deny that akratic satisficing is ever rational, they must show either that acting against one's own decisions is always irrational, or that virtuous actions always implement one's own decisions. Although I think that many Aristotelians are committed to both claims, I don't propose to establish either of them here. Instead, I wish to argue that antiperfectionism is not an Aristotelian virtue – indeed, it is not even a coherent notion on an Aristotelian view – and therefore that Swanton's proposed defense of the rationality of akratic satisficing is out of bounds for Aristotelians.

In Swanton's Stockerian analysis of akratic satisficing, we take for granted that (a) "all things considered his life would be better if he were not self-indulgent," and it follows that his life would be better if he were not self-indulgent *now*. Swanton then claims (c) "now he wants to lead the kind of life where he is not so hard on himself," – that is, he wants the kind of life in which he indulges himself from time to time – in particular, now. This claim, however, seems to reflect a conception of the best life that permits the occasional minor, harmless self-indulgence, in contrast to the conception that seems to be expressed in (a), which prohibits self-indulgence altogether.[38] Now surely he cannot rationally accept both conceptions of the best life, not least of all because they issue conflicting prescriptions in this case. The second conception seems much more plausible (and more Aristotelian, too), and this fact might lead us to wonder why anyone would think that it is better never to be self-indulgent.

If this is right, then we should say one of three things about this case: (1) If the man accepts both conceptions of the best life, then he is irrational for maintaining a contradiction, viz. that one should and should not sometimes indulge oneself.[39] This possibility, however, seems unlikely. (2) If he accepts the extreme conception of the good life that denies him the least little indulgence, then we should say he has a false view about flourishing. In that case, his actions cannot strictly be virtuous at all, much less express the virtue (if there is one) of antiperfectionism. This is so because his enkratic (or non-akratic) actions will direct him toward his false conception of flourishing and thus fail to contribute to his actual flourishing. His akratic actions, in turn, will not be systematically directed toward the correct conception of flourishing in the way required for action to be virtuous. Indeed, if he performs akratic actions with any frequency, an Aristotelian may doubt whether he can have any virtues, because he would exhibit thereby a lack of practical wisdom.[40] (3) If instead he accepts the more plausible conception of flourishing that permits occasional self-indulgence, then his judgment (a) that it would be best never to indulge himself is mistaken and somewhat difficult to explain. Even if the judgment in (a) is better expressed as the view that it would be best if he did not indulge himself *now*, he has made a mistake in reasoning. That mistake would show that he lacked complete *phronesis*, I suppose, because he has reasoned incorrectly about what flourishing requires him to do in this case. His action, then, could not be fully virtuous, diverging as it does from what the phronetic person would do, in particular diverging in the reasoning that produces the action.[41]

It could be that I have misunderstood this case, and Swanton's immoderate satisficer thinks something like this: "Self-indulgence, though not wrong in every case, is usually wrong and would be wrong now. Still, it is so demanding to live up to one's own conception of flourishing; it would not be a grave shortcoming to indulge myself just this once." Let's suppose that his indulgence would indeed be wrong now. I think that this form of reasoning – which could constitute a form of what people often mean nowadays by 'rationalization' – is common enough, but it betrays one of two things. Either we should say that the man has a much less demanding notion of flourishing than he thinks he has; or he is akratic and has developed a vice of not attempting to correct himself. Or perhaps both are true. In any case, it seems that this is not a case in which a satisficer exhibits Aristotelian virtue.

I claimed earlier that the idea of a virtue of antiperfectionism is incoherent on an Aristotelian view. The reason is this: The virtues are the excellences possessed by a person who flourishes. Flourishing is living well, perhaps as well as possible. Hence, if the occasional harmless self-indulgence is part of or consistent with flourishing, as seems likely, then *phronesis* will permit, and perhaps sometimes even require, virtuous people to indulge themselves from time to time. As a result, the very activity that purports to exhibit antiperfectionism will be sought by those who pursue flourishing – presumably "perfectionists." This point is quite general and applies to any antiperfectionist activity, feeling, or trait: If that activity fits coherently into a good life, as any virtuous activity must, then the "perfectionist" may pursue it.[42] If not, then the activity is not virtuous. Hence, no Aristotelian can acknowledge a virtue of antiperfectionism.

A similar argument might reject the concept of rational supererogation. The concept of rational supererogation is applicable only where it is possible to fail to perform the action that rationality deems "best," and yet to act in a way that is still rationally permissible. Once again, the idea is that sometimes we admire those who adhere so strictly to the demands of rationality, even where their actions seem above and beyond what rationality requires. From an Aristotelian perspective, this situation cannot occur, at least not as envisioned by a defender of rational supererogation.[43] My action is completely rational only if it is directed in the (or a) proper way (and it is no simple matter to specify that) toward my flourishing. But the conception of "the best possible life" must be one that I am capable of achieving and not overly demanding, or else it is not truly the best possible life *for me*, that is, for the kind of living thing I am. My actions that fail in some respect or other – perhaps I act akratically from time to time – are to that degree irrational, though they may possess some measure of rationality, as when akratic action reflects a correct decision. That partial rationality may be important to my progress toward flourishing, but it does not make the action "rationally permissible." And so virtuous action and flourishing can never be, for an Aristotelian, rationally supererogatory. That category seems to lack application.

Recall that the context of this discussion is the question of whether satisficing is a constituent of flourishing. Swanton's and Stocker's arguments about satisficing's expressing a virtue of antiperfectionism made this a live option. But an Aristotelian conception of flourishing seems to deny the possibility of such a virtue. I argued earlier that satisficing is of strictly instrumental value, and if this conclusion is correct then satisficing, however useful, cannot itself be a constituent of flourishing. But even if that argument is unsound, we have reason to doubt that satisficing is a virtue. That leaves open the possibility that satisficing represents some other kind of constituent of flourishing, and if proponents of this sort of view wish to defend it, they will need to articulate the link between satisficing and a good life.

Conclusion

The answer to my title question is: Of course Aristotle could satisfice. As a descriptive matter, we all satisfice frequently. No doubt we usually act rationally when we do so. The interesting normative questions are, when is it rationally permissible to satisfice, and how does satisficing fit into the account of practical reason? I have tried to sketch part of an answer to these questions here, contrasting a broadly Aristotelian conception of the virtues and of practical reason with the thinking of several contemporary theorists. I have argued that satisficing is not intrinsically moderate or temperate, and that for an Aristotelian it does not express antiperfectionism (even if there were such a virtue). I might also allude to a point Schmidtz makes in this context, which is that nothing in the satisficing rule requires that the satisficer choose a moderate threshold: One's idea of what is satisfactory in some particular context might be outrageously immoderate. Finally, because satisficing is a cost-saving strategy that has only instrumental value, no one rationally chooses it for its own sake.[44] Hence, satisficing is not itself virtuous, nor does its employment by itself express virtue. As I have said, however, virtuous people do satisfice, when the strategy's cost savings are worthwhile and when using the rule is consistent with virtuous action.

Some recent work on satisficing has sought to develop connections between satisficing and virtue, or particular virtues. I have discussed Swanton, Schmidtz, Stocker, and Slote, but none of them, as far as I know, accepts an Aristotelian conception of the virtues or practical reason. So why should they care if their ideas concerning satisficing cannot in every detail be accommodated within an Aristotelian view?

Perhaps they won't. My point, however, has not been to criticize their work. Their efforts to distance themselves from Aristotle – explicit in some cases, tacit in others – are intelligible in light of the obscurity of much of Aristotle's theory and the implausibility of some of the rest. Their discussions of satisficing, in contrast, are relatively clear and propounded in the context of addressing some particular worry in the theory of practical reason or ethics. In those contexts, the idea of pursuing what is "good enough" is theoretically attractive and might do useful work in an Aristotelian theory. The question has been: How can the notion of satisficing be articulated in the way most at home within an Aristotelian theory? I have tried to show that, even despite the opacity of central Aristotelian theses, a suitable conception of satisficing will likely not be one that makes satisficing itself a virtue or an element of flourishing.

Notes

1. H. A. Simon, *Administrative Behavior*, 3rd ed., The Free Press, 1976, xxvi–xxvii.
2. Simon, *Administrative Behavior*, 81ff.
3. The *locus classicus* of Plato's view is, of course, the *Republic*, book V and especially book VI.
4. Christine Swanton, "Satisficing and Virtue," *Journal of Philosophy* 90 (1993): 33–48.
5. Michael Slote, *From Morality to Virtue*, Oxford University Press, 1994.
6. David Schmidtz, *Rational Choice and Moral Agency*, Princeton University Press, 1995.
7. Christine Korsgaard, *The Sources of Normativity*, Cambridge University Press, 1996.
8. Michael Slote, *Beyond Optimizing*, Cambridge: Harvard University Press, 1989, especially chapters 5 and 6. For a sophisticated defense of radical satisficing, see Michael Weber's contribution to this volume.
9. Slote, *Beyond Optimizing*, chapter 5.
10. Schmidtz, *Rational Choice and Moral Agency*, 38.
11. Michael Byron, "Satisficing and Optimality," *Ethics* 109 (1998): 67–93.
12. Swanton, "Satisficing and Virtue," 40.
13. Swanton, "Satisficing and Virtue," 41, original emphasis.
14. Unless otherwise indicated, all quotations from Aristotle are cited by Bekker number from Aristotle, *Nicomachean Ethics*, tr. Terence Irwin, 2nd edition, Hackett, 1999.
15. Swanton, "Satisficing and Virtue," 40.
16. Swanton, "Satisficing and Virtue," 42–3.
17. The emphasis on "solely" here calls attention to the fact that we can act for the sake of more than one end at once, as when I buy a particular kind of sandwich both to satisfy my hunger and to promote health.
18. Some interpreters maintain otherwise: They claim that reasons get their status from promoting flourishing, conceived as a single, all-encompassing ultimate end. I don't think Aristotelians as such are committed to this claim, though I cannot defend the position here.
19. I do not mean merely being *called* a teacher or being appointed to a certain position. To actually be a teacher, one must teach.
20. "Every craft and every line of inquiry, and likewise every action and decision, seems to seek some good; that is why some people were right to describe the good as what everything seeks. But the ends [that are sought] appear to differ; some are activities, and other as products apart from the activities" (1094a1–6). When the activity itself is the end, the means constitute the end. When the end is a product apart from the activity, clearly such products are

the causal consequences of the activity, such that the activity is a mere means to the end.

21. Elizabeth Anscombe discusses the concept of 'intention' by suggesting that we report our reasons for acting in response to "why" questions. Sometimes, though, we act for no reason, in the sense that there is no suitable intention to be reported, as in the case of absent-minded tearing of paper. See G. E. M. Anscombe, *Intention*, Ithaca, N.Y.: Cornell University Press, 1957.

22. Cf. Aquinas, *Summa Theologiae* I–II, 49, 3.

23. It is helpful in this context to recall Aquinas's distinction between 'human actions' and 'actions of a human', where he distinguishes the former on the grounds that they exhibit rationality through being willed for the sake of some end; cf. *ST* I–II, 1, i. Only human actions may be virtuous or vicious, according to Aquinas, and so he too would claim that all virtuous actions have an intended end.

24. Jonathan Dancy describes a case of attending the funeral of a distant friend of the family and expressing sympathy because it seems the right thing to do, yet without really aiming to console anyone. Here the goal seems to be merely expressing the sympathy; Dancy claims he would not count his expression a failure if no one was consoled by it. See his *Moral Reasons*, Blackwell, 1993, 35. Dancy's own view of this example is that it is "non-purposive," because he claims that he is "not interested in doing a bit of sympathy-expressing." I think, however, that as he describes the case, his action *is* purposive, that its purpose is to express sympathy, and that "doing a bit of sympathy-expressing" is *exactly* what he wants to do (and nothing more). I cannot develop the point further here.

25. Aristotle does claim that actions like murder and theft are always wrong; cf. 1107a9ff. But it seems likely that these actions are wrong by definition, as incorporating in their very concepts the notion of unjustified or wrongful action. The interesting normative question in such cases is not whether a particular instance of murder is wrong but whether a particular homicide is to be counted as an instance of murder.

26. One might argue that satisficing need not be merely instrumentally valuable if it were a component of flourishing and valued for its own sake. This suggestion strikes me as a bit odd: The idea seems to be that along with one's health, family, career, hobbies, and so on, one might include satisficing among the constituents of a good life. Aside from the surface implausibility of this claim, it seems to me wrong-headed in another way. The constituents of flourishing are ends, about the means to which we deliberate. But no one had even heard of satisficing prior to Simon's coining the term. It makes much more sense (to me, at any rate) to think that satisficing might be a tool that we all used without knowing it than to think of it as an end that we (all?) pursued without knowing it.

27. This conclusion generalizes a point I have made elsewhere with respect to satisficing and theories of instrumental rationality; see my "Satisficing and Optimality."

28. Schmidtz, *Rational Choice and Moral Agency*, 36.

29. Satisficing *might* be rational; on the other hand, I might be mistaken to judge that it is.

30. The claim that the practical syllogism begins with a premise concerning flourishing is controversial; indeed, it is a minority view. Jonathan Lear, among others, articulates a more widely held view, according to which the practical syllogism begins with a premise concerning the immediate end of action (a good meal, a ticket to the opera, a pair of shoes) and proceeds to an action that leads to that end. Such an account makes good sense of the practical syllogism as used in deliberation, because it captures the search for suitable means; but the practical syllogism has an additional function. It can also be used to justify action: A complete justification of any particular action will include not only reference to the immediate end sought but also an account of the relationship – if any – between that end and flourishing. The interpretation I favor incorporates the deliberative function of the practical syllogism and its justificatory function and is thus preferable in virtue of its scope. Alasdair MacIntyre develops an account of this sort in *Whose Justice? Which Rationality?*, University of Notre Dame Press, 1988, chap. 8. I am not claiming that the ultimate end subsumes all reasons for action, only that it is always in point to inquire about the relationship between one's action and immediate end on the one hand, and one's ends and flourishing on the other. The virtuous person will have a correct account of these matters. That seems to be the salient point for discussing the relationship between satisficing and *phronesis*.

31. Scott MacDonald, "Ultimate Ends in Practical Reasoning: Aquinas's Aristotelian Psychology and Anscombe's Fallacy," *Philosophical Review* 100 (1991): 31–65.

32. Schmidtz, *Rational Choice and Moral Agency*, 93.

33. If one reads Aristotle differently and does not endorse the idea of an inclusive end, then it is even less plausible to think that the theory adopts a maximizing conception of practical reason. For if our final ends cannot be commensurated in any systematic way, then clearly there can be no metric along which they might be maximized.

34. Michael Stocker, *Plural and Conflicting Values*, Oxford University Press, 1990.

35. Swanton, "Satisficing and Virtue," 44; note that the characterization of this person as an "immoderate satisficer" is Swanton's, not mine.

36. Swanton, "Satisficing and Virtue," 45.

37. Swanton, "Satisficing and Virtue," 45.

38. Is the desire mentioned in (c) merely a "local" desire, such that it would be a mistake to read into the fact that "he wants to lead the kind of life where he is not so hard on himself" a conception of the good? To answer this question, it seems natural to ask why the man would want to lead an easier life. The most sensible answer, it seems to me, is that he judges such a life to be better, or best, and so adopt it as a partial conception of the good. Why else would he want to lead an easier life? How could it have *strictly* instrumental value?

39. Could the man simply have conflicting desires, as one finds in various sorts of dilemmatic situation? It's not irrational to have conflicting desires (desires such that if one is satisfied then the other cannot be), and if that's the proper

description of the man's situation, then my charge of irrationality would be deflected. But it seems to me that Swanton characterizes the man's desires so that they embody judgments about what would be better or best, and that some of those judgments are all-things-considered judgments. See also the previous note. If this line of thought is correct, then the desires are not lower-level, stand-alone desires that might conflict without compromising the man's rationality.

40. One need not adopt Aristotle's so-called "unity of the virtues" thesis in order to accept my argument here. All that's needed is the principle that the possession of *phronesis* is a necessary condition of the possession of any other complete virtue. I take it that this principle is the less controversial half of the "unity of the virtues" thesis. See book 7 of the *Nicomachean Ethics*.

41. Again assuming the principle relating *phronesis* to the virtues articulated in the previous note.

42. This argument is oversimplified. Not all activities fit into any one good life, and some activities can be virtuous, vicious, or indifferent depending on who does them and how. But I hope I have said enough to show that a purported virtue of antiperfectionism will not allow on an Aristotelian account an action that would otherwise be unjustified.

43. One might wonder whether Aristotle's comments about the lack of *akribea* (exactitude) in ethics, in book 1 of the *Nicomachean Ethics*, might open the door to supererogation. The idea would be that, because perfect virtue need not in every case determine a single course of action as the best, one might act with perfect virtue and fail to do what is best. In that case, virtue seems to allow supererogation. My own interpretation of Aristotle's remark is that it concerns not the virtues but rules, with the implication that rules are true "generally and for the most part" rather than universally. Consequently, wisdom is always required for the application of ethical precepts, first in order to know which one is relevant to a given case, second to know whether it applies in that case, and third to know what to do in the exceptional case where the rule fails to govern. Even if that reading is mistaken, to say that virtue leaves open which action is best is not to say that choosing an appropriate action is doing less than the best. Rather, in some cases there is more than one best action. And if so, then again the schema leaves no conceptual space for supererogation. This argument is sketchy, and I look forward to elaborating it elsewhere.

44. This claim seems to me true of the conception of satisficing that I have discussed here, though not necessarily of other notions, including others in this volume.

11

How Do Economists Think About Rationality?

Tyler Cowen

1. Introduction

It is commonly believed that the rationality postulate, whatever that may mean, stands at the core of economic theory and much of social science research. Many economists go so far as to *define* their science in terms of the rationality assumption. I therefore try to spell out how working economists approach rationality, with the goal of explaining the practice of economic science to philosophers and other social scientists.

I do *not* survey the enormous literature on the methodology of economics.[1] Much of this literature focuses on philosophy of science rationales (or lack thereof) for rationality assumptions. The writers debate instrumentalism, the use of rhetoric to discuss rationality, whether assumptions need be realistic, and whether economic propositions are or should be falsifiable, to name a few of the better-known issues. These debates have generated insight, but taken alone they give a misleading picture of what economists do. Often they focus on economics as a whole – or on one or two fields – rather than on the increasingly diverse ways in which contemporary economists conduct their research.[2]

Philosophers, on the other hand, commonly believe that economic logic focuses on instrumental rationality, as exemplified by a Humean ends-means logic. That is, economics focuses on how to use means to achieve given ends, but it cannot judge the quality or rationality of those ends. Philosophers have put forth alternative notions of rationality, including "practical reasoning," procedural rationality (do our mental processes for forming values make sense?), and expressive rationality (do we have the right ends or values?). From a philosophical perspective, economic rationality is only one small part of rationality, and for this reason economics appears radically incomplete as a "final theory of the world," whatever its other virtues may be.[3]

I approach the rationality postulate from a differing perspective. In particular, I stress that there is no single, monolithic economic method or approach to rationality. Labor economists, finance theorists, experimental economists, and macroeconomists, among others, all think of rationality and use the rationality postulate in different ways. I explicate modern economic method by searching out and identifying the *differences* across fields, rather than by forcing everything into an account of the underlying unities.

Within economics, competing notions of the rationality postulate vie for graduate students, external funding, journal space, Nobel prizes, public attention, policy influence, and other rewards. A particular approach to the rationality postulate proves useful to the extent that it helps a new field get off the ground, generate useful results, help formulate policy, show intuitive resonance, command attention, and so on. We should think of this competitive process as fundamental to contemporary economics – more fundamental than any single account of rationality that might be provided.

We frequently observe some rationality concepts displacing others. The rational expectations assumption gained in prestige in the 1970s and 1980s and now has a secure foothold. In more recent times it has been challenged by behavioral assumptions and quasi-rationality. In the past twenty years, empirical labor economics and experimental economics have risen greatly in status. Computational economics can be seen as knocking at the door, though it remains inaccessible to most economists, and in the eyes of many outsiders it has not generated new and unique results. Most generally, the number of available rationality concepts has multiplied since the development of basic consumer theory early in the twentieth century, which reflects both scientific advance and a more intense competitive process.

Starting from these points, I seek to integrate the perspectives of the practitioner and the methodologist, and to explain to non-economists how economists use the rationality postulate. Section 2 presents some basic ways of thinking about rationality postulates and what role they might play in economics. Section 3 considers how contemporary economists actually use rationality postulates in differing fields of economics. Section 4 considers the implications of this diversity, and for how we should understand criticisms of economics.

2. How Might Economists Be Thinking About Rationality?

We see at least five basic ways of interpreting rationality postulates. I call these description, transitivity only, tautology, normative, and pragmatic. In section 3 I will illustrate each with particular applications. Note that the five categories may overlap to some degree.

Description

In this view the rationality postulate describes individual behavior and has definite empirical implications. These implications are in principle falsifiable. For the time being, and perhaps forever, the rationality postulate best describes economic behavior. Note that this view may attach varying substantive meanings to the empirical content of the rationality concept.[4]

Transitivity Only

Some economists believe that rationality requires only the postulate of transitivity of preference. Transitivity, in this context, stipulates that if A is preferred to B, and B is preferred to C, then A is preferred to C. In other words, preferences can be represented by a global rank ordering. Typically it is left open whether transitivity must *always* be satisfied, or if we require only that transitivity be true "often enough." Note that the transitivity only view can be a special case of the first "descriptive" view – at least if we interpret transitivity as an empirical property rather than a logical one.

Tautology

Any and all behavior can be described as rational, provided we are willing to manipulate the theory enough to avoid any testable implications. The rationality postulate therefore involves no substantive commitment to any empirical claims. A strong version of this view postulates that rationality is a useful tautology; a weaker view postulates that it is an arbitrary use of terms offering no particular advantage.

Pragmatic, or Useful Organizing, Category

This view rejects foundationalist approaches to rationality. We do not necessarily know exactly what the rationality postulate does or means. Nonetheless, economists who use the rationality postulate come up with better work and better ideas than those who do not. It is a useful heuristic for the economist. The rationality postulate is part of a research strategy for generating new ideas, regardless of its descriptive or logical status.

Normative

Individuals are not always rational, but rationality is an ideal that we should strive to achieve. Economic theory can be used to improve the quality of decision making. Note that this approach can be combined with any number of more substantive commitments to what rationality means.

3. Rationality Postulates in Economics

With these basic ideas in place, let us now consider some of the roles they play, in various combinations and permutations, in economic research. I consider several fields in the discussion that follows, including macroeconomics, theory of the consumer, expected utility theory, finance, empirical labor economics, and experimental economics. I do not mean to suggest that every practitioner in a cited area holds the same views. Rather, I consider a "typical" use of the rationality concept, as it might be found in the specified field or subfield of economics. Again, I am referring primarily to research practice rather than to the methodological literature.

Theory of the Consumer Under Certainty

The theory of consumer behavior under certainty provides the first few chapters of most microeconomics texts. It concerns how to represent preference orderings, relative price effects, income effects, indifference curves, and so on. These results stand at the base of many other propositions in economic theory.[5]

Strictly ordinal utility theory, under conditions of perfect certainty, typically treats the rationality postulate as a tautology. For any observed market behavior, we can try to redescribe that behavior *ex post* in terms of an underlying ordinal utility function. Virtually nothing could refute the hypothesis that individual behavior can be described in such terms. The theory of "revealed preference" tells us that observed market demands can be retranslated into underlying utility functions under a wide variety of assumptions. Over time, economists have worked hard at relaxing the assumptions behind consumer theory. Originally, assumptions such as continuity and divisibility were important, but now consumer theories have been developed that dispense with those assumptions while still delivering the standard results of neoclassical theory. Even observed "in-transitivities" can be redescribed as "changing preferences over time." Note that this basic theory does not assume that individuals are selfish but accommodates altruistic motives regularly.[6]

Theory of the Consumer Under Uncertainty
The theory of choice under uncertainty started with von Neumann–Morgenstern subjective expected utility theory and has since expanded to cover various modifications of that basic approach. For our purposes, I will speak simply of the von Neumann–Morgenstern approach as a more general appellation, even though many modern researchers reject the original axiomatic formulation of the theory.

In contrast to the theory under certainty, economists typically do not treat their theories of expected utility as tautologies. To the extent that empirical tests reject the axioms, there are grounds for rejecting the theory. Those who work with narrower versions of the von Neumann–Morgenstern approach typically admit that some degree of falsification has occurred. They do not defend the theory on tautological grounds but rather question whether some equally tractable alternative has been developed and whether the extant alternatives in fact yield better predictions across the board.

Several axioms of the von Neumann–Morgenstern approach are subject to falsification. Most notorious in this regard is the so-called "independence axiom." The independence axiom typically specifies that an additional percentage chance of some outcome has the same utility value to an individual, whether it is added to a 30, 40, or 50 percent probability of the outcome in question. In other words, mutually exclusive world-states ("what I could have had") should not influence the value of what I have, according to this postulate.

This axiom is contradicted by the evidence, whether we look at questionnaires or experiments with real dollar prizes. Notice, for instance, that the phenomenon of "nerves" often falsifies the independence axiom. If I move from a .99 chance of a good outcome to a 1.0 chance of that same outcome (certainty), I can stop worrying about what will happen. This extra 1 percent, in this context, may be worth more than moving from an .01 chance to an .02 chance. For some individuals, the move from .00 to .01, or to some smaller positive increment, is especially important. This can be taken to represent the value of hope and may explain why so many people play the lottery. Similarly, regret may falsify the independence axiom. If we feel bad about what we could have had but did not get, then the values of mutually exclusive world-states will influence one another.[7]

Note that even here we could try to define the expected utility axioms as tautologies. Assume, for instance, that an individual values the "move from .00 to .01 chance of becoming a millionaire" more than the "move from .90 to .91 chance of becoming a millionaire." This would appear to falsify the independence axiom. Yet such behavior is consistent with the independence axiom *if* we specify the relevant outcomes differently. Perhaps "the chance of becoming a millionaire" is not the relevant outcome. Instead, imagine that the relevant outcome is "the chance of becoming a millionaire, plus the hope that is enjoyed in the process of waiting to discover one's fate." The moves from .00 to .01 and from .90 to .91 thus represent different outcomes, and valuing them differently can be fully rational. Under this approach, no observed behavior could refute the independence axiom.

Taking this logic further, any apparent violation of the independence axiom could be taken to mean that we had not specified the appropriate outcomes or world-states correctly. Under this maneuver, however, the definition of an outcome varies with the probability of that outcome. For technical reasons, this interdependence of outcomes and probabilities would make expected utility theory intractable, because an outcome could never be defined as separate from its probability. Common judgment holds that expected utility theory would cease to be a useful tautology if it were treated in this fashion.

Note that the "tautologizing moves" in choice theory under certainty are seen as less destructive of tractability. They may decrease the usefulness of the theory, but they pose no immediate technical problem comparable to the intermingling of outcomes and probabilities, as we find in the theory of choice under uncertainty. For this reason, economists treat the theory of consumer behavior under uncertainty as having falsifiable axioms to a greater extent than they do the theory of choice under certainty.

Some choice theorists have attempted to reconstruct expected utility theory without the independence axiom.[8] In this theory, expected utility is linear in the probabilities only locally, not globally. Yet even this theory admits of possible empirical refutation. It implies particular attitudes toward how gambles are resolved over time and how individual preferences will change with the temporal resolution of uncertainty. Although these propositions are considered difficult to test, they are not tautologies either.

For these reasons, few economists interpret expected utility theory as a tautology. Instead, expected utility theory is considered as either a testable hypothesis, a normative standard, or a useful analytical category, depending on the field of investigation. When economists do choice theory, especially in a laboratory setting, the expected utility approach serves as a testable hypothesis, to be either supported or falsified by the data.

For more general theoretical purposes, the expected utility hypothesis is a useful building block for presenting some larger idea. In labor economics, for instance, it is commonly postulated that workers choose some degree of shirking, depending on their chance of being caught and fired. Expected utility theory, especially in its simplest forms, is used to represent this problem. Most of the economists who use expected utility theory in this way do not believe that it is descriptively true. Nonetheless, they hold it to be the most tractable and convenient approach at hand. They regard the theory as both falsifiable and false, yet useful nonetheless. The empirical failings of expected utility theory are considered inessential to the basics of work/shirk decisions.

Expected utility theory also can be used normatively. The experimental literature now shows that people do not satisfy the independence axiom across probabilities. Nonetheless, a normative theorist still might believe that people *ought* to satisfy such axioms. The entire field of risk analysis tries to help people make better decisions under uncertainty. Risk analysis has been used to advise the U.S. Department of Defense, to help adjudicate lawsuits, to make securities markets more efficient, and to help companies make decisions about how to invest and when to buy insurance. Normative risk analysis forms a substantial part of applied economics – often in the context of consulting – even when it does not show up in academic research more narrowly defined.

Macroeconomics

A large body of macroeconomics uses the assumption of rational expectations, henceforth RE. Although a majority of working macroeconomists do not accept the empirical validity of RE, most of the important work in macroeconomics over the past thirty years has used the RE assumption. Rationality, for macroeconomists, refers primarily to rationality of expectations, rather than to some property of preferences.

RE has been defined in several ways that may be coextensive. Under one account, RE means that individuals understand the "true model" of the economy; in other words, trading individuals have the understanding of a fully accomplished macroeconomist. Under another account, individual forecasts of economic variables are correct on average. This can mean either that the errors of an individual average out to zero over time, or that at any point in time, individual forecasts are scattered around the true variable but with a correct mean. Finally, RE may mean that errors are serially uncorrelated over time. That is, if I guess too high one period, that has no predictive power for whether I guess too high or too low the next period. Again, this proposition can hold for either individuals or groups.[9]

Economists put these assumptions into macroeconomic models for several reasons. First, some economists believe that those assumptions are roughly true. A more common view is that they provide a kind of modeling discipline. The view is commonly voiced that "errors can be used to explain anything." By forcing the theorist not to rely too heavily on errors, the RE assumption makes it harder to come up with *ad hoc* models. Finally, the RE assumption may be useful as a foil, to see what a world without systematic errors would look like. By comparing this idealized picture with the real world, we may get a better sense of whether systematic errors are central to the phenomenon of business cycles and other economic problems.

The RE assumption has received a wide variety of tests. When we look at questionnaires about expectations, RE commonly fails to predict measured expectations. Similarly, RE fails tests in the laboratory setting. Some RE predictions, however, are commonly (though not always) validated at the macroeconomic level. It appears that the money supply does not affect real output, once we take interest rates into account, and that budget deficits do not cause real interest rates to rise.[10] Both of these predictions follow from some standard RE models, though of course the studies test several hypotheses jointly, rather than just RE taken alone.

Rationality, in the form of RE, is considered testable, both in principle and in reality. Failing the tests lowers the status of the RE assumption without making it worthless altogether. RE thus has descriptive, pragmatic, and normative components, to refer to the categories outlined above.

Theory of Finance
Financial economics has one of the most extreme methods in economic theory, and increasingly one of the most prestigious. Finance concerns the pricing of market securities, the determinants of market returns, the operating of trading systems, the valuation of corporations, and the

financial policies of corporations, among other topics. Specialists in finance can command high salaries in the private sector and have helped design many financial markets and instruments. To many economists, this ability to "meet a market test" suggests that financial economists are doing something right.

Depending on one's interpretation, the theory of finance makes either minimal or extreme assumptions about rationality. Let us consider the efficient markets hypothesis (EMH), which holds the status of a central core for finance, though without commanding universal assent. Like most economic claims, EMH comes in many forms, some weaker, others stronger. The weaker versions typically claim that deliberate stock picking does not on average outperform selecting stocks randomly, such as by throwing darts at the financial page. The market already incorporates information about the value of companies into the stock prices, and no one individual can beat this information other than by random luck (or perhaps by outright insider trading).

Note that the weak version of EMH requires few assumptions about rationality. Many market participants may be grossly irrational or systematically biased in a variety of ways. It must be the case, however, that their irrationalities are unpredictable to the remaining rational investors. If the irrationalities were predictable, rational investors could make systematic extra-normal profits with some trading rule. The data, however, suggest that it is hard for rational investors to outperform the market averages. This result suggests that extant irrationalities are either very small or very hard to predict, two rather different conclusions. The commitment that *one* of these conclusions must be true does not involve much of a substantive position on the rationality front.

The stronger forms of EMH claim that market prices accurately reflect the fundamental values of corporations and thus cannot be improved upon. This claim does involve a distinct and arguably stronger commitment to a notion of rationality.

Strong EMH still allows that most individuals may be irrational, regardless of how we define that concept. These individuals could literally be behaving on a random basis, or perhaps even deliberately counter to standard rationality assumptions. It is assumed, however, that at least one individual does have rational information about how much stocks are worth. Furthermore, and most important, it is assumed that capital markets are perfect or nearly perfect. With perfect capital markets, the one rational individual will overwhelm the influence of the irrational on stock prices. If the stock ought to be worth \$30 a share but irrational "noise traders" push it down to \$20 a share, then the person who knows better will keep on buying shares until the price has risen to \$30. With perfect capital markets, there is no limit to this arbitrage process. Even if the person who knows better has limited wealth, he or she can borrow against the value of the shares and continue to buy, making money in the process and pushing the share price to its proper value.

So the assumptions about rationality in strong EMH are tricky. Only one person need be rational, but through perfect capital markets, this one person will have decisive weight on market prices. As noted previously, this can be taken as either an extreme or modest assumption. Although no one believes that capital markets are literally perfect, they may be "perfect enough" to allow the rational investors to prevail.

"Behavioral finance" is currently a fad in financial theory, and in the eyes of many it may become the new mainstream. Behavioral finance typically weakens rationality assumptions, usually with a view to explaining market anomalies. Almost always these models assume imperfect capital markets in order to prevent a small number of rational investors from dwarfing the influence of behavioral factors. Robert J. Shiller claims that investors overreact to small pieces of information, causing virtually irrelevant news to have a large impact on market prices. Other economists argue that some fund managers "churn" their portfolios – trade for no good reason – simply to give their employers the impression that they are working hard. It appears that during the Internet stock boom simply having the suffix "dot com" in the firm's name added value on share markets and that after the bust it subtracted value.[11]

Behavioral models use looser notions of rationality than does EMH. Rarely do behavioral models postulate outright irrationality; rather, the term "quasi-rationality" is popular in the literature. Most frequently, a behavioral model introduces only a single deviation from classical rationality postulates. The assumption of imperfect capital markets then creates the possibility that this quasi-rationality will have a real impact on market phenomena.

The debates between the behavioral theories and EMH now form the central dispute in modern financial theory. In essence, one vision of rationality – the rational overwhelm the influence of the irrational through perfect capital markets – is pitted against another vision – imperfect capital markets give real influence to quasi-rationality. These differing approaches to rationality and the corresponding assumptions about capital markets are considered to be eminently testable.

Empirical Labor Economics

Empirical labor economics has been one of the most successful areas in neoclassical economics over the past fifteen years. Largely through careful use of panel data sets, economists have generated much knowledge about wages, labor supply decisions, the effects of the welfare state, and the nature of unemployment, among other topics.[12]

Empirical labor economists tend to be among the least theoretical of economists and tend to be the most likely to defer to the data. Labor economics offers few (if any) *a priori* propositions. Even traditional supply and demand patterns are difficult to forecast. We cannot say *a priori* whether an increase in wages causes people to work more (being paid more money per hour, the substitution effect) or to work less (they have more money and can now consume leisure, the income effect). The operation of the law of demand is contingent in similar fashion. Under some circumstances, a rise in real wages can *increase* the demand for labor rather than lower it (as standard demand theory would otherwise predict). A hypothesis known as efficiency wage theory stresses how higher wages can make workers more productive, either by making them happier, or by making them more afraid to shirk. Employers therefore may demand more labor for higher wages, at least along some margins.

Given the difficulty of establishing clear theoretical predictions, labor economists tend to be among the most positivistic of economists. They consider the test to be everything, and theory to tell us little. A typical piece of labor economics writes down some utility function for laborers and thus assumes a kind of rationality. This utility function, however, usually has few testable implications on its own other than implying that individuals prefer income and leisure. This is more of a concrete statement about preferences than about rationality. In other cases, labor economists may use subjective expected utility theory for reasons of convenience, but without possessing any deep commitment to the underlying theoretical apparatus. Therefore we can think of labor economics as involving minimum assumptions about rationality and as relying almost entirely on the data for its substantive hypotheses. Theory certainly helps labor economists interpret the data, but this theory is remarkably thin with regard to its assumptions about rationality.

Game Theory

In game theory, notions of rationality are highly specific, and economists debate the propriety of one notion against another. Such debates are central to the theoretical enterprise.

To see how this works, let us step back for a moment for some context. In most (non-game-theoretic) economic models, individuals are assumed to play what are called "dominant strategies." A dominant strategy unambiguously maximizes the individual's return, such as when an individual maximizes utility or a firm maximizes profit. Exercising a dominant option of this kind is uncontroversial in economic theory, even though at a deeper level economists may disagree about what an institution seeks to maximize (profit, revenue, prestige, etc.). Once the maximand is given, individuals will pursue the dominant strategy. In other words, more is preferred to less.

When we move to game theory and the world of strategic interdependence, dominant strategies frequently do not exist. The payoff of a given strategy depends on what the individual expects others to do. Often no single strategy yields higher returns for every possible response from others. So getting a good return depends on making accurate predictions about the behavior of others; of course, these same others are trying to make accurate predictions about their opponents as well.

At this point, game theory resorts to *equilibrium concepts* to resolve games. The most famous of these is the Nash equilibrium, which describes a series of moves as an equilibrium only when neither player has an incentive to deviate from his or her strategy, taking the strategy of the others as given. Nash equilibrium thus represents one attempt of game theory to model the notion of rationality in a game. In more complicated games, game theorists resort to such notions as "subgame perfection," "time consistency," "perfect Bayesian equilibrium," and many others. In each case, these concepts attempt to define rationality for the purpose of "solving" the game or games. Note also that the solution concept can be viewed in positive terms, in normative terms, or more abstractly as possessing certain formal properties, without necessarily being either predictive or normative.

Debates about rationality arise for two reasons. First, many common solution concepts are implausible. Second, a solution concept may imply multiple equilibria.

To start with plausibility, Nash equilibria appear unlikely in many contexts. If we consider a multi-period Prisoners' Dilemma, played ten times, the Nash concept usually predicts defection in the first round.[13] Yet even most game theorists do not play this strategy of immediate defection when asked to play the game for real money. Economists therefore have tried to come up with richer notions of equilibrium that can account for the predictive limitations of the Nash concept.[14]

In many games we find a multiplicity of Nash equilibria, often an infinite or near-infinite number of such equilibria. The simplest way of generating multiple equilibria is to set up a coordination game with two possible points of high return. Large numbers of equilibria arise most easily when we consider trigger and response strategies. For instance, if an individual plays "if you defect, I will defect for seven successive periods with p = 0.9," it may also be an equilibrium strategy to play the same but with p = 0.90001, with p = 0.90002, and so on. Many games have an infinite number of possible equilibria.

When multiple Nash equilibria exist, the game-theoretic notion of rationality does not, taken alone, yield unique predictions. Economists have developed "refinement concepts," which seek to discriminate among the various Nash equilibria (or other multiple equilibria, derived from other solution concepts) and to elevate one as the uniquely rational outcome. Some of these refinements are highly complex and consist of classificatory criteria that have no clear intuitive referents. Other refinement concepts deliberately introduce bounded rationality and ask which equilibria could be computed by persons in the real world. These debates have given rise to a voluminous and complex literature, and there is no general agreement concerning the best refinement concept.

Game theory has shown economists that the concept of rationality is more problematic than they had previously believed. What is rational depends not only on the objective features of the problem but also on what agents believe. This short discussion has only scratched the surface of how beliefs may imply complex or multiple solutions. Sometimes the relevant beliefs, for instance, are beliefs about the out-of-equilibrium behavior of other agents. These beliefs are hard to model, or it is hard to find agreement among theorists as to how they should be modeled.

In sum, game theorists spend much of their time trying to figure out what rationality means. They are virtually unique among economists in this regard. Game theory from twenty years ago pitted various concepts of rationality against one another in purely theoretical terms. Empirical results had some feedback into this process, such as when economists reject Nash equilibrium for some of its counterintuitive predictions, but it remains striking how much of the early literature does not refer to any empirical tests. This enterprise has now become much more empirical and more closely tied to both computational science and experimental economics.

Experimental Economics

Experimental economists test economic propositions in a controlled laboratory setting with real dollar prizes. By using controlled experiments
in this regard, experimental economics comes closer to the methods of
many of the natural sciences.[15]

Experimental economics typically treats *all* propositions about rationality as up for grabs. The ability to perform controlled experiments
relieves experimental economics from the necessity to start with unques-
tioned assumptions. Virtually every economic assumption about individual behavior has been subject to test in a laboratory setting. Furthermore,
virtually all of these assumptions have been falsified.

Some of the most radical experiments appear to have falsified the
assumption of transitivity. Individuals can be induced to show preferences that cycle indefinitely. Other experiments have focused on what is
called "preference reversal." These experiments ask individuals whether
they prefer prize x or prize y. Shortly thereafter, these same individuals are asked whether they prefer some probability of x or the same
probability of y. The same individuals who prefer x to y often prefer
the probability of y to the probability of x. Preference reversal, like violations of transitivity, suggests there is no well-defined preference ordering. It appears to undercut any well-specified notion of instrumental
rationality.[16]

Experimental economics, however, does not necessarily imply nihilistic
conclusions. Much of the literature shows how markets can operate even
when individuals are not rational in ways assumed by standard theory. To
provide a simple example, laboratory markets rapidly reach a coherent
equilibrium, even when the traders fail numerous other tests of individual rationality, including transitivity. These results contradict mainstream
analysis, which treats individual rationality as an underpinning of market
operation. The results imply that markets have some means of working
even when rationality is not present, which implies that standard theory,
in addition to its failings on the rationality question, does not provide a
good account of markets.

Twenty or thirty years ago, experimental economics was considered to
be a highly speculative method of investigation. Many economists thought
it was outright dubious. Today, experimental methods are used commonly
at the highest levels of the profession. Most issues of the *American Economic
Review*, the profession's flagship journal, contain at least one experimental piece.

Experimental economics is also tied closely to game theory, though the two branches of economics often conflict. Experimentalists know the failings of game theory and hope to fill in the empty boxes with results from the laboratory. The experiments typically find more cooperation than game-theoretic accounts would have predicted. Experimentalists wish to introduce a desire for cooperation into economics, whereas game theorists are more skeptical about the lab results, often stressing the differences between the experiments and real-world conditions.

Of all the branches of economics, experimental economics probably goes furthest in the empirical direction with regard to rationality. Experimental economics regards all or most stipulations of the rationality postulate as empirical in nature and as potentially falsifiable. The surprising lesson is that what we assume about rationality does not seem to matter for many economic contexts. Markets economize on rationality, whatever that concept may mean, more than neoclassical economics usually implies.

Economic Imperialism

Some economists argue that the economic method should be extended to many or all of the other social sciences, such as political science, sociology, and anthropology. This movement has already made strong progress in political science, has made some inroads in sociology, and is starting to influence anthropology.

Gary Becker's work on the economics of the family is a paradigm example of economic imperialism. Becker has sought to bring the understanding of the family under the rubric of economic reasoning. For each family member he postulates a utility function and constraints, and then he uses various models to examine family interactions. Using this method, Becker and other researchers have studied the effects of familial division of labor, familial altruism, government policies toward children, and government welfare policies.[17]

Becker's work has proven among the most controversial applications of rationality postulates. Applying rationality postulates to the family differs from most other parts of economics. Most significantly, the economist cannot resort to the usual assumption of profit maximization, as is applied to business firms. The objective function of the family is less well specified, and it is harder to link to any empirically measurable variable. In addition to its economic functions, the family provides love, affection, the chance to raise children, and many other personal goals. Furthermore, though families engage in many implicit forms of trading, they eschew explicit trading for many choices. Most families do not bid as to who gets to watch their favorite television program on a given evening. Economic models are well suited to handle trade, but they have a harder time defining the operation of nontrade allocative mechanisms.

I am not aware of a philosophically sophisticated defense of economic imperialism (advocates tend to believe in the primacy of practice), but the following defense might be offered in response to these problems. Rational choice explanations, in the realm of economic imperialism, are most defensible when we think of them as complements to alternative approaches rather than substitutes. This will weaken some of the more extreme pretensions of the imperialistic approach but also place it on sounder footing.

We start with the notion of explanation in general, however that term might be understood. Trying to explain family outcomes is bound to be problematic, for the reasons specified previously. The vagueness of family "objectives" is not just a problem for economic modes of reasoning; it renders all explanation more difficult. Given these problems, however, rational choice approaches do make a particular claim about how to approach explanation. Specifically, when offering an explanation, it is useful to break that explanation into two parts: claims made about preferences and claims made about constraints. With this breakdown in place, we have a rational choice attempt at explanation, motivated by the pragmatic grounds discussed earlier in this chapter. The rational choice approach may help us generate new ideas about the family and new ways of testing old ideas.

If we translate this method into the context of the family, the rational choice theorist believes that this parsing will yield useful results. Insight may arise through (at least) three mechanisms. First, the categories may allow us more easily to observe connections between apparently unrelated events. Some of the problems of the family, for instance, such as "moral hazard," may resemble the problems of the welfare state. Second, the categories may make causal chains easier to isolate. An understanding of division of labor in the household, for instance, may help us understand when dowry payments are likely to be positive or negative. Third, the categories may make it easier to test hypotheses against the data, however problematic this enterprise may be. Andrei Shleifer, for instance, considers whether older individuals use their bequests to manipulate the behavior of the young; his basic insights came out of a rational choice model.[18]

Fixed Preferences

Some researchers treat the constant preference assumption as part of the core of rationality and the economic approach, especially as applied to other disciplines. Economists typically assume that preferences are constant over time. George Stigler and Gary Becker go further and insist that this practice defines the economic or rational choice method. Although most economists reject this extreme view, in practice economists remain skeptical of explanations that invoke changing preferences. It is commonly argued that changing preferences can be used to "explain anything."[19]

This view is not a rationality postulate in the full-blown sense of the word. Nonetheless, in the eyes of some, it is an important auxiliary hypothesis for what it means to apply a theory of rationality. In this view, adherence to a rationality-based approach must rule out changing preferences, because a rational choice model – if based on the idea of given preferences – could not explain how preferences could ever change.

Economists are more likely to accept explanations based on varying preferences across individuals than explanations based on changing preferences for a single individual. Principal-agent models, for instance, commonly postulate one person who is risk-neutral and another who is risk-averse. Similarly, it is obvious that some people like classical music, others like rock and roll, and so on. Even in these cases, however, Stigler and Becker stake out an extreme position. They suggest that the idea of differing human capital endowments be used in lieu of the concept of changing preferences. In their terminology, all individuals have the same tastes for music, but some individuals have better complementary endowments in their human capital for enjoying classical music. Most other economists see this difference as a semantic one rather than a real one. Thus they will accept varying preferences across different individuals, but they are reluctant to accept changing preferences over time for a single individual.

Even changing preferences are making inroads in the research community. Fischer Black invoked changing preferences as a fundamental cause of business cycles. Contemporary consumer theory considers individuals with non-hyperbolic discounting, in other words individuals who seek to postpone their pains and commitments as they draw near. The Christmas boom in economic activity also seems hard to explain without invoking changing preferences across the seasons. The same might be said for fashion cycles, or increasing demand for safety as most individuals, especially males, age. Note that a purely economic approach would imply that the young would take the fewest risks, because they have the

most years left to lose. The data show convincingly that young males take
the most risks and take fewer risks as they age.[20]

The stable preference assumption may have been an unfortunate
addition to the basic economic method. Economists typically reject
preference-based explanations on the grounds that "anything can be explained by changing preferences." Furthermore, changes in constraints
are seen as potentially measurable and thus offering potentially testable
hypotheses, whereas changes in tastes are seen as harder to pin down.
These criticisms, however, are misleading for at least two reasons. First, we
often have actual data about preferences and preference changes, against
which preference-based explanations can be tested. Second, many economic phenomena *cannot* be explained easily on the preference side, no
matter how much wiggling and squirming is done. An increase in the
real wage rate, for instance, will cause many entrepreneurs to substitute
machinery for labor. This phenomenon can be explained easily on the
constraint side, but not easily on the preference side. Examples of this
kind could be multiplied. Invoking changing preferences is therefore not
a universal license for abuse.[21]

Satisficing

The early work of Herbert Simon, Richard Cyert, and James March led
to the idea of "satisficing." Satisficing refers to the idea that individuals
do not seek the best outcome but rather stop once they find an outcome
that is "good enough." The concept of satisficing came originally from
the realization that most maximizing problems are extremely complex
and often lead to simple "rule of thumb" solutions.

Many economists do not regard the satisficing postulate as an independent alternative to a rationality assumption. Consider a simple example
of what might be called satisficing: An individual is searching in a gro-
cery store for a good piece of fruit – say, a cherry. Most people would not
spend their day searching through the entire bin of cherries. Rather at
some point they will be content to pick a cherry that is "good enough."
It is easy to see how this example can be reinterpreted as an application
of rationality. The searching individual will face an opportunity cost of
time, and the benefits of getting a good cherry are only so large. The
individual will make some calculation, either explicit or implicit, about
how much time is worth devoting to the cherry search. It is well known
that an optimal strategy often consists of a "stopping rule." That is, the
individual should stop searching and pick the best option available, after
some finite period of time.[22]

Defenders of the satisficing approach do not regard this criticism as decisive. In their view, satisficing has more predictive power, even if it does not have well-defined microfoundations. Some taxi drivers, for instance, simply may stop taking fares once they have accumulated a certain amount of money for the evening.

The economists who oppose the satisficing model typically point out that we can always define such behavior as rational in one set of terms or another. We could say, for instance, that an "income effect" has kicked in. Once the driver has a certain amount of money, he may prefer to consume leisure instead of working. Defenders of satisficing, however, may still claim superior predictive power for their approach. Some taxi drivers may still behave in closer accord with the satisficing model. The mainstream model implies that high income or wealth – regardless of its source – causes the taxi driver to work less. But if the taxi drivers receive more money from some other source, perhaps a gift, they often drive their cab just as much. So perhaps it is not the "income effect" (or whatever other mechanism might be postulated) at work. The taxi drivers may be making context-laden decisions that are best described by the satisficing construct. Many drivers might have an inclination to stop once they have accumulated a certain quantity of fares on a given evening. They feel they have done "a good night's work" and feel no need to bring home more money that evening.

Computation
The past two decades have brought increasing interest in computational models in economics. Computational models have a number of roots, but in part they attempt to improve on the satisficing concept. Satisficing approaches typically postulate an absolute stopping rule at some point. Computational approaches attempt to derive the point at which an individual will stop calculating, depending on the complexity of the problem at hand. So we can think of computational approaches as providing microfoundations for satisficing. Under these microfoundations, however, we do not always generate a fixed stopping rule, as under satisficing.

Rather than allowing all solutions to a problem, the computational research agenda focuses on which of these solutions might be computable to rational agents with limited abilities. Kenneth Binmore has applied this point to the choice among solution concepts in game theory (see the discussion of game theory above), and Thomas Sargent has tried to integrate the idea of computability into monetary theory and macroeconomics.

Sargent has also worked to integrate the idea of economic computation with the theory of artificial intelligence.[23]

Computational theories, like experimental economics, have not arisen in a vacuum. In part they are designed to address some of the weaknesses in previous accounts of rationality. For instance, Binmore's computational approach tries to resolve the problems of game theory, as discussed previously. Sargent's computational work attempts to work around the limits of rational expectations in macroeconomics.

Note that the work on computation moves closer to what philosophers sometimes call procedural rationality. Rationality now becomes defined in terms of some computational algorithm.

Most work in computational economics is new and highly mathematical, still resists easy summary, and is relatively inaccessible to non-experts (which includes this author). Nonetheless it is easy to see how the emphasis on computability puts rationality assumptions back on center stage and further breaks down the idea of a monolithic approach to rationality. The choice of computational algorithm is not given *a priori* but is continually up for grabs. Furthermore, the choice of algorithm will go a long way toward determining the results of the model. Given that the algorithm suddenly *is* rationality, computational economics forces economists to debate which assumptions about procedural rationality are reasonable or useful ones.

The mainstream criticism of computational models, of course, falls right out of these issues. Critics believe that computational models can generate just about "any" result, depending on the assumptions about what is computable. This would move economics away from being a unified science. Furthermore, it is not clear how we should evaluate the reasonableness of one set of assumptions about computability as opposed to another set. We might consider whether the assumptions yield plausible results, but if we already know what a plausible result consists of, it is not clear why we need computational theories of rationality.

To make matters even more difficult, human beings appear to have vastly different computational abilities in different activities and different spheres of life. To give a simple example, most individuals have relatively good abilities to remember faces and voices and to sort through various aspects of interpersonal relationships. It has proven difficult to get computers to perform these same tasks as well. In more abstract, less personal contexts, individuals do not have nearly the same abilities. Few can perform complex long division unaided. This point implies that computational theories of rationality will probably fail to settle on a single, simple account of how computational rationality proceeds.

Currently computational theories of rationality are an open box. It is not clear how they will develop. Nonetheless, they illustrate the growing diversity of rationality concepts within economics.

4. Conclusion

Our examination of how economists use the rationality postulate suggests diversity more than anything else. Economists accept no single set of assumptions about rationality, nor any one set of attitudes about the role of rationality assumptions in economic theory and practice. Rather, we have seen the rationality postulate – and attitudes toward it – evolve in different directions in different fields of economics. Some fields view the rationality postulate quite broadly, whereas other fields identify it with some particular assumptions (macroeconomics). Some fields regard rationality as a tautology (consumer behavior under certainty), whereas others regard it as potentially testable (consumer behavior under uncertainty). Game theory places great importance on the rationality concept, as does computational economics, whereas empirical labor economics and experimental economics imply that the rationality concept does not matter so much.

We therefore need an account of the rationality postulate that can explain its varied uses across fields and subfields of economics. To return to our list in section 2, the first three views (tautology, transitivity only, and descriptive) must appear incomplete. They may account for how rationality is used in particular instances, but without providing an account of rationality in economics more generally. The most serious contender thus remains the pragmatic view that rationality and various rationality assumptions serve as useful organizing categories. Given the plurality of investigative methods in economics, this result will imply that particular rationality assumptions take numerous forms.

This look at the rationality postulate may not satisfy those critics who, in any case, do not like the content of economic theory. But at the very least the rationality postulate is a less vulnerable target of criticism than is usually thought. I do not mean to suggest that economic uses of the rationality postulate cannot be improved upon. I have, however, attempted to revise the picture of the rationality postulate as an easy whipping boy for critics. Economic practice, in this regard, is more sophisticated than the views of any single economist. This is an appropriate result for a science that emphasizes invisible hand mechanisms and the limitations of central planning. I see many things wrong with contemporary economics, but the rationality postulate is not near the top of my list. I hope that this chapter induces some of the critics of economics to be more blunt and more specific about their objections.

I believe that economists hold a default view about their own use of rationality concepts, although they seldom articulate it. They see the rationality concepts in use as the result of a competitive process – and thus the best available practice, at least given our current state of scientific information. A rationality concept, in this regard, is like a market price or a management practice. Not every price or practice is optimal when compared with full information, but the competitive process nonetheless gives us as good a menu of choice as we are likely to have. It provides the best available options, relative to the imperfections in our information. I believe this optimistic view, whether right or wrong, is the underlying reason why practicing economists pay so little heed to methodology.[24]

This underlying model of economic science has a surface simplicity. If we refer to rationality postulates as "inputs" into scientific research, a competitive process (under certain conditions) allocates inputs efficiently. Economists, who tend to accept efficiency as a relevant standard, therefore believe that this competitive process yields an approximation of good science, and this belief involves the rationality postulate in its diverse forms.

I do not raise this possibility to evaluate it but rather to note that any effective criticism of economics must start with the institutions that produce (and evaluate) economics. Methodological criticisms alone, especially if they focus on rationality, are unlikely to be persuasive. In the meantime, we should de-emphasize monolithic attempts to characterize (or criticize) the method of economics and recognize the strongly plural character of research practice.

Notes

The author wishes to thank Bryan Caplan, Robin Hanson, and Alex Tabarrok for useful comments.
1. For relevant treatments and surveys, see, for instance, Bruce J. Caldwell, *Beyond Positivism: Economic Methodology in the Twentieth Century*, New York: Routledge, 1994; and Daniel M. Hausman, *The Inexact and Separate Science of Economics*, Cambridge University Press, 1992.

2. Melvin Reder, *Economics: The Culture of a Controversial Science,* University of Chicago Press, 1999, lays more stress on practice than do most writers on economic method.

3. For a presentation of this view, see Shaun Hargreaves Heap, *Rationality in Economics,* New York: Blackwell, 1989. The moral general philosophic literature on rationality is vast. For some recent perspectives, see David Schmidtz, *Rational Choice and Moral Agency,* Princeton University Press, 1995; Robert Audi, *The Architecture of Reason: The Structure and Substance of Rationality,* Oxford University Press, 2001; and Elijah Millgram, *Varieties of Practical Reasoning,* Cambridge: MIT Press, 2001.

4. See, for instance, James C. Cox, "Testing the Utility Hypothesis," *Economic Journal* 107 (1997): 1054–78.

5. The reader who wishes further detail should consult Hal Varian, *Microeconomic Analysis,* New York: Norton, 1992.

6. On revealed preference, see Paul Samuelson, "A Note on the Pure Theory of Consumer's Behavior," *Econometrica* 5 (1938): 353–4. On relaxing assumptions behind existence proofs, see, for instance, Andreu Mas-Colell, "The Price Equilibrium Existence Problem in Topological Vector Lattices," *Econometrica* 54 (1986): 1039–54.

7. The Allais paradox provides the best-known counter to the independence axiom. In the Allais paradox, individuals are first asked to rank gamble A against gamble B. If the individual chooses A, the independence axiom implies that same person should prefer C over D. Yet we systematically observe individuals preferring A over B, and D over C. See Mark J. Machina, "Expected Utility without the Independence Axiom," *Econometrica* 50 (1982): 277–324.

8. See Machina, "Expected Utility without the Independence Axiom."

9. For a discussion of different forms of rational expectations, see Tyler Cowen, *Risk and Business Cycles: New and Old Austrian Perspectives,* New York: Routledge, 1997, 8–9, which also provides more detailed citations to the literature.

10. See, respectively, Robert B. Litterman and Laurence Weiss, "Money, Real Interest Rates, and Output: A Reinterpretation of Postwar U.S. Data," *Econometrica* 53 (1985): 129–56; and Paul Evans, "Interest Rates and Expected Future Budget Deficits in the United States," *Journal of Political Economy* 95 (1987): 34–58.

11. See Robert J. Shiller, *Irrational Exuberance,* New York: Broadway Books, 2000. Richard H. Thaler, *Quasi Rational Economics,* New York: Russell Sage Foundation, 1994, presents many behavioral themes.

12. By its very nature, empirical labor economics cannot be presented in any canonical form, nor is it typically found in book-length treatments. The best source is the articles published in the *American Economic Review* in the last fifteen years, under the editorship of Orley Ashenfelter, himself an empirical labor economist.

13. The so-called "folk theorem," which allows for cooperation, kicks in only when the number of rounds is large and the discount rate is small.

14. These attempts have spawned a huge literature. See, for instance, John C. Harsanyi and Reinhard Selten, *A General Theory of Equilibrium Selection in Games*, Cambridge: MIT Press, 1988.

15. On experimental economics, see, for instance, John H. Kagel and Alvin E. Roth, eds., *The Handbook of Experimental Economics*, Princeton University Press, 1995.

16. See David M. Grether and Charles R. Plott, "Economic Theory of Choice and the Preference Reversal Phenomenon," *American Economic Review* 69 (1979): 623–38.

17. See Gary S. Becker, *A Treatise on the Family*, Harvard University Press, 1993. For a more general treatment of economic imperialism, see Gerard Radnitzky and Peter Bernholz, eds., *Economic Imperialism: The Economic Approach Applied Outside the Field of Economics*, New York: Paragon House, 1987.

18. On these points, see Theodore C. Bergstrom, "A Fresh Look at the Rotten Kind Theorem – and Other Household Mysteries," *Journal of Political Economy* 93 (1985): 1045–76; and Douglas B. Bernheim, Andrei Shleifer, and Lawrence H. Summers, "The Strategic Bequest Motive," *Journal of Political Economy* 34 (1985): 1045–76.

19. See George S. Stigler and Gary J. Becker, "De Gustibus Non Est Disputandum," *American Economic Review* 67 (1977): 76–90.

20. On some of these ideas, see Fischer Black, *Exploring General Equilibrium*, Cambridge: MIT Press, 1995; and Robert Barsky and Jeffrey Miron, "The Seasonal Cycle and the Business Cycle," *Journal of Political Economy* 97 (1989): 503–34.

21. Bryan Caplan, "Stigler-Becker versus Myers-Briggs: Why Preference-Based Explanations Are Scientifically Meaningful and Empirically Important," working paper, George Mason University, 2001, argues that economists should be willing to consider varying tastes across individuals, and sometimes changing tastes over time.

22. For a philosophic examination of satisficing, see Michael Slote, *Beyond Optimizing*, Harvard University Press, 1989. Michael Byron, "Satisficing and Optimality," *Ethics* 109 (1998): 67–93, provides a critique of the philosophic underpinnings of many satisficing models.

23. See Kenneth Binmore, "Modeling Rational Players, Part I," *Economics and Philosophy* 3 (1987): 179–214; Kenneth Binmore, "Modeling Rational Players, Part II," *Economics and Philosophy* 4 (1988): 9–55; and Albert Marcet and Thomas J. Sargent, "Convergence of Least-Squares Learning in Environments with Hidden State Variables and Private Information," *Journal of Political Economy* 97 (1989): 1306–22.

24. Sherwin Rosen, "Austrian and Neoclassical Economics: Any Gains From Trade?" *Journal of Economic Perspectives* 11 (1997): 139–52, comes closest to stating this view. See Leland B. Yeager, "Austrian Economics, Neoclassicism, and the Market Test," *Journal of Economic Perspectives* 11 (1997): 153–65 for a response.

Bibliography

Adler, Matthew D., and Eric A. Posner, "Implementing Cost-Benefit Analysis When Preferences Are Distorted." In Matthew D. Adler and Eric A. Posner, eds., *Cost-Benefit Analysis: Legal, Economic, and Philosophical Perspectives.* Chicago: University of Chicago Press, 2001, 269–311.

Anderson, Elizabeth, "Reasons, Attitudes, and Values: Replies to Sturgeon and Piper." *Ethics* 106 (1996): 538–54.

Anscombe, G. E. M., "Modern Moral Philosophy." *Philosophy* 33 (1958):1–19.

Aristotle, *Nicomachean Ethics.* In Richard McKeon, ed., *The Basic Works of Aristotle.* New York: Random House, 1941.

Arrow, Kenneth J., "Utilities, Attitudes, Choices: A Review Note." In *Individual Choice Under Certainty and Uncertainty.* Cambridge, Mass.: Harvard University Press, 1984, 55–84.

Audi, Robert. *The Architecture of Reason: The Structure and Substance of Rationality.* New York: Oxford University Press, 2001.

Barsky, Robert, and Jeffrey Miron, "The Seasonal Cycle and the Business Cycle." *Journal of Political Economy* 97 (1989): 503–34.

Becker, Gary S. *A Treatise on the Family.* Cambridge, Mass.: Harvard University Press, 1993.

Bergstrom, Theodore C., "A Fresh Look at the Rotten Kind Theorem – and Other Household Mysteries." *Journal of Political Economy* 93 (1985): 1045–76.

Bernhaim, Douglas B., Andrei Shleifer, and Lawrence H. Summers, "The Strategic Bequest Motive." *Journal of Political Economy* 34 (1985): 1045–76.

Binmore, Kenneth, "Modeling Rational Players, Part I." *Economics and Philosophy* 3 (1987): 179–214.

"Modeling Rational Rational Players, Part II." *Economics and Philosophy* 4 (1988): 9–55.

Black, Fischer, *Exploring General Equilibrium.* Cambridge, Mass.: MIT Press, 1995.

Bratman, Michael E., "Reflection, Planning, and Temporally Extended Agency." *Philosophical Review* 109 (2000): 35–61.

Broome, John, *Weighing Goods: Equality, Uncertainty, and Time.* Oxford: Basil Blackwell, 1991.

Butler, Joseph, *Fifteen Sermons.* Oxford: Clarendon Press, 1874.

Byron, Michael, "Satisficing and Optimality." *Ethics* 109 (1998): 67–93.

Caldwell, Bruce J., *Beyond Positivism: Economic Methodology in the Twentieth Century.* New York: Routledge, 1994.

Caplan, Bryan, "Stigler-Becker versus Myers-Briggs: Why Preference-Based Explanations Are Scientifically Meaningful and Empirically Important." Working paper, George Mason University, 2001.

Cowen, Tyler, *Risk and Business Cycles: New and Old Austrian Perspectives.* New York: Routledge, 1997.

Cox, James C., "Testing the Utility Hypothesis." *Economic Journal* 107 (1997): 1054–78.

Daniels, Norman, "Wide Reflective Equilibrium and Theory Acceptance in Ethics." *Journal of Philosophy* 76 (1979): 266–82.

Darwall, Stephen, "Rational Agent, Rational Act." *Philosophical Topics* 14 (1986): 33–57.

Dreier, James, "The Structure of Normative Theories." *The Monist* 76 (1993): 22–40.

"Accepting Agent Centred Norms: A Problem for Non-Cognitivists and a Suggestion for Solving It." *Australasian Journal of Philosophy* 74 (1996): 409–22.

Elster, Jon, *Sour Grapes.* New York: Cambridge University Press, 1983.

Ulysses and the Sirens: Studies in Rationality and Irrationality. New York: Cambridge University Press, 1984.

Evans, Paul, "Interest Rates and Expected Future Budget Deficits in the United States." *Journal of Political Economy* 95 (1987): 34–58.

Foot, Philippa, "Utilitarianism and the Virtues." In Samuel Scheffler, ed., *Consequentialism and Its Critics.* New York: Oxford University Press, 1988, 224–42.

Natural Goodness. New York: Oxford University Press, 2001.

Gardiner, Stephen M., "Aristotle's Basic and Non-Basic Virtues." In D. N. Sedley, ed., *Oxford Studies in Ancient Philosophy* XX. New York: Oxford University Press, 2001, 261–95.

Gauthier, David, *Morals by Agreement.* Oxford: Clarendon Press, 1986.

Gibbard, Allan, *Wise Choices, Apt Feelings.* Cambridge, Mass.: Harvard University Press, 1990.

Grether, David M., and Charles R. Plott, "Economic Theory of Choice and the Preference Reversal Phenomenon." *American Economic Review* 69 (1979): 623–38.

Hampton, Jean, "The Failure of Expected Utility Theory as a Theory of Reason." *Economics and Philosophy* 10 (1994): 195–242.

Harsanyi, John C., and Reinhard Selten, *A General Theory of Equilibrium Selection in Games.* Cambridge, Mass.: MIT Press, 1988.

Hausman, Daniel M., *The Inexact and Separate Science of Economics.* New York: Cambridge University Press, 1992.

Heap, Shaun Hargreaves, *Rationality in Economics.* Oxford: Basil Blackwell, 1989.

Herman, Barbara, *The Practice of Moral Judgment.* Cambridge, Mass.: Harvard University Press, 1993.

Horney, Karen, *Neurosis and Human Growth: The Struggle Toward Self Realization.* New York: Norton, 1970.

Howard-Snyder, Frances, and Alastair Norcross, "A Consequentialist Case for Rejecting the Right." *Journal of Philosophical Research* 18 (1993): 109–25.

Hume, David, *Treatise of Human Nature.* L. A. Selby-Bigge, ed. New York: Oxford University Press, 1968.

Hurka, Thomas, "Two Kinds of Satisficing." *Philosophical Studies* 59 (1990): 107–11.

"Consequentialism and Content." *American Philosophical Quarterly* 29 (1992): 71–8.

Hurley, S. L., *Natural Reasons: Personality and Polity.* New York: Oxford University Press, 1989.

Hursthouse, Rosalind, *On Virtue Ethics.* New York: Oxford University Press, 1999.

Jackson, Frank, "Decision-Theoretic Consequentialism and the Nearest and Dearest Objection." *Ethics* 101 (1991): 461–82.

Jeffrey, Richard C., *The Logic of Decision,* 2nd ed. Chicago: University of Chicago Press, 1983.

Kagan, Shelly, *The Limits of Morality.* New York: Oxford University Press, 1989.

"Does Consequentialism Demand Too Much?" *Philosophy and Public Affairs* 13 (1984): 239–54.

Kagel, John H., and Alvin E. Roth, eds., *The Handbook of Experimental Economics.* Princeton, N.J.: Princeton University Press, 1995.

Kahneman, Daniel, et al., "When More Pain Is Preferred to Less: Adding a Better End." *Psychological Science* 4 (1993): 401–5.

Korsgaard, Christine, *The Sources of Normativity.* New York: Cambridge University Press, 1996.

Levi, Isaac, *Hard Choices: Decision Making Under Unresolved Conflict.* New York: Cambridge University Press, 1986.

Litterman, Robert B., and Laurence Weiss, "Money, Real Interest Rates, and Output: A Reinterpretation of Postwar U.S. Data." *Econometrica* 53 (1985): 129–56.

Little, Margaret Olivia, "Virtue as Knowledge: Objections from the Philosophy of Mind." *Nous* 31 (1997): 59–79.

MacDonald, Scott, "Ultimate Ends in Practical Reasoning: Aquinas's Aristotelian Psychology and Anscombe's Fallacy." *Philosophical Review* 100 (1991): 31–65.

Machina, Mark J., "Expected Utility without the Independence Axiom." *Econometrica* 50 (1982): 277–324.

MacIntyre, Alasdair, *After Virtue.* Notre Dame, Ind.: University of Notre Dame Press, 1984.

Whose Justice? Which Rationality? Notre Dame, Ind.: University of Notre Dame Press, 1988.

Marcet, Albert, and Thomas J. Sargent, "Convergence of Least-Squares Learning in Environments with Hidden State Variables and Private Information." *Journal of Political Economy* 97 (1989): 1306–22.

March, James G., "Bounded Rationality, Ambiguity, and the Engineering of Choice." In J. G. March, ed., *Decisions and Organizations.* Oxford: Basil Blackwell, 1988, 266–93.

Martineau, James, *Types of Ethical Theory*. Oxford: Clarendon Press, 1886.

Mas-Colell, Andreu, "The Price Equilibrium Existence Problem in Topological Vector Lattices." *Econometrica* 54 (1986): 1039–54.

McDowell, John, "Non-Cognitivism and Rule-Following." In *Mind, Value, and Reality*. Cambridge, Mass.: Harvard University Press, 1998, 198–218.

Mendola, Joseph, "Gauthier's Morals by Agreement and Two Kinds of Rationality." *Ethics* 97 (1987): 765–74.

Mill, John S., *Utilitarianism*. Indianapolis: Hackett, 1979.

Millgram, Elijah, *Varieties of Practical Reasoning*. Cambridge, Mass.: MIT Press, 2001.

Mulgan, Timothy, "Slote's Satisficing Consequentialism." *Ratio* 6 (1993): 121–34.

Nagel, Thomas, *Mortal Questions*. New York: Cambridge University Press, 1979.

The View from Nowhere. New York: Oxford University Press, 1986.

Nietzsche, Friedrich, *Beyond Good and Evil*. trans. R. J. Hollingdale. New York: Penguin Books, 1973.

Zarathustra. trans. Walter Kaufmann. In *The Portable Nietzsche*. New York: Penguin Books, 1976.

On the Genealogy of Morals. trans. Douglas Smith. Oxford: World's Classics, 1996.

Nozick, Robert, *Anarchy, State, and Utopia*. New York: Basic Books, 1974.

The Examined Life. New York: Simon & Schuster, 1989.

Nussbaum, Martha C., "Aristotelian Social Democracy." In R. Bruce Douglas, Gerald M. Mara, and Henry S. Richardson, eds., *Liberalism and the Good*. New York: Routledge, 1990, 203–52.

"Non-Relative Virtues: An Aristotelian Approach." In Martha C. Nussbaum and Amartya Sen, eds., *The Quality of Life*. New York: Oxford University Press, 1993, 242–69.

Pettit, Philip, "Satisficing Consequentialism." *Proceedings of the Aristotelian Society* suppl. 58 (1984): 165–76.

Plato, *The Republic*. tr. Richard W. Sterling and William C. Scott. New York: Norton, 1985.

Pollock, John L., "A Theory of Moral Reasoning." *Ethics* (1986): 506–23.

Radnitzky, Gerard, and Peter Bernholz, eds., *Economic Imperialism: The Economic Approach Applied Outside the Field of Economics*. New York: Paragon House, 1987.

Railton, Peter, "Facts and Values." *Philosophical Topics* 14 (1986): 5–29.

Rawls, John, *A Theory of Justice*. Cambridge, Mass.: Harvard University Press, 1970.

Raz, Joseph, *The Morality of Freedom*. Oxford: Clarendon Press, 1986.

Practical Reason and Norms. Princeton, N.J.: Princeton University Press, 1990.

Reder, Melvin, *Economics: The Culture of a Controversial Science*. Chicago: University of Chicago Press, 1999.

Resnik, Michael, *Choices*. Minneapolis: University of Minnesota Press, 1987.

Richardson, Henry S., "Commensurability." In Lawrence Becker, ed., *Encyclopedia of Ethics*, 2nd ed. New York: Routledge, 2001, 258–62.

Practical Reasoning About Final Ends. New York: Cambridge University Press, 1994.

Rosen, Sherwin, "Austrian and Neoclassical Economics: Any Gains from Trade?" *Journal of Economic Perspectives* 11 (1997): 139–52.

Samuelson, Paul, "A Note on the Pure Theory of Consumer's Behavior." *Econometrica* 5 (1938): 353–4.

Scheffler, Samuel, *The Rejection of Consequentialism*. Oxford: Clarendon Press, 1982.

Human Morality. New York: Oxford University Press, 1992.

Schmidtz, David, "Rationality within Reason." *Journal of Philosophy* 89 (1992): 445–66.

Rational Choice and Moral Agency. Princeton, N.J.: Princeton University Press, 1995.

Sen, Amartya, *Choice, Welfare, and Measurement*. Cambridge, Mass.: MIT Press, 1982.

Seung, T. K., and Daniel Bonevac, "Plural Values and Indeterminate Rankings." *Ethics* 102 (1992): 799–813.

Shiller, Robert J., *Irrational Exuberance*. New York: Broadway Books, 2000.

Simon, Herbert A., "A Behavioral Model of Rational Choice." *Quarterly Journal of Economics* 69 (1955): 99–118.

"Theories of Decision Making in Economics and Behavioral Science." *American Economic Review* 49 (1959): 253–83.

Models of Thought. New Haven, Conn.: Yale University Press, 1979.

Models of Bounded Rationality: Behavioral Economics and Business Organization, vol. 2. Cambridge, Mass.: MIT Press, 1982.

Administrative Behavior: A Study of Decision-Making Processes in Administrative Organizations. New York: The Free Press, 1997.

Slote, Michael, "Satisficing Consequentialism." *Proceedings of the Aristotelian Society* 58 supp. (1984): 139–63.

Goods and Virtues. Oxford: Clarendon Press, 1983.

Common-Sense Morality and Consequentialism. New York: Routledge, 1985.

"Moderation, Rationality and Virtue." In Sterling M. McMurrin, ed., *The Tanner Lectures on Human Values* VII. Salt Lake City: University of Utah Press, 1986, 56–99.

Beyond Optimizing: A Study of Rational Choice. Cambridge, Mass.: Harvard University Press, 1989.

From Morality to Virtue. New York: Oxford University Press, 1994.

Morals from Motives. New York: Oxford University Press, 2001.

Smart, J. J. C., and Bernard Williams, *Utilitarianism: For and Against*. New York: Cambridge University Press, 1973.

Smith, Holly, "Deciding How to Decide: Is There a Regress Problem?" In M. Bacharach and S. Hurley, eds., *Foundations of Decision Theory*. Oxford: Basil Blackwell, 1991, 194–219.

Smith, Michael, *The Moral Problem*. Oxford: Basil Blackwell, 1994.

Sobel, David, "Subjective Accounts of Reasons for Action." *Ethics* 111 (2001): 461–92.

Sosa, David, "Consequences of Consequentialism." *Mind* 102 (1993): 101–22.

Stigler, George S., and Gary J. Becker, "De Gustibus Non Est Disputandum." *American Economic Review* 67 (1977): 76–90.

Stocker, Michael, "Desiring the Bad: An Essay in Moral Psychology." *Journal of Philosophy* 76 (1979): 738–53.

Plural and Conflicting Values. New York: Oxford University Press, 1990.

Sumner, L. W., *Welfare, Happiness, and Ethics*. Oxford: Clarendon Press, 1996.

Swanton, Christine, "Satisficing and Virtue." *Journal of Philosophy* 90 (1993): 33–48.

———. "A Virtue Ethical Account of Right Action." *Ethics* 112 (2001): 32–52.

Taylor, Charles, *Sources of the Self: The Making of Modern Identity*. Cambridge, Mass.: Harvard University Press, 1989.

Thaler, Richard H., *Quasi Rational Economics*. New York: Russell Sage Foundation, 1994.

Ullmann-Margalit, Edna, and Sidney Morgenbesser, "Picking and Choosing." *Social Research* 44 (1977): 757–85.

Varian, Hal, *Microeconomic Analysis*. New York: Norton, 1992.

Velleman, David, "Well-Being and Time." *Pacific Philosophical Quarterly* 72 (1991): 48–77.

Walzer, Michael, *Just and Unjust Wars: A Moral Argument with Historical Illustrations*. New York: Basic Books, 1977.

Weber, Michael, *Satisficing: The Rationality of Preferring What Is Good Enough*. Ph.D. dissertation, University of Michigan, 1998.

Williams, Bernard, "Persons, Character and Morality." In *Moral Luck*. New York: Cambridge University Press, 1981, 1–19.

Wolf, Susan, "Moral Saints." *Journal of Philosophy* 79 (1982): 419–39.

Yeager, Leland B., "Austrian Economics, Neoclassicism, and the Market Test." *Journal of Economic Perspectives* 11 (1997): 153–65.

Zagzebski, Linda, *Virtues of the Mind: An Inquiry into the Nature of Virtue and the Ethical Foundations of Knowledge*. New York: Cambridge University Press, 1996.

Index